FIELDING, DICKENS, GOSSE, IRIS MURDOCH
AND OEDIPAL *HAMLET*

Also by Douglas Brooks-Davies

Number and Pattern in the Eighteenth-Century Novel: Defoe, Fielding, Smollett and Sterne
Spenser's 'Faerie Queene': A Critical Commentary on Books I and II
The Mercurian Monarch: Magical Politics from Spenser to Pope
Pope's 'Dunciad' and the Queen of Night
Henry Fielding, *Joseph Andrews* and *Shamela* (editor)
Henry Fielding, *Jonathan Wild* and *A Journal of a Voyage to Lisbon* (editor)
Edmund Spenser, *The Faerie Queene: A Selection* (editor)
Edmund Spenser, *The Faerie Queene, Books I to III* (editor)

FIELDING, DICKENS, GOSSE, IRIS MURDOCH AND OEDIPAL *HAMLET*

Douglas Brooks-Davies
*Senior Lecturer in English Literature
University of Manchester*

St. Martin's Press   New York

© Douglas Brooks-Davies 1989

All rights reserved. For information, write:
Scholarly and Reference Division,
St. Martin's Press, Inc., 175 Fifth Avenue, New York, NY 10010

First published in the United States of America in 1989

Printed in the People's Republic of China

ISBN 0–312–02393–6

Library of Congress Cataloguing-in-Publication Data
Brooks-Davies, Douglas.
Fielding, Dickens, Gosse, Iris Murdoch, and Oedipal Hamlet.
Bibliography: p.
Includes index.
1. English prose literature—History and criticism.
2. Oedipus complex in literature. 3. Shakespeare,
William, 1564–1616. Hamlet. 4. Shakespeare, William,
1564–1616.—Influence. 5. Fielding, Henry, 1707–1754.
Tom Jones. 6. Dickens, Charles, 1812–1870. Great
expectations. 7. Gosse, Edmund, 1849–1928. Father and
son. 8. Murdoch, Iris, Black prince. I. Title.
PR756.O43B7   1989   828'.08   88–18170
ISBN 0–312–02393–6

To Lucy and Michael
for their friendship

Gentle to me and affable hath been
Thy condescension, and shall be honour'd ever
With grateful Memorie.

Contents

List of Abbreviations viii

Preface ix

Introduction xi

1 Fielding's *Tom Jones*: Encountering the King 1
   1.1 Secrets 6
   1.2 Father Time 14
   1.3 Ruling Fathers 24
   1.4 The Authorial Father 40
   1.5 The Ghostly Mother 48

2 Dickens: *Great Expectations* and the Ghost of the Father 60
   2.1 Photographs and Ghosts 61
   2.2 Reaching for the Mother 73
   2.3 Extending the Circumference 89
   2.4 Completing the Circle 107

3 Edmund Gosse's *Father and Son*: Remembering the Mother 115
   3.1 The Knot Secured 119
   3.2 Severing the Father 127
   3.3 Father Adam, Mother Ophelia 135
   3.4 Naming Hamlet 146

4 Iris Murdoch's *The Black Prince*: Overthrowing the Tyrant and Inscribing the Feminine 151
   4.1 Apollo, Marsyas, and Hamlet 154
   4.2 Ophelia's Sisters 163
   4.3 Arrival at the Past 169

Notes 180

Select Bibliography 203

Index 207

Abbreviations

The following abbreviations have been used

CQ	Critical Quarterly
DAI	Dissertation Abstracts International
DNB	Dictionary of National Biography
DSA	Dickens Studies Annual: Essays on Victorian Fiction
ECS	Eighteenth-Century Studies
E in C	Essays in Criticism
ELH	English Literary History
HLQ	Huntington Library Quarterly
MLN	Modern Language Notes
N and Q	Notes and Queries
NCF	Nineteenth-Century Fiction
NLH	New Literary History: A Journal of Theory and Interpretation
PLL	Papers on Language and Literature
PMLA	Publications of the Modern Language Association of America
PQ	Philological Quarterly
SE	The Standard Edition of the Complete Psychological Works of Sigmund Freud, gen. ed. James Strachey in collaboration with Anna Freud. 24 vols. London: Hogarth Press and the Institute of Psychoanalysis, 1953–74
SEL	Studies in English Literature, 1500–1900
SP	Studies in Philology
UTQ	University of Toronto Quarterly

Note: All *Hamlet* quotations in my text are from *Hamlet*, ed. Harold Jenkins. The Arden Shakespeare. London and New York: Methuen, 1982.

All quotations from *The Black Prince* by Iris Murdoch © 1973 by Iris Murdoch, reprinted by permission of Viking Penguin Inc.

Preface

I offer in this book a series of extended reinterpretations of four texts, three novels and an autobiography, each of which demonstrates an allusive commitment to *Hamlet*. The chapters may be read as separate essays, but readers who pursue them in sequence will detect a developing argument about the role of the Oedipus complex in the creative male psyche and the myths it perpetrates about the feminine. Each of my three male authors, I argue, uses *Hamlet*, with greater or lesser degrees of subtlety, as a focus for Oedipal anxiety, revisiting the play for his own psychologically, historically, and socially determined ends; while Iris Murdoch in the *Black Prince*, the subject of chapter 4, proposes a radical, even feminist, re-vision of *Hamlet* that recognises and then rejects virtually everything embodied in the three preceding *Hamlet*-based texts.

The nature of my readings has led me to use some at least of the insights afforded by the neo-Freudians and post-structuralists, and the Introduction is intended as a primer, for those who are unfamiliar with them, to the Lacanian and other assumptions which my interpretations take for granted; I have, however, deliberately avoided the rather prickly vocabularies associated with these methodologies because they seem, for my purposes, unnecessarily forbidding, a way of rendering formidable what could be said more simply and accessibly.

I would like to thank the Registrar of the University of Manchester and my colleagues in the English Department for granting me sabbatical leave in the Lent term of 1986, during which much of this book was written. Damian Grant, with characteristic generosity, lent me books from his seemingly bottomless treasure chest of works on literary theory; Patrick Swinden, equally generously, gave me a copy of his unpublished essay on *The Black Prince*; Mary Lago read and commented on a draft of the Edmund Gosse chapter with a thoroughness and wisdom for which a mere formal acknowledgement is paltry recompense.

For the most part the book was developed from ideas formulated through tutorial discussions and seminars. Chapter 1 benefitted in its early stages from the interest of Laura Lilik, and chapter 2 grew from a Dickens tutorial one gloomy February morning in 1984 and would not have taken the shape it has had not Jackie Curthoys, Denis Hall, Alan Greene and Mark Fairey persuaded me to continue. I doubt, however, that they thought I would continue at such length. The Iris Murdoch chapter was tested against the scepticism and engagement of my final year seminar group on contemporary women novelists at Manchester during 1987. I am grateful to the whole of that pioneering group, but to Catherine Knight and Andrew Hartley, whose conversations about, and own work on, Iris Murdoch revealed an understanding and commitment that I found at once stimulating and humbling, I send my special thanks and thoughts. Mary Syner produced an immaculate typescript from my scrappy and piecemeal manuscript, amid her other duties in the English Departmental office. My thanks to her for her patience and efficiency.

It is a great pleasure, finally, to thank Peter Howe who, in return for drafts of typescript and Ancient Mariner-like insistence on my part for conversation on the topics of this book, gave me the gifts of time, knowledge, and friendship.

Manchester   Douglas Brooks-Davies

Introduction

When Joe asks, after attending Wopsle's performance of *Hamlet*, 'if the ghost of a man's own father cannot be allowed to claim his attention, what can, Sir?' (*Great Expectations*, chapter 27), he raises a question that is central to his own life and even more so to that of Pip, whom he is addressing. For *Great Expectations* is one of Dickens's supreme ghost stories, a fiction about the return of the dead that announces its subject in the opening chapter when the convict Magwitch leaps out from behind a grave stone only to shamble away through 'the hands of the dead people' into the blackness of the evening and of the marshes. Whatever other interpretation one may like to place upon him, Magwitch is, in that undeniable language which narrative at its best often shares with dreams, the 'ghost of [Pip's] own father'. He looms into the narrative while Pip is crying over the graves of his parents, bullying, threatening, yet physically pathetic and stained, totally 'other': one who has crossed into that unimaginable territory from whose bourn, according to Hamlet even though his father has already proved him wrong, no traveller returns, and who carries on him the taints and marks of that ultimate horrifying unknowable, the secret of non-being, that erasure of self which is death.

The mature Pip who recounts the experiences of his early life is thus exploring what Freud would later call the landscape of the 'uncanny',[1] the boundaries of which in Pip's case are marked by his parental graves and also by Satis House, whose inhabitant is a ghostly spinster of a mother with overtones of that most terrifying of nineteenth-century nightmare figures, the living entombed, the person buried alive who taps messages to the world beyond her confining walls to which no one will listen.

There are similar preoccupations in Fielding's *Tom Jones*, Gosse's *Father and Son* and Iris Murdoch's *The Black Prince*. In fact, all the works discussed in this book are concerned with the Oedipal triangle of mother-son-father and with that area of the ghostly in which the unconscious mind and the memory combine to produce and symbolise the repressed only to disclose that what has been repressed is fear of death focused on images of the absent mother and father. This is, of course, the area where Lacanian psychoanalysis, post-structuralism, and feminism are likely to find themselves competing with and complementing each other with the jargon of their various discourses. I have tried to avoid the jargon while benefitting from the insights I have gained from reading Lacan, Derrida, Barthes, Luce Irigaray, Hélène Cixous, and the many English and American critics in their traditions who have enlivened and permanently enriched my understanding of how literature may be seen to announce itself and make its effects.[2]

The readings that follow are predicated upon the metaphorical validity for these particular works of the idea of infant bonding with the mother and consequent hostility to the father. For those unfamiliar with Lacan's restatement and amplification of Freud's definition of the Oedipus complex, it is worth stating here that Lacan insists on the absolute quality of the female as well as male human being's desolation at maternal absence. This is a deprivation announced initially by the severing of the umbilicus and later reinforced by the arrival of paternal authority with its demand that the child confront and acknowledge the fact of sexual difference in the form of genital maleness and femaleness. According to Lacan, before the ego starts to develop, the child is 'one' with its mother, lacking any defined sense and centre of self (at this point it inhabits what Lacan terms the 'imaginary order'). While still biologically dependent on its mother and within this phase, the child begins to enter the 'mirror stage', which entails building up images of itself from external phenomena. The first focus of attention here is the mother's body which, however, is supposedly recognised as simultaneously self and not-self, something to which the child belongs and with which it identifies but from which it knows it is separate. The intrusion of the father guarantees the child's sense of apartness and awareness of separation and the sense of loss that this recognition entails. For Lacan as for Freud, then, the father represents Law in its specific sense of prohibition against incest and codification of socially acceptable patterns of behaviour. His presence also pushes the libidinal desire, which Freudians and neo-Freudians alike perceive in the infant's relationship with its mother, into the deepest recesses of the unconscious.

Lacan also sees this Freudian model as crucial to the acquisition of language, which occurs at around the point when the 'imaginary order' of union with the mother is succeeded by what he calls the 'symbolic order', which is marked simultaneously by the appearance of the father and of linguistic awareness. Language is thus, for

Lacan, paternal; to be articulate is to enter the domain of the father. But, by definition, language is also identified with mother-loss and the admission of difference. Combining Freud and Saussure, Lacan comes up with a variant of the ancient idea of language itself as an image of loss and absence: in the Judaeo-Christian tradition the Tower of Babel marks our distance from God and paradise; in Lacanian thinking language is based on recognition of the *difference* of one sign from another and the *absence* of the signified object. Further, all that language can signify in this new postlapsarianism is loss, for linguistic signs can name but never possess the objects of its utterer's attention which are, by definition, merely metaphorical substitutes for the primally lost mother.

I have grossly oversimplified here. Nevertheless, this view of language, whatever one's reservations about it, is at least suggestive in relation to Bradley's vow of silence in *The Black Prince* and to the young Edmund's reluctance to speak in *Father and Son*. Both, on a strictly Lacanian interpretation, would be reinforcing their bond with the mother by refusing to enter the linguistic realm of the father, and although in both instances I have adopted a slightly different reading, the general relevance of Lacan's thinking in these, as in other matters, will be clear, making him and Freud the main (if not the only) phantoms lurking behind my particular text. Appropriating their fictions and metaphors where relevant as a shorthand method of exploring the ways in which *Hamlet* functions as a Darwinian parent text to individual works by Fielding, Dickens, Gosse and Murdoch, I try to maintain overall an individualistic and historically-based approach which nevertheless is prepared to risk itself in the direction of deconstructionist speculation.

This is not a book about *Hamlet* or critical attitudes to *Hamlet*. And the *Hamlet* it focuses on, as will by now be apparent, is neither Wilhelm Meister's heroic melancholic nor the Mallarmean doubter nor the Laforguean reformist but, simply, Hamlet the Oedipal obsessive.[3] Without wishing to argue that *Hamlet* is solely or even largely Oedipal, I suggest that it was intuitively perceived by Fielding, Dickens, and Gosse as a dramatic and textual representation of Oedipal anxiety which they subsequently felt compelled to revisit in written texts of their own. Briefly (to invoke Lacan again), *Hamlet* seems to have functioned for these writers as a signifier (or chain of signifiers) which is so closely related to the Oedipal signified (murdered yet intrusive father, maternal deprivation because of Gertrude's marriage to Claudius, and so forth) that it demanded absorption into those other vastly complex chains of signifiers *Tom Jones, Great Expectations* and *Father and Son*, in which it would be re-formed and the signified, accordingly, more riddlingly repressed and diverted. In other words, like all texts, they are designed to disclose and obscure, to suggest answers and assert secrecy simultaneously.

The case of *Father and Son* is fascinating from this point of view because it mentions Hamlet only once, so that his (or its) naming can be seen almost as a Freudian slip marking a return of the repressed that reveals suddenly, in all its nakedness, the centrality to the text of the otherwise almost unnoticeable presence of the ghostly father as Law, as agent of repression, and as claimant to the mother's body. In other words, once Hamlet is named most of the other words and images ('signifiers') in Gosse's work are seen to signify in relation to it as the work's arch — albeit largely secret — signifier. We are alerted by it to the significances of its ghosts and murders and the narrative weight, belied by the patrilinear title, bestowed upon the mother, and to the metaphorical engagement between *Hamlet* and Philip Gosse's key contribution to the evolution debate, *Omphalos*, which is mentioned and described in chapter 5 of *Father and Son* and again 'signifies', in the Lacanian sense, exactly that infinite grief at maternal absence that *Hamlet* also (read in this way) expresses.

It is at least interesting, and probably more than a coincidence, that each of my three male re-visions of *Hamlet* has as its central character a boy orphan, each of whom, by a process that Karl Miller has made us familiar with, surrounds himself with doubles who are sometimes benign and sometimes malignly demonic validations or countermanders of the precarious 'self' that is the focus of the narrative.[4] This principle, again, is authorised by *Hamlet*, the complexity of whose doublings was first elaborated upon in Ernest Jones's *Hamlet and Oedipus*.

The theme of the orphan means in turn that *Tom Jones, Great Expectations,* and *Father and Son* are, like *Hamlet*, parentalian fictions, that is, works which, like *Hamlet*, honour and in a way raise a memorial to the dead father, paying tribute at least as much as they Oedipally vilify him for the loss of the mother.[5] Each is thus, as I describe it, a ghost story balanced on the edge of that abyss of ambiguity that the ghost himself embodies by reminding us of rituals of 'obligations towards ancestors' while generating a fear

Introduction

that means, psychologically speaking, 'the overpowering of consciousness by the autonomous contents of the unconscious' symbolised in this instance by the father.[6] To express it slightly differently, the ghost demands a rationally performed ritual enacted in accordance with cultural and anthropological requirements on the one hand and threatens erasure of that performing self on the other.

These three works are also linked by their attitude to Ophelia. It is she who becomes their emblem of maternal absence and desire, bearing the burden simultaneously of elegiac lament and pornographic rejoicing as the fictions' son-lover views her death as an image of loss and as an opportunity for possession in the manner of Browning's 'Porphyria's Lover'.[7] Yet this is to oversimplify, for *Tom Jones* feels obliged to rescue her, in the form of Sophia, from the more oppressive aspects of male dominance even as it celebrates her incarceration and violation by her sadistic Jacobite of a father and the obscene Lord Fellamar. Even Dickens, who seems to have been psychologically more attracted to the morbid aspects of Ophelia and pruriently fascinated by the topography of the dead female body, nevertheless moves beyond the merely pornographic (his presentation of Miss Havisham) by giving Pip and Magwitch aspects of Ophelia themselves, as if making them compensate for Oedipal guilt by identifying with the female victim. Gosse, also morbidly fascinated by her madness and manner of suicide, achieves a still more radical reinstatement of Ophelia. Conforming overall to Freudian expectation by using her as a symbol of maternal absence and deprivation, he resurrects her in the form of two surrogate mothers, mad Miss Flaw and the nameless girl who plunges into the pool at his baptism and who symbolically transfers her billowing Ophelian robes to the presiding clergyman. This transvestite moment enables the son to shift back from the realm of his father to that of his mother, to identify himself as feminine in an essential sense that is consonant with the Freudian notion of our yearning to be at one with the mother.

This book finishes with a detailed reading of what is the supremely (not because it is the only) significant novel on the *Hamlet*-Oedipus theme by a woman novelist, Iris Murdoch's *The Black Prince*. Murdoch, inheriting a tradition of male-dominated criticism and allusive appropriation of Shakespeare's play, focuses on the figures of Ophelia, Gertrude, Hamlet and Old Hamlet in order to demonstrate by imitation the level of Oedipal anxiety

Hamlet encodes for certain males and the depths of patriarchal conspiracy it can be seen to conceal. Adopting one of her characteristic stances, that of male first-person narrator, she narrates, in effect, her own autobiography of sexual difference. Interestingly, Deborah Johnson, whose feminist reading of Iris Murdoch was published just as I was finishing this book, detects, as I do, an analogy between Murdoch's assumption of the male persona here and in her other fictions and Luce Irigaray's theory of imitation of the male — his language, his habits, his structures — in order to expose them and redeem them for the principle of the feminine.[8] In the case of *The Black Prince* Murdoch inhabits a male mind that revels in *Hamlet*-centred Oedipal fantasies and subtly deconstructs it by revealing its limitations and claiming alternative iconographic, narrative and linguistic spaces for woman. The crucial point here is that *The Black Prince* is selfconsciously 'about' the role of the artist and that Bradley Pearson's central image of the artist is Shakespeare simultaneously as Hamlet and *Hamlet*, prostrating himself before the Apollonian father-god of his creativity. The novel can be read straightforwardly as an account and justification of male orthodoxy. It can and must (if we follow through the implications of male-imitation) be read as a re-vision of Apollonian mythic structures and of *Hamlet* on behalf of the female artist Julian (the girl who acted Hamlet at school and dresses as Hamlet for Bradley), who ends the novel by claiming words as the province of the feminine by defining them as the 'ultimate matrix' of spirit.

This is not to say that Murdoch then goes on to pioneer obviously feminine areas in the ensuing novels. She is too close to Plato, concepts of male deity, and the idea of a (male) priesthood for that. In *The Black Prince* she states her case for the feminine in a form at once stark and astonishingly complex, but it is a case that is in the end ambiguous. For if she exposes the pernicious implications of male hegemony in philosophy, literature, and other arts, she nevertheless registers a keen fascination with male fantasies and an acceptance of male structures. Despite the implicit radicality of *The Black Prince*, then, its author is a realist. She assumes the coexistence of male and female and is interested in the tensions engendered by that coexistence and in the consequent psychology of male creativity. Some sentences from near the end of her *The Fire and the Sun: Why Plato Banished the Artists* show, briefly, what I mean:

[Plato] was also the master, indeed, the inventor, of a pure calm relaxed mode of philosophical exposition which is a high literary form and a model forever. Of course he used metaphor, but philosophy needs metaphor and metaphor is basic: how basic is the most basic philosophical question. Plato also had no doubt a strong personal motive which prompted him to write. Socrates (*Theaetetus* 210C) called himself a barren midwife. Plato often uses images of paternity. Art launches philosophy as it launches religion, and it was necessary for Plato, as it was for the evangelists, to write if the Word was not to be sterile and the issue of the Father was to be recognised as legitimate.[9]

The questions raised here in terms of sexual politics are legion, but the main one concerns that old area of male anxiety, legitimacy. A father names, and so legitimises, a child, but the paternity and hence legitimacy of that child is in fact a maternal secret. This, if I understand the implications of Murdoch's own metaphor correctly, makes *writing* a feminine activity, since its function is to legitimise 'the issue of the Father'. Taking the metaphor a stage further, we could say that for Murdoch the Word itself, as child, is really in the possession of the mother. But I suspect that Murdoch would not go so far. It is enough for her that she has emphasised an area of male anxiety without appropriating the Word totally for the feminine. Julian's claim on words as matrix (womb) is thus uncharacteristically rash,[10] a vision unsubstantiated by the eight novels which have followed *The Black Prince* so far. Its emotional validity is, nonetheless, unquestionable in the context of the Oedipal nightmare from which she has escaped just as the novel's case against the Oedipal *Hamlet* as a whole is unanswerable.

Julian's liberation lies at the end of this study, though, for it is an achievement which, however limited, has to be measured against the weight of the opposition, the imprisoning forces of male orthodoxy. For, whatever their humanitarian credentials, Fielding, Dickens, and Gosse were all on the side of that paternal Law which demands Ophelia as victim and scapegoat; that same Law which, codified in literary-historical terms, produces Harold Bloom's *Anxiety of Influence* with its definition of literary 'succession' as a battle for supremacy against fathers, and admirers of Bloom like Wendell Stacy Johnson, who detects in Bloom's book a significance far greater than the literary-historical.[11]

I begin, then, with Fielding, a writer who was firmly (though not so firmly as some) entangled in the net of Oedipal anxiety and who, as the discoverer of 'a new Province of Writing', found himself charting territory in which he kept on bumping up against the ghosts of his fathers and mothers. His narrator's stance is one that Julian would recognise as being rather similar to that of Bradley Pearson.

1
Fielding's *Tom Jones*: Encountering the King

For a comic novel *Tom Jones* is extremely dark. Tom, the foundling, is shadowed by his half-brother Blifil almost from the beginning; the villagers' concerted attempts to discover parents for him are more grimly desperate than they are comically redemptive; Allworthy, in effect the adoptive father, nearly dies in Book V; Tom is expelled unjustly from his home in the following book to pursue a long pilgrimage that, although it will end in his gaining a home, is pursued against the backdrop of the bloody 1745 Jacobite rebellion against George II and has as its guide-posts the gratuitous enmity of Northerton. Then there is the sombre midnight autobiography of the Old Man of the Hill, who pops up like some *eminence grise* to support the authorial assertion in VIII.1 that ghosts are permissible in 'modern' works; the sexual encounter with Mrs Waters (who, however, turns out to be Tom's supposed mother, so that the guilt of the broken incest taboo haunts him for a while); the miserable affair with the middle-aged and foul-breathed Lady Bellaston (why does Fielding introduce this extraordinarily unsympathetic detail?); the arranged rape of Sophia; and Tom's imprisonment for supposed murder. Meantime Sophia travels a rather similar route, fleeing her manic father when he insists that she marry the hating and hateful Blifil, and encountering a sister spirit in her cousin Harriet Fitzpatrick who narrates an autobiography not unlike her own concerning a tyrannical gaoler of a man (husband this time, not father); constant oppression; the death of her only consolation, a little baby, and so on. After Tom's expulsion the season suddenly changes to winter and most of the narrated events take place during long winter nights which are relieved only by the specious comfort of the warm and noisy barn in which the magisterial king of the gypsies performs momentarily and anachronistically before disappearing into the void of history (XII.12); and by the joyless masquerade where Tom, searching for Sophia, is trapped by Lady Bellaston and where the lights, arranged so cunningly by the impresario Heidegger, merely serve to illuminate a spiritually empty space and reveal the absence of deity (XIII.7), maternal or paternal.

This is, of course, a partial view of the novel. Yet it is true to those registers of the narrating voice that become particularly strained when they talk of the Jacobite rebellion, of parent-child relationships, and of death: those very registers, in fact, which are strained to their limits in XVI.5 when Tom and his companion Partridge attend a performance of *Hamlet* with David Garrick in the lead role and such an extraordinary mixture of emotional response is recorded that it is all too clear that the play has focused into the minutest detail the novel's darkest and most problematic concerns.[1] For although Jones 'expected to enjoy much Entertainment in the Criticisms of *Partridge*' and Partridge does indeed 'afford . . . great Mirth . . . to all who sat within hearing', it is unease, even distress, rather than laughter, that are generated by the episode.[2] Partridge knows, for instance, what a ghost is, and that he is not seeing one in Act I when the 'Man . . . in the strange Dress' enters. But when Garrick's Hamlet is so afraid, he knows that it is a ghost after all as play becomes psychological reality: *'Follow you?* I'd follow the Devil as soon. Nay, perhaps, it is the Devil — for they say he can put on what Likeness he pleases. — Oh! here he is again. – *No farther*! No, you have gone far enough already; farther than I'd have gone for all the King's Dominions'.

Now Partridge has early on been certified as a lunatic or – apparently the same thing – a superstitious Jacobite.[3] This should trigger an instant laughter response in us, as it does in the Hanoverian Jones, to most things he says. He is, after all, daft to believe in ghosts. Or is he? How serious was Fielding when, in *Tom Jones*, VIII.1, he speculated on the admissibility of the supernatural in modern fictions and decided that 'the only supernatural Agents which can in any Manner be allowed to us Moderns are Ghosts', and followed that by recounting a particularly horrible case of murder, of which he had personal knowledge, two days after which the murderer, Fisher, went 'with some young Ladies to the Play of *Hamlet*; and with an unaltered Countenance heard one of the Ladies, who little suspected how near she was to the Person, cry out, Good God! if the Man that murdered Mr. *Derby* was now present!' (VIII.1)?[4] The authorial voice is deeply serious and committed here, and it is this voice that speaks in the chapter that is given over entirely to *Hamlet*. Tom's reactions are, in this instance at least, naïve, and Partridge's about right. Ghosts in some form do walk, or at the very least the idea of ghosts is a valid one. Have Tom and Partridge not both met, on Mazard Hill at night, an old man so strangely attired that Partridge's conviction that he must be a ghost rings truer than Tom's rationalistic denial?[5] It is certainly true that the Old Man of the Hill, who makes his appearance at the end of the book in which Fisher watches *Hamlet*, bears a significant analogical relationship with the ghost of Old Hamlet himself as he walks onto the stage in xvi.5 'in the strange Dress', and it is a relationship perceived by Partridge rather than Tom because, it may be, Tom is at this stage of his pilgrimage still rather too busy burying what *Hamlet* can teach him to resurrect from his unconscious mind. The pilgrimage, in other words, may cease when the novel's dialogue with *Hamlet* has been played through.

The ghost of Old Hamlet urges a greater and continuing presence on the Old Man of the Hill with his tale of sibling rivalry, woman hatred, a dead father, and engagement in the events of James II's reign that culminated in the ejection of the Stuarts and the arrival, in 1688, of William of Orange and constitutional monarchy. Old Hamlet, too, talks of sibling rivalry, exemplifies the deadness (and/or awful livingness) of a father, generates an appalling misogyny, and all within a political discourse as Fortinbras challenges for the Danish crown. Tom has a manic half-brother, is fighting for one king against another, and has not only a dead father but a dead mother as well. Or did he, as a foundling, ever have any parents? Where exactly does he stand in relation to women? Is there an answer in the presence of *Hamlet* to the fact that he runs away from the Man of the Hill to make love to his supposed mother, Jenny Waters? Is his laughter at Partridge's response to *Hamlet* so loud that it enables him not to listen?

If this sounds like a series of questions leading to a 'now read on', then in a way it is. *Hamlet* resonates in the most subtle and unexpected ways through *Tom Jones*, revealing the deepest authorial doubts, ambiguities, and anxieties and, by that very fact, Fielding's questioning and liberal humaneness. My *Tom Jones* may not be all that different from William Empson's common sense *Tom Jones* after all,[6] even though the reading offered here concentrates on features of the text which many have ignored or silently glossed over: in the case of the *Hamlet* chapter the status of the ghost, of course; but also the desperate ambiguity, in the context of recent memories of the '45, of Partridge's comment quoted earlier that

Hamlet had already followed the ghost too far, 'farther than I'd have gone for all the King's Dominions'. Which king, and how do we know he is a king? And, in connection with this, the further implied question, what is the relationship between kings and fathers?

I also take seriously Partridge's reaction to the ghost's reappearance in Act III, given the novel's preoccupation with woman abuse in the cases of Squire Western, Mr. Fitzpatrick, Blifil, and others. For what is portrayed here is a paradigm of patriarchal misogyny as the ghost sets Hamlet off vilifying Gertrude again and Hamlet transfers his energies to Partridge: 'Ay, no wonder you are in such a Passion; shake the vile wicked Wretch to Pieces. If she was my own Mother I should serve her so. To be sure, all Duty to a Mother is forfeited by such wicked Doings'. There would seem, at this rate, to be no hope for women at the mouths and hands of men, no way of preventing Sophia from becoming Ophelia.

Then again, the novel demands that we enquire into the analogy between Fisher as spectator of *Hamlet* and Claudius as spectator of 'the Play, which *Hamlet* introduces before [him]', yet another scene selected for our consideration in *Tom Jones's* much-cut performance. Finally, the paragraph on 'the Grave-digging Scene' requires that it, too, should engage our attention as it 'engaged the Attention of *Partridge*'. Maybe it is not making Fielding sound too much like Dickens to suggest that there is more than meets the eye in Partridge's reaction to Yorick:

> Upon *Hamlet's* taking up the Skull, he cry'd out, 'Well, it is strange to see how fearless some Men are: I never could bring myself to touch any Thing belonging to a dead Man on any Account. — He seemed frightned enough too at the Ghost I thought.

Tom, after all, 'belongs' to a dead man.

Tom Jones is so deeply concerned with the parentless status of the foundling that it generates virtually the whole of the novel's narrative structure. Although *Hamlet* is the main clue here, there is significant support from another play that is admitted into the text, again on two occasions, Thomas Otway's *The Orphan*. The title in itself may seem vibrant enough; but the way *Tom Jones* uses it is even more so, for it is invoked in those textually sensitive areas, the Man of the Hill's tale (VIII. 10) and the complementary tale of Mrs Fitzpatrick (XI.5). On both occasions the same passage is alluded to, Chamont's vision (or is it reality?) of a 'wrinkled hag, with age grown double', the consequence of his dream of Monimia with two 'wanton' lovers. And this dream admits one further, primal, text into *Tom Jones*, that of *Oedipus Tyrannus*. For after the dream Chamont

> rose and called for lights, when, oh, dire omen!
> I found my weapon had the arras pierced
> Just where that famous tale was interwoven,
> How th'unhappy Theban slew his father.[7]

Tom Jones links *Hamlet* and *Oedipus Tyrannus* in the most teasing and baffling of ways.[8] And while the following account does not pursue what might be hypothesised to be the 'psychogenesis' of *Tom Jones*, it is worth recalling that some of the features of the narrative that might otherwise be, or appear to be, inexplicable, like the affair with Lady Bellaston, could be the product of such familiar psychological devices as repression and substitution on Fielding's part. It is also at least worth acknowledging that the novel's preoccupation with filial relationships and the last of a series of battles between Catholic Stuart and Protestant Hanover could well be primarily locatable in Fielding's own troubled boyhood. The treacheries of the Stuart father-kings, against whom Fielding reacted so violently as pamphleteer and journalist during and after the '45, may have raised suppressed memories of his father's treatment of him and his siblings after their mother's death. For the father's rapid remarriage and return to Henry's real mother's home led to documented disturbance in the boy's behaviour, presumably at least in some sense Oedipal in origin, as he fought the father to validate his mother's memory in the presence of the stepmother. If we add to this that the stepmother was an Italian and a Roman Catholic, then we may sense a more than political origin to his fascination with the exiled Stuarts who, having received succour abroad (in France) for two generations and more, and still as committed to their Catholicism as they had ever been, were once more threatening invasion and claiming their inalienable right to rule. In Fielding's personal and in the nation's political life absent fathers with Catholic affiliations were making, and had made, unwelcome returns.[9]

Tom Jones's commitment to *Hamlet* emphasises the primal drama of fathers and sons and mothers (and daughters), as does its less obvious indebtedness to *Oedipus Tyrannus*. Both plays assist the novel in exposing the patriarchal dynamics of kingship and, apparently another but really the same, problem, that of authorial authority. *Tom Jones* raises, in fact, the question fundamental to many male creators: how far does an Oedipal text compromise its author? And it raises it in this particular form: how does the author present and sustain himself given that his fiction is itself preoccupied with such self-referring questions as: which king?; who is my father?

From this point of view the presence of *Hamlet*, as well as that of *The Orphan* and *Oedipus Tyrannus*, in *Tom Jones* might be interpreted as evidence of the anxiety of influence as the avowedly paternal and absolutist author busily assimilates and comically reworks and undoes texts which question the status of parenthood and children, kill fathers, question them, deny them, want to be buried with them. It is *Hamlet*, though, which most obviously probes and undermines paternal authority and thus the authority of the male self, as Partridge reveals in a brilliant deconstructive manoeuvre by leaving the performance of that play convinced that 'the King' is the best actor. Who does he mean? The ghost? The player king? Fortinbras? Claudius? After all, 'Any Body may see he is an Actor' (xvi.5). Any *body*? At the end of *Hamlet*, strewn as the stage is with corpses?

Partridge speaks for all of us here as we scrutinise *Tom Jones* through the lens — or maybe it is a mirror — provided by *Hamlet*.

1.1 SECRETS

> Horatio: This to me
>   In dreadful secrecy impart they did,
>   And I with them the third night kept the watch,
>   Where, as they had deliver'd, both in time,
>   Form of the thing, each word made true and good,
>   The apparition comes.
>
>   (*Hamlet*, i.ii)

The History of Tom Jones, a Foundling is devoted to the disclosure of 'the Secret of [Tom's] Birth' (xviii.10). This is one of the last occasions that the word is used in this novel which has been so preoccupied with the apparent unknowableness of Tom's genesis that *secrets* and *secrecy* have taunted us throughout its considerable length: 'if the Historic-Muse hath entrusted me with any Secrets, I will by no means be guilty of discovering them till she shall give me leave' (II.6); Allworthy may or may not be the Partridges' 'secret Benefactor' (*ibid.*); Sophia's love for Tom is a 'Secret' prematurely revealed to her Aunt Western (VI.5); Lady Bellaston 'had little further Design than to secure within her own House the Repository of a Secret' (xv.10), and so on. Yet in one way what seems to be the novel's major secret, which all the others mime or parody, is 'known', or inferrable, from early on. There are strong clues in the discovery of the infant Tom in Allworthy's house and in Bridget's affection towards him that she is his mother; and Jenny Jones, Tom's supposed mother, knows the real father: 'I must on my Knees intreat you, not to persist in asking me to declare the Father of my Infant. I promise you faithfully you shall one Day know; but I am under the most solemn Ties and Engagements of Honour, as well as the most religious Vows and Protestations, to conceal his Name at this Time' (I.7). She keeps this promise in XVIII.7. If the discovery and subsequent marriage to Sophia seem a little glib, a mere conforming to the artifice of comic norms and a myth of eternal return, at another level they announce the end of a riddling attempt to ponder the relationship between paternity and filial identity. Tom can marry and have children because his mother and father have been identified and he has a name.

But even in saying this do we not sense the depths of Fielding's diversionary tactics when confronting the filial-parental dilemma? Tom never really has a father. He died before the child was born; he is mentioned only once in the novel. His name, Summer, means nothing to us in terms of plot and nothing to Tom, in practice, in terms of name. Tom, as far as we are concerned, retains the putative matronymic Jones. We are never invited to think of him as Tom Summer. Indeed, the title of his *History* actually prohibits our doing so, insisting as it does that Tom is, and always will be, *Tom Jones* and *a Foundling*.

The novel's biggest secret, then, is that it pretends: pretending to forget that Oedipus himself was a foundling it posits that if you have, in effect, no parents, there can be no parental-filial dilemma. Thus the act of separation from the parents takes on primary importance. Tom's secret is born with him, literally: the secret of his parenthood; the secret of separation. For Latin *secretus* means *concealed* or *hidden* as an extension of the original meaning *separated, sundered* (from *secerno*).[10] But since the Oedipal myth is initiated by sundering (Oedipus is abandoned and subsequently fostered, ignorant of his real parents; in order to avoid fulfilling Apollo's prophecy of murder and incest he travels the long road to Thebes), *secret* becomes in *Tom Jones* a terrifying revealing word, pointing as it does to the impossibility of concealing the fact that by *secrecy* the whole Oedipal drama was set in motion. Similarly, in *Hamlet* 'secrecy' is, with deep irony, demanded for what is known to many if not all:

Hamlet: But you'll be secret?
Horatio: }
Marcellus: } Ay, by heaven
Hamlet: There's never a villain dwelling in all Denmark
But he's an arrant knave.
Horatio: There needs no ghost, my lord, come from the grave
To tell us this.

(I.v.126ff)[11]

Within this overall framework of secrecy in its two meanings, *Tom Jones* considers another problem: that the foundling motif with its myth of separation also raises the anxiety that being parentless, while apparently solving the Oedipal problem, means that you are unknowable. After all, society expresses its anxiety that children must belong to parents by trying to trace familiar features from the moment of birth. Within the novel even Allworthy feels happier when he thinks he knows who Tom's mother is, not only because that establishes one certainty, but also because the mother can lead to the father. In *Tom Jones* the anxiety begets extraordinary happenings: both Allworthy and Partridge are proposed, accepted, and castigated as paternal candidates, and then the text itself seems to suggest that the secret of Tom's birth must be knowable by reduplication. Hence Captain Blifil's entry into the narrative to marry Bridget Allworthy, Tom's biological mother, and beget Tom's half-brother, Blifil, in a strange scrambling of the Cain-Abel, Claudius-Old Hamlet, Hamlet-Laertes doublings and differentiations.

But this manoeuvre in turn simply emphasises the secret of guilt — Tom's, the author's, the male reader's own — by answering the question 'who is this foundling who claims to have no father?' by transforming him into his own evil double and giving him the father one must always biologically have. The twist is that he inhabits godfather Allworthy's household and is presented in the psychologically intolerable but inevitable form of misogynistic tyrant who hates and virtually kills his own brother (Dr Blifil, I.13) and dies in the garden like Old Hamlet (another incident recalled in XVI.5 as Partridge tells of Hamlet's 'own Father's Spirit, and how he was murdered in the Garden') while mentally killing off Allworthy. So *Tom Jones* opens with a non-father and proceeds rapidly to a paternal grave while the mother, Bridget, cries out 'Somebody hath murdered him' (II.9). Some of the darkness of *Tom Jones* is transparently Oedipal.

Young Blifil is not, however, just Tom's guilty and manically vengeful double. His name indicates that he diminishes Tom, that the fiction of having no parents, so apparently liberating, is in fact tormenting because it suggests also that the non-existent parents might not want him. For *Blifil* is the *foolish* or *insipid son* (Latin *bliteus-filius*), taunting his twinned half-brother with a dreadful suspicion that he is a negligible nobody, an insipid nothing.[12]

This sounds more like Sterne than Fielding, and yet there the central doctrinal statement is, at the beginning of II.2 as Blifil's father buttonholes Allworthy, just after young Blifil's birth and Tom's baptism, to utter this rationale for the young Blifil's dedication to Tom's annihilation:

> He gave him frequent Hints, that to adopt the Fruits of Sin was to give countenance to it. He quoted several Texts (for he was well read in Scripture) such as, *He visits the Sins of the Fathers upon the Children; and the Fathers have eaten sour Grapes, and the Children's Teeth are set on edge,* &c. Whence he argued the Legality of punishing the crime of the Parent on the Bastard. He said, 'Tho' the Law did not positively allow the destroying such base-born Children, yet it held them to be the Children of no body; that the Church considered them as the Children of no body . . .'.

In his Calvinist mania the Captain identifies Tom as a reprobate and denies women altogether.[13] And yet his outburst has an appallingly simple logic that opens up vertiginous possibilities: the foundling bastard has no parents; it is the child of no body; if the parents have no body then the child could never have been conceived or born. The child does not exist.

A problematic text like *Tom Jones* compounds its problems rather than resolving them, hence the supplementary joke that Captain Blifil is also practising a trick learned from Odysseus's encounter with Polyphemus.[14] As this wily dark father zooms off into his own fantasising orbit, however, Bridget's maid Deborah, perplexed by the enormity of the problem of no body, decides to find or fabricate one by becoming the biblical Deborah, 'a mother in Israel' (Judges 5:7) and announcing herself pregnant with Partridge: 'she had now, as she *conceived*, fully detected the Father of the Foundling' [author's italics]. This is in the same chapter as, and an obvious counter to, the Captain's 'no body' proposition; but even this brave attempt to rescue Tom from the grip of the Blifils by generating Partridge and thus validating Tom is doomed to failure because Partridge is found guilty of paternity and disappears ('*Partridge*, having now lost his Wife, his School, and his Annuity, and the unknown Person having discontinued the last-mentioned Charity, resolved to change the Scene, and left the Country, where he was in Danger of starving with the universal Compassion of all his Neighbours'; II.6). He does not re-appear until VIII.4 (the book of ghosts and of the Man of the Hill) and when he does he has a different name and profession. As the barber Benjamin (son of whose right hand born of whose sorrow? (Gen. 35:18)) he is only a very minimal somebody; and for six books — a whole third of the novel — he has been nobody.

The idea of the nobody who is nothing persists in *Tom Jones* as a worrying possibility, as we shall see (below, section 1.4). Meantime the very existence of Tom within his fiction seems to give the lie at the common sense level to the notion of his own and his parents' non-existence, and so the novel, having established the maternal role of Jenny Jones and causing her to disappear too, concentrates busily on multiplying fathers (Allworthy, Partridge) in dizzying pseudo-proof of the fact that Tom had, and maybe still has, a father even at the very moment that Captain Blifil's tombstone at the end of Book II teases with the fact of paternal death. And are we not in the world of Beckett when we detect the fine threat in the opening lines of the epitaph (II.9)?:

> Here lies
> In Expectation of a joyful Rising,
> The Body of
> Captain JOHN BLIFIL

This threat that dead fathers won't lie down (as they refuse to in

Hamlet) engenders a macabre sense that every 'father' who appears in *Tom Jones* is a ghost, a joyfully prancing Captain Blifil, a sense reinforced by our discovery that Tom has, all along, been searching for a body, or at least for a name to attach to the paternal nobody that has lain buried for some twenty-one years. The Captain's assertion about Tom's bastardy has made sense after all: he is the child 'of no body' because the father is, like Yorick, merely bones, and since Tom never saw him his idea of him can only be ghostly. In the end Tom is, like Hamlet, both somebody and nobody, and his fiction is generated by a stichomythia between these two puzzled aspects of his 'self'.

If you are the child of nobody you have no mother either, and so maternal ghosts haunt the novel, too, telling Tom that his mother is dead and simultaneously inviting him to hear her voice so that her discovery will release him from the other side of the Oedipal bind and become recognised as a husband by Sophia. The obvious maternal ghost is Lady Bellaston (section 1.5, below). Less obviously, and yet equally, ghostly is Jenny Waters, with whom Tom has gone to bed and who, as Jenny Jones, was accused of being Tom's mother at the beginning of the novel. Now, in xviii.7, she becomes the medium through whom the real mother's secret is revealed, and also a ghost. Jenny discloses the true father's identity and the mother's as well, simultaneously dispelling the incest threat and focusing Allworthy, finally, as Tom's most un-Claudius-like uncle, by unburdening herself to Allworthy of 'a Story . . . which I am concerned falls to my Lot to unfold to you'. A page later she urges the attentive and 'aghast' (ghost stricken) Allworthy to 'have Patience . . . and I will unfold to you the whole Story'. She is a ghost by virtue of her parody of Old Hamlet ('lend thy serious hearing/To what I shall unfold'; 'I could a tale unfold whose lightest word/Would harrow up thy soul'), and her ghostliness achieves at once the pushing of the Oedipally taboo mother into the past where she emotionally belongs and the verification of Tom as somebody. For this ghost is fleshly and female and knows 'the great Secret' of Tom's birth, and in revising Old Hamlet's unfolded tale recapitulates the writing of *The History of Tom Jones*, momentarily, from the female viewpoint, thus undoing the power of the fathers.

This revision is fascinating not just in itself but for its consequence. For although it clarifies by placing everyone in correct familial alignment with everyone else (Allworthy as an uncle rather than father, and so forth), the information it conveys turns out to be emotionally unacceptable to Allworthy and, perhaps, to Fielding too, so Allworthy insists on going over the tale yet again, and this time it is he who takes on the tones and phrases of Old Hamlet. Jenny's ghostly voice had established him in the subsidiary role of uncle. Allworthy counters by asserting his Old Hamlet-like grip on Tom's life. This is in xvIII.10, the first meeting between Tom and Allworthy since Tom's banishment in Book VI. No sooner have they greeted each other than Allworthy feels obliged to deliver a sermon that is noticeably indebted to the ghostly Old Hamlet's long speech in I.v:

> You say, however, you have seen your Errors; and will reform them. I firmly believe you, my dear Child; and therefore, from this Moment, you shall never be reminded of them by me. Remember them only yourself so far, as for the future to teach you the better to avoid them; but still remember, for your Comfort, that there is this great Difference between those Faults which Candour may construe into Imprudence, and those which can be deduced from Villainy only. The former, perhaps, are even more apt to subject a Man to Ruin; but if he reform, his Character will, at length, be totally retrieved . . . . But Villainy, my Boy, when once discovered, is irretrievable: the Stains which this leaves behind, no Time will wash away. The Censures of Mankind will pursue the Wretch, their Scorn will abash him in Public; and if Shame drives him into Retirement, he will go to it with all those Terrors with which a weary Child, who is afraid of Hobgoblins, retreats from Company to go to Bed alone. Here his murdered Conscience will haunt him. Repose, like a false Friend, will fly from him. Where-ever he turns his Eyes, Horror presents itself; if he looks backward, unavailable Repentance treads on his Heels; if forward, incurable Despair stares him in the Face; till, like a condemned Prisoner, confined in a Dungeon, he detests his present Condition, and yet dreads the Consequence of that Hour which is to relieve him from it.   xvIII.10

While ostensibly and carefully discriminating Tom from Blifil, Allworthy, who had mysteriously returned to London with Blifil while *Hamlet* was being performed before Tom and Partridge (xvI.6), accuses, blurring Abel and Cain, insisting that Tom *is* somehow Blifil, and he does so in words which recall Old Hamlet's tale of murder, the prison house, the punishment that must be left to heaven while conscience pricks and stings Gertrude on earth, and of remembrance ('Remember me . . . Remember thee?') and villainy (which prompts Hamlet's 'O villain, villain, smiling damned villain . . . '). Allworthy's picture here actually precipitates the solution to the dilemma, however, by enabling Tom to differentiate himself from Blifil. Allworthy, censorious, the demanding patriarch, tries to drag him back into the old ways; Tom pushes forward as he pleads for mercy for the Blifil whom Allworthy, rather practised in this kind of thing, now disowns: 'let me beseech you, Sir . . . to reflect on the dreadful Consequences of driving him to violent and sudden Despair. How unfit, alas! is this poor Man to die in his present situation' (xviii.11). Yet even as Tom pleads, it is as if he is supplicating again for himself before the implacable father, as if the Blifil self exists whenever Allworthy is in evidence. And that, in turn, does not bode well for the end of the novel. Squire Western is tamed (though his presence in the house is probably far less tolerable than we are asked to believe); but what about Allworthy?

> *Allworthy* was likewise greatly liberal to *Jones* on the Marriage, and hath omitted no Instance of shewing his Affection to him and his Lady, who love him as a Father. Whatever in the nature of *Jones* had a Tendency to Vice, has been corrected by continual Conversation with this good Man, and by his Union with the lovely and virtuous *Sophia*.   xviii.13

There is an awfulness here. The patriarch has obviously continued his ghostly sermon well beyond the marriage, resolutely declining silence or unobtrusiveness. With the other fathers under control this one obstinately remains, trying to reduce Tom to a nobody yet again by mortifying his youthful self so that he can become merely the image of Allworthy, the reflection of that image who insists on being his father: 'He hath also, by Reflexion on his past Follies, acquired a Discretion and Prudence very uncommon in one of his lively Parts'.[15]

This is the novel's final statement, and it undermines the comic resolution which has been included in xviii.7 to displace Oedipal guilt over patricide with a statement of the inevitability of paternal death in terms of the seasonal cycle. Tom's real father was named Summer, and, says Jenny to Allworthy:

that Mr. *Summer*, the son of your Friend, educated at your Expence, who, after living a Year in the House as if he had been your own Son, died there of the small Pox, was tenderly lamented by you, and buried as if he had been your own; that *Summer*, Sir, was the Father of this child.

As she recounts these details Jenny's narrative takes on the hypnotic rhythms of a litany: Summer, son, friend, living, son, died, lamented, buried, Summer, father, child. At the wintry end of *Hamlet*, Horatio becomes a midwife to 'deliver' an epitome 'of carnal, bloody, and unnatural acts, / Of accidental judgments, carnal slaughters, / Of deaths put on by the cunning and forc'd cause' (v.ii.386–8). *Tom Jones* tries to end with the delivery of the secret of an old birth and with an infant girl and boy (Tom's and Sophia's children) in accordance with the comic secret known within Hamlet's black world to the gravedigger, who sings about youth and love while he digs up old bones in order to create yet another grave from which, as he understands it, life will spring. *Tom Jones* tries, but it does not succeed. The icy clutch of the ghostly fathers remains rather too strong.

1.2 FATHER TIME

> *Hamlet*: Why, e'en so, and now my Lady Worm's, chopless, and knocked about the mazard with a sexton's spade. Here's fine revolution and we had the trick to see't.
>
> (*Hamlet*, v.i)

Tom's greatest riddle has to do with knowing the self in relation to various shadow fathers and mothers produced by the flickering lights of his unconscious mind. Fielding's game is to let that unconscious apparently run free, to see what it will engender given the liberating fact that Tom is a foundling. Authorial games are directed by the teleology of their perpetrator's own unconscious, though, as Oedipus is by Apollo's prophecy; so that the liberating fantasy turns out to be anything but liberating as Fielding's preoccupation with paternal treachery and abandonment produces a fictional world dominated, like Hamlet's, by paternal death. Captain Blifil dies; Allworthy nearly dies; Summer is dead. And very shortly after Tom has been expelled by Allworthy he meets a father who is one of the living dead. This is the Man of the Hill who, since Tom encounters him in what is explicitly the Book of Ghosts, is Tom's first major equivalent to Old Hamlet's ghost.

Book VIII is the Book of Ghosts because of its opening chapter, 'A wonderful long Chapter concerning the Marvellous', which tells us, as we have seen, that 'the only supernatural Agents which can in any Manner be allowed to us Moderns are Ghosts'; because of Partridge's superstitions about 'Ghosts, Devils, [and] Witches' (viii.10); and because of his ghost story in viii.11. The book's narrative opens with the expatriate Tom, recovering from being belaboured over the head with a bottle by Ensign Northerton, being attended by the barber, Benjamin, who turns out to be his supposed father, Partridge. But Partridge knows he is not Tom's father and 'absolve[s] [him] from all filial Duty' (viii.6) while simultaneously inflicting another father, in the shape of Allworthy, on him (viii.7). As Tom loses one father he gains another because, it seems, male human nature abhors a paternal vacuum. The problem is that Allworthy has just nearly died and, in a kind of mock fulfilment of Captain Bilfil's threat from the tombstone, joyfully risen again. That rising has led to the deeply puzzled Tom's accusation and expulsion as a 'Reprobate' (vi.11) — an outcast, somebody sundered (once more) from the parental body and name. More than that, Latin *reprobus* also means *spurious*; a charge which again leaves Tom a placeless nobody. The risen father who has disavowed Tom is now insisted on by Partridge as being the biological father. Conflicting thoughts and fantasies about paternal death lead, first, to the emergence of the political theme into the novel (Jacobites versus Hanoverians, father kings and pretenders versus elective monarchs) and, second, to the Man of the Hill, another 'dead father' who comes, ghostlike, to speak to Tom of Oedipal hatred, misogyny, and kings.

Just over half way through the Book of Ghosts, then, Partridge and Tom find themselves, at night, 'at the Bottom of a very steep Hill' (viii.10). Tom insists on going to the top and Partridge determines to accompany him, for 'his chief Fear was that of Ghosts, with which the present Time of Night, and the Wildness of the Place, extremely well suited'. The Man of the Hill soon appears in the narrative, but only after further omens in the form of an allusion to Thomas Otway's tragedy *The Orphan*; a potted biography in which the Man is made to seem like a ghost (he 'seldom walks out but by Night, for he doth not care to be seen . . . I have lived with him above these thirty Years, and in all that Time he hath hardly spoke to six living People'); and his rescue from robbers by Tom, ominous because of its half-echo of Oedipus's murder of his father, reputedly killed by robbers.[16]

At this point the Old Man is described:

> *Partridge* no sooner saw the Gentleman, than the Strangeness of his Dress infused greater Terrors into that poor Fellow, than he had before felt either from the strange Description which he had heard, or from the Uproar which had happened at the Door.
>
> To say the Truth, it was an Appearance which might have affected a more constant Mind that that of Mr. *Partridge*. This Person was of the tallest Size, with a long Beard as white as Snow. His Body was clothed with the Skin of an Ass, made something into the Form of a Coat. He wore likewise Boots on his Legs, and a Cap on his Head, both composed of the Skin of some other Animals.

On one level he is a wild man modulated into the type of the stoic contemplative.[17] At a more profound level he is Allworthy understood as the usurping murderer Claudius at the moment when Hamlet perceives him as the 'king of shreds and patches' (III.iv.103). Tom's fantasy has conjured up a paternal ghost, like that of Old Hamlet, that is encountered 'in the dead waste and middle of the night' (I.ii.198–200), then, because of his unjustified accusation and expulsion by Allworthy, has proceeded to identify it with its dark double. Uncle Allworthy, kind and nurturing then brutally punitive, becomes Uncle Claudius.

There is one other curious detail which seems to reinforce the Man's tale's deep centrality to Tom's fatherless history. It is, that the Man lives on Mazard Hill. A mazard is a skull, and Tom's skull has been reputedly cracked by Northerton towards the end of Book VII. A doctor has pronounced him to be in great danger (VIII.3) but Partridge, as barber surgeon, has made his entry into Tom's history in order to give a second opinion. He says: 'when I see into your Skull, I will give my Opinion of your Case' (VIII.6). Partridge touches the living skull; the Old Man lives on the secular Golgotha of Skull Hill. It is as if Partridge, once thought of as Tom's father and disinherited by his own father (VIII.4), has helped activate the Old Man out of Tom's broodings on his reprobate status. And in doing so he becomes, fleetingly, a strangely haunted Hamlet to Tom's Yorick, anticipating the moment when, at the performance of *Hamlet*, he will cry out, as '*Hamlet* tak[es] up the Skull [of Yorick] . . . "Well, it is strange to see how fearless some Men are: I never could bring myself to touch any thing belonging to a dead Man on any Account. — He seemed frightned enough too at the Ghost, I thought"'. Hamlet's holding of the skull sets off a train of memories of childhood and paternal death; Partridge's handling of Tom's skull seems to awaken similar but even more painful memories.

The Man is, then, a complicated phenomenon and his hill is the gigantic black projection, in the numerical centre of the novel,[18] of Tom's own mazard as it responds to having been battered by Allworthy's nearly fatal illness and his own subsequent banishment from the paternal domain. Not surprisingly the Man's tale, however simple its structure, is complex in its implications.

Main clues to the significance of the tale lie in the Man's jealousy of his elder brother because he had all the mother's affection ('my Mother . . . never loved me'), and his guilt over stealing from a friend and thus grieving 'one of the best of Fathers'. The enmity towards the elder brother is clearly Oedipal and relates back within the novel to the enmity between Tom and Blifil.[19] The Man's tale unfolds in a familiarly riddling and self-referential way: he succumbs while at Oxford to a companion with the Blifil-like 'diabolical' passion for 'destroying and ruining the Youth of inferior Fortune'. Deeply in debt he thinks of self-annihilation, of becoming the nobody he believes he is in his mother's eyes ('Self-murder itself became the Subject of my serious Deliberation') and then steals from his friend (another brother surrogate) by unlocking his escritoire. He is subsequently gaoled and 'removed by *Habeas Corpus* to *Oxford*' but released when no witnesses appear against him.

We have met *habeas corpus* earlier in the novel in connection with Northerton's supposed murder of Tom at the end of Book VII, and there the allusion to it was phrased in such a way as to evoke even earlier jokes about paternal bodies and no-bodies ('The first Thing done, was securing the Body of *Northerton*' (vii.12); 'But whether *Northerton* was carried away in Thunder or Fire, or in whatever other Manner he was gone; it was now certain, that his Body was no longer in Custody' (vii.14)). The phrase catches Partridge's imagination now and engenders a ghost story within the Man's story that takes us back, symbolically at least, to Hamlet's father again as he comments, in connection with the lack of witnesses, that perhaps the Man's friend forebore prosecution because he 'did not care to have [his] Blood upon his Hands, and he was in the right on't. If any Person was to be hanged upon my Evidence I should never be able to lie alone afterwards for Fear of seeing his Ghost'. We think of *Hamlet*, particularly since the play has been mentioned in VIII.1 in connection with Fisher's murder of Mr Derby, and we continue to think of *Hamlet* as Partridge tells his tale of Frank who was responsible for the conviction of a horse thief. Frank was 'had up for a Witness' and the thief was found guilty and hanged. As a result Frank 'never was in the dark alone, but he fancied he saw the Fellow's Spirit' and his fears were confirmed one night after his drunken nocturnal skirmish with a calf.

Tom laughs and even 'the Stranger' smiles, but Partridge, who knows what is inside skulls obsessed with fathers, is indignant. Frank, the supposed 'free one', has, after all, been responsible for a death and feels himself, however unjustly, implicated in guilt.[20] We sense almost subliminal echoes of Tom's dilemma (supposedly free as a foundling but in fact embroiled in dark fantasies about dead, absent parents) and the echoes are reinforced by a legal phrase which Partridge pauses over. After the thief was committed to prison the Justice 'bound *Frank* in a Recognizance, I think they call it, a hard Word compounded of *re* and *cognosco*; but it differs in its Meaning from the Use of the Simple, as many other Compounds do'. If *habeas corpus* recalls the quest for bodies, then *recognizance*, legally 'an obligation to act', means at root *to know again*, *re-cognition*, and the *re-cognition* that *Tom Jones* is so obsessed with is of course paternal re-cognition.[21] Not surprisingly, then, the Man's story soon comes up with just such a re-cognition. Tom had rescued him from thieves; way back in the past this ghostly father had rescued his own father from thieves. The Man narrates how the rescued man, still apparently a stranger:

> having had his Eyes for some time stedfastly on me, . . . threw himself back in his Chair, crying, O my Son! my Son! and then fainted away.
> Many of the People present imagined this Accident had happened through his Loss of Blood; but I, who at the same Time began to recollect the Features of my Father, was now confirmed in my Suspicion, and satisfied that it was he himself who appeared before me. I presently ran to him, raised him in my

Arms, and kissed his cold Lips with the utmost Eagerness. Here I must draw a Curtain over a Scene which I cannot describe: For though I did not lose my Being, as my Father for a while did, my Senses were however as overpowered with Affright and Surprize, that I am a Stranger to what past during some Minutes, and indeed till my Father again recovered from his Swoon, and I found myself in his Arms, both tenderly embracing each other, while the Tears trickled a-pace down the Cheeks of each of us.

VIII.13

In this rescue there is an almost overt paternal death wish, the kind of thing that, in a fiction, is often handled through the distancing device of a tale within a tale, and in life through a dream. 'Affright' suggests an unwelcome apparition, and the periphrasis for the swoon, 'I am a Stranger to what past', suggests a disowning of the father and that a consequence of that disowning is that the Man himself will be for ever an outcast, a reprobate (the narrative insists, whenever he speaks, that the Man is called 'the Stranger'). Finally, when the son runs to the father 'and raise[s] him in [his] Arms', this filial resurrection is undercut by the curiously necrophiliac 'and kissed his cold Lips with the utmost Eagerness'. They are cold because he has fainted (surface meaning); he kisses them so eagerly because they are cold with the chill of death (unconscious meaning).

Interwoven through all this is the Man's attitude to women. Rejected by his mother, betrayed by his 'female Companion' after the burglary he performed at Oxford, he hates all women and refuses to listen to his father's suggestion that he should 'think of Marriage' now that his mother is dead and he has returned to live at his father's house. (His former gaming companion Watson tries to keep him in London with a timely but unheeded warning: he 'dissuaded me from burying myself, as he called it, out of a simple Compliance with the fond Desires of a foolish old Fellow' (VIII.13)).[22] After four years the father dies and is replaced by the hated elder brother who, as a passionate huntsman, is presumably to be seen as a type of the tyrannical Nimrod.[22]

Life now becomes intolerable and the Man leaves for Bath to take the waters, for 'my violent affliction, added to a sedentary Life, had thrown me into a kind of paralytic Disorder'. He has, in effect, died with the father, but revives with the aid of water and Watson, for on his second day in Bath he is seated by the river under some willows when:

> I heard a Person on the other Side the Willows, sighing and bemoaning himself bitterly. On a sudden, having uttered a most impious Oath, he cried, 'I am resolved to bear it no longer,' and directly threw himself into the Water. ... An Angler ... immediately came up, and both of us together, not without some Hazard of our Lives, drew the Body to the Shore.

This male Ophelia is alive and turns out to be Watson, the agent of the Man's resurrection from his disorder. But just at the point where we suspect that he has risen only to descend into the same mustily claustrophobic and repetitively self-involved gyrations that he has already performed before us, the narrative changes direction. News of Monmouth's Protestant rebellion against Catholic James II means that family politics now become national politics (VIII.14). The Man and Watson join the rebel forces, and after Monmouth's defeat at Sedgemoor the Man is betrayed by his friend to the king's forces but escapes, at length arriving at the solitary place where he now lives:

> The first Person with whom I took up my Habitation was the Mother of this old Woman, with whom I remained concealed, till the News of the glorious Revolution put an End to all my Apprehensions of Danger, and gave me an Opportunity of once more visiting my own Home . . . . [My brother] was selfish and ungenerous. I could not look upon him as my Friend, nor indeed did he desire that I should; so I presently took my Leave of him, as well as of my other Acquaintance; and from that Day to this my History is little better than a Blank.

The Man, born in 1657, is now himself 88, for it is 1745 and Bonnie Prince Charlie's forces are on the march and Tom has joined the King's troops against them. He is frozen in time like Miss Havisham, his life a perpetual brooding over 1688, the year of the Glorious Revolution which ousted James and enthroned the constitutional Protestant William III in his place. Politically, he appears to be on what Tom regards as the correct side, which is strange given the revealingly black psychology of his tale. How, then, are his politics and psychology to be reconciled?

The answer is that he sides against the patriarchal James in continuation of his Oedipal struggle with his father. With his own father dead and his hated brother in his place he strikes out against the father king by championing an outsider, James's brother's bastard son, James, Duke of Monmouth, as an ultimate assertion of his contempt for father, patriarchal rules of heredity, and the validity of patriarchally aligned genealogical tables. The rebellion fails and the man lies low for three years while the father king rules the motherland again. He emerges from hiding late in 1688 with the flight of that king to France, and yet his subsequent life is nothing but solitude and morose withdrawal — in his own words, 'a Blank'. This death-in-life, which Tom discovers him still perpetuating, is an elaborate version of the 'paralytic Disorder' he suffered after his father's death and brother's succession to the paternal home. I have just said that the paralysis suggests that he dies with the father. Another interpretation might be that his brother's rise to power in the family hierarchy confirms the Man's sense of unworthiness, his feeling that he is a nobody, so that he literally invalidates himself by paralysis. The anti father-king rebellion of 1685 had stirred him to life again as Watson (who encourages him to reject the paternal values) did in Bath, but it fails and he becomes static once more, now hiding with a woman whom he can think of only as a mother: 'The first Person with whom I took up my Habitation was the Mother of this old Woman' (viii.14). When the Revolution comes he attains a state of armistice with the brother and yet withdraws into his black and ghostly night because even this Revolution perpetuated a king, and kings, in the Old Man's crazed mind, must always be fathers and therefore guilt-inducing and intolerable. He now approximates to Partridge's Frank, once apparently a free spirit until 'bound in a Recognizance' and subsequent superstition and guilt. Frank fears retributive ghosts and murders a calf; the Man fears humanity and battles with the memory of the father and mother who reduced him to a haunted and haunting wreck.

The murderous depths of the Man's battle with the parents can be reconstructed from a passage at the end of Book VIII. His tale has been concluded because it is dawn and ghosts must disappear when they 'scent the morning air' (*Hamlet*, i.v.58). In a final exchange Tom reproves the Man for his misanthropy and misogyny and the Man replies:

'My first Mistress and my first Friend, betrayed me in the basest

Manner, and in Matters which threatened to be of the worst of Consequences, even to bring me to a shameful Death.'

'But you will pardon me,' cries *Jones*, 'if I desire you to reflect who this Mistress, and who that Friend was. What better, my good Sir, could be expected in Love derived from the Stews, or in Friendship first produced and nourished at the Gaming-Table! To take the Characters of Women from the former Instance, or of Men from the latter, would be as unjust as to assert, that Air is a nauseous and unwholesome Element, because we find it so in a Jakes. I have lived but a short Time in the World, and yet have known Men worthy of the highest Friendship, and Women of the highest Love.'

Tom perceives for a moment with wonderful clarity exactly where the Man's problems lie, but the Man cannot listen because to him all men are the primally treacherous father and all women the primally treacherous mother. '*First* Mistress' and '*first* Friend' are substitutes for the parental pair who have set off in the Man's cracked mazard vision after vision of male traitors coupled with whorish females while he lives under the Oedipally maternal care (we recall the relevant passage from *The Orphan*) of the aged daughter of the woman with whom he first took lodging.

And so, speaking in the darkness, the Man is a ghost. Or is his long nocturnal tale perhaps a dream in which truths have emerged that are to be submerged or half-forgotten by the light of day? Certainly, Tom will not hear nor see so clearly for a very long time. Yet the quality of the reader's perception of the tale is even more dreamlike than Tom's because we are privy to a clue that is unavailable to him. This is the mention of *Hamlet* in Book VIII's preliminary chapter on ghosts. From 'that memorable story of the Ghost of *George Villers*' in Clarendon's *History of the Rebellion*[23] we move swiftly to 'the History of *Fisher*' as an instance of human depravity. In 'order to possess himself of what remained in' the escritoire of his friend and benefactor Mr Derby, Fisher concealed himself and then:

came suddenly from his lurking Place, and walking softly behind his Friend into his Chamber, discharged a Pistol Ball into his Head. This may be believed, when the Bones of *Fisher* are as rotten as his Heart. Nay, perhaps, it will be credited that the Villain went two Days afterwards with some young Ladies to the

Play of *Hamlet*; and with an unaltered Countenance heard one of the Ladies, who little suspected how near she was to the Person, cry out, Good God! if the Man that murdered Mr. *Derby* was now present! Manifesting in this a more seared and callous Conscience than even *Nero* himself; of whom we are told by *Suetonius*, 'that the Consciousness of his Guilt after the Death of his Mother became immediately intolerable, and so continued; nor could all the Congratulations of the Soldiers, of the Senate, and the People, allay the Horrors of his Conscience.'

Nero slept with his mother, murdered her, and was tormented by her image, as Hamlet remembers on his way to his mother's room (III.ii.384–5), and as Fielding reveals here in a passage which seems to be the most striking instance in *Tom Jones* of the parallel between dream-work and the 'work' of the creating literary mind. Nero, already mentioned a couple of paragraphs earlier, reappears as a kind of double of Fisher, and the intervening mention of *Hamlet* suggests an Oedipal reading of this whole section — that the male is separable into matricidal (Nero) and patricidal selves (Fisher) because the murder of Derby is parallel to Nero's murder of Agrippina.

But what we as readers are privileged to know, that Tom does not as he endures the Man's long tale, is that the Man of the Hill's crime of stealing from his friend's escritoire (VIII.11) is Fisher's crime. Dream-work logic would indicate that the violated friend is a substitute for the father and/or hated elder brother and that the Man is both Fisher and Nero in his emotional relationship with father and mother.

It comes as a shock, though, to discover (or rediscover) the games dream-work and the work of fiction play with fact. For the Derby murder actually took place some twenty years before the composition of *Tom Jones*, on 10 April 1727, and Fielding knew of it, presumably from his friend Richard Willoughby who was Fisher's landlord in London at the time of the murder and the key witness at his trial.[24] Now this Richard Willoughby is the 'Justice *Willoughby* of *Noyle*' before whome the horse thief is carried in Partridge's ghost story in VIII.11 and who 'bound *Frank* in a Recognizance': the binding that released guilt and a ghost that, via the Man's tale and the preliminary chapter to Book VIII, have their origin in Fisher and Nero and *Hamlet*. The terrible question arises, has Fielding revealed to the light of day and the scrutiny of the critic the origin of the guilt within himself? He hated his father overtly after his mother's death and at a crucially formative period in his life. Does the dream world of Book VIII play its familiar game with names and initials and let slip the dreadful possibility that the authorial unconscious has determined an identification of the murdering lawyer H F (Henry Fisher) with that lawyer-turned-novelist H F (Henry Fielding)?

At any rate, that paternal ghost the Man of the Hill unfolds a hair-raising tale from the depths of his dark prison house. As he stands outside time his voice reaches back to the beginning of Oedipal history, telling of the perpetual battle between fathers and sons and of the agonised filial battle against being a nobody and a blank.

1.3 RULING FATHERS

Marcellus: Is it not like the King?

(*Hamlet*, 1.i)

Perhaps Fielding did not know that the murderer Fisher was jestingly reputed to have been one of the Young Pretender's followers in the '45.[25] Even so, the joke is a remarkably apposite one for this phase of our reading of *Tom Jones* since it links private and public, father hatred and the father king, in much the same way as Fielding does in the novel. For when the Man of the Hill's 'Discourse' with Watson becomes political, the politics merely extend his quarrel with his father and brother. As we have seen, he can make one rebellious gesture against the Catholic *pater patriae* but he appears to be inhibited from actually supporting his elected successor William III. William's accession is marked by the Man's final break with his brother and his life-long decision to live in the wilderness with a maternal keeper. However bloodless, the 1688 Revolution re-enacts in the Man's mind the crime of king-and-father killing. It confirms the Man in his Oedipal guilt (hence the maternal keeper) while leaving him subject, intolerably, to a surrogate king-father.

What the Man also does is to offer us the rudiments of a psychology of Jacobitism. For although he has pathologically forced his own history into a 'blank', failing to fight against the Jacobites in 1715 and indeed never even having heard that there was a rebellion then (VIII.14), he voices vehement anti-Stuart feelings which are vital to our reading of the novel. Significantly, this part of the Man's ruminations constitutes the most heavily revised section of *Tom Jones*: an infallible sign of Fielding's interest and maybe even of his anxiety. As the Man speaks against the father-king he also attacks his father.

In the first edition the Man merely directs attention to James II's Catholicism and his absolutist denial of liberty: 'how little he valued either his Royal Word, or Coronation-Oath, or the Liberties and Rights of his People. But all had not the Sense to foresee this at first; and therefore the Duke of *Monmouth* was weakly supported' (VIII.14). This is strangely muted, almost as if, when confronted with enunciating objections to the father-king, the voice falters and stumbles over the treacherous, lumpen, words.

The revisions for the third edition of a few months later expand the attack on James. The voice is not that of the Fielding of *The True Patriot* and *The Jacobite's Journal* addressing those readers who may already, in the brief intervening years between 1745 and late 1749, have found their own memories becoming blank in respect of the treacheries of the Stuart fathers. Or is it the voice of a Fielding who, for some reason we shall never know, found himself at the mercy of his unconscious, and bitterly, irrepressibly, angry again over the treachery of his own father and the Catholic stepmother he forced upon him, and decided to let that voice rasp and rip in the Man's Oedipal tale?

Anyway, what we now hear is a thunderingly anti-Catholic voice that is also, unlike the voice of the first edition, insistently anti-papal.[26] The couple of references to popery or papists in the first edition are now multiplied and rendered infinitely more vehement: James 'declared War against the Protestant Cause. He had brought known Papists into the Army . . . . Popish Priests swarmed thro' the Nation . . . . Our own Clergy were forbid to preach against Popery', and so on. The political problem enshrined in the references to the Pope predates the reformation, of course, and it is the problem of temporal allegiance: Pope or sovereign? But is not the embittered voice of the Old Man, now an authorial dummy, ghosted by that of a bemused son? Papa is both Pope and Daddy, the gigantic father hated and feared by Protestants. As Fielding's anger rises, though, so too does our awareness of his anxiety over the emotional pull to the father-king and the papal father. The context of this anti-Jacobite rhetoric within the Man's tale suggests that Fielding locates Jacobitism as the province of the psychologically regressed, those who have not developed a right relationship with their parents. He knows that 'the Tyranny of the Pope . . . was abolished by *Henry* the Eighth' and therefore that what those who espoused the '45 were expressing was a collective Oedipal death wish. But what he also knows is how strong that wish is in himself, with what incredible difficulty his Hanoverian stance, his active espousal of elective monarchy (the opposite of the Man's withdrawal into solitude and silence under William) were won from the blinding emotions of father hatred on the one hand and father love, the desire for complete annihilation into the person of the father, on the other.

The revisions inevitably introduce God, the last resort of a patriarchal male trying to accommodate this searing complex of emotions: 'as our Duty to the King can never be called more than our second Duty, he had discharged us from this, by making it incompatible with our preserving the first, which is surely to Heaven'. Thus one can break with the father but not break with the Father; and this leaves Fielding free, through the Man, to label the father a tyrant and, in doing so, release the full venom of father-hatred: James 'declared himself, in fact, as absolute as any Tyrant ever was or can be'.

The label *tyrant* has a long and anguishing history, telling of bonds recognised and repudiated, of hatred and the crying need to be free. In Fielding's own history this passage from *The Jacobite's Journal* reveals, almost, all:

> Can the most rank Jacobite be stupid enough to flatter himself, that the Freeborn People of *England*, remarkable above any other Nation for good Sense and Love of Liberty, will ever be brought to swallow that monstrous Absurdity, so repugnant to the Common Sense of Mankind, so derogatory to the native Freedom of Human Creatures, so opposite to all the Principles of our Constitution, and so contrary to the express Declaration of Holy Writ —*That Kings are by Divine Appointment, and consequently their Title indefeasible.* If they are so, let them produce their Charter, and at least condescend to tell us the Marks, by which we may discover the Real from the Counterfeit. If they cannot do this, let them be assured that, in the mean time, as we were born free, we will maintain our Liberty . . . . We will entertain more honourable Conceptions of that Eternal Being, the supremely merciful God, than ever to let that become an Article of our Belief;

the very Mention of which fills us with Horror, — That the greatest Tyrants that ever plagued Mankind, in all their horrible Impieties, in all their excessive Cruelties, in all their foul Murders, in all their abominable Lusts, in all their monstrous Villainies, in all their general Devastations, in every Act of publick Oppression, or private Injustice, — acted by Divine Appointment, — A most daring and impious Assertion. – Let the Jacobites duly consider of it, and they will be filled with Confusion at its Blasphemy. For to what doth this blasphemous Assertion amount to less, than that the supreme all-merciful God hath given a Divine and Indefeasible Right to Kings to murder out of Wantonness their own Subjects . . . .[27]

As the passage continues, and as we brood over *Tom Jones*, it seems less and less clear that 'we [are] born free'. For the father tyrant is the parental father waiting to kill us before we kill him, historically alive for generation after generation, dominating our mental life even as we repudiate him. Nero receives a fair amount of space in this section of this number of the *Journal* as he does in *Tom Jones*, VIII.1 where, we have seen, he is linked with Fisher and *Hamlet* and, eventually, with the Old Man of the Hill himself. Fielding can never in the end, it seems, make Milton's wonderfully simple, knot-cutting, distinction: 'Fathers and kings are very different things: Our fathers begot us, but our kings did not', and so his attacks on Jacobites and tyrants are expressions of his constant battle with the dark father within.[28] His support for the Hanoverian father marks a considerable victory for reason over mystery and all the instinctual and emotional forces that signify or induce regression; but the text of *Tom Jones* shows just how emotionally limited that support was.

Thus, Tom can speak authoritatively for the Hanoverian author in VIII.9 when he rejects Partridge's credulous reporting of the opinions of a Catholic priest and of the prophecies and omens relating to the outcome of the '45:

'With what Stuff and Nonsense has thou filled thy Head?' answered *Jones*. 'This too, I suppose, comes from the popish Priest. Monsters and Prodigies are the proper Arguments to support monstrous and absurd Doctrines. The Cause of King *George* is the Cause of Liberty and true Religion. In other Words, it is the Cause of common Sense, my Boy . . .'.

Protestant libertarianism's luminous 'common Sense' displays the counterfeits for the pretenders they are – just for a moment. After all, the Old Man is about to appear and to confuse things dreadfully, and the sacred force of the pull of the dark places will be felt even more strongly in Book XII when Tom and Partridge encounter the gypsies. There, in xii.12, we will see that the Fielding who can tease Partridge for his belief in ghosts and witches and can state with brilliant succinctness the perception that Stuarts and Stuart lovers have a tradition of Nero-like misogyny starting with James I, will also succumb with quiet awe to the epiphanic mystery of the absolutist gypsy king.

Like the Man of the Hill, the gypsy king is encountered at night. The weather is foul and Partridge feels himself 'bewitched' as he sees lights and hears music amid 'such Darkness [as] was never seen upon Earth'. He obviously suspects that he has stumbled upon some terrifying *Walpurgisnacht* ritual: 'They can be nothing but Ghosts or Witches, or some Evil Spirit or other, that's certain'. But Partridge, intuitively right about the ghostly mustiness of the Man of the Hill, is wrong this time. The lights and noise are coming from a barn, and when he and Tom enter, Tom is approached by a patriarch as different as can be from the Man of the Book of Ghosts:

> a venerable Person approached him with many friendly Salutations, rather of too hearty a Kind to be called courtly. This was no other than the King of the *Gypsies* himself. He was very little distinguished in dress from his Subjects, nor had he any *Regalia* of Majesty to support his Dignity; and yet there seemed (as Mr. *Jones* said) to be somewhat in his Air which denoted Authority, and inspired the Beholders with an Idea of Awe and Respect xii.12

One critic has convincingly detected a double for Fielding the author here.[29] For the moment, and remaining with the novel's politics, we concentrate on the way Hanoverian (Fielding-Tom) is drawn to the king even while disclaiming by admitting the possibility of delusion: 'tho' all this was perhaps imaginary in *Jones*, and the Truth may be, that such Ideas are incident to Power, and almost inseparable from it'. (Fielding deliberately slides away from the problem by reporting Tom after the event. What we need to know is if this was his reaction at the time of meeting the 'venerable Person' before he knew his position in the gypsy hierarchy.)

There is, however, no delusion. The king is recognisable as a king and, moreover, as a gypsy (Egyptian) he is at the end of a long line of benevolent absolutists. So attractive is this example of absolutism devoid of its regalia of mystification and the obligation to be tyrannical that Fielding is moved, *in propria persona*, to celebrate the advantages of absolute monarchical power:

> no limited Form of Government is capable of rising to the same Degree of Perfection, or of producing the same Benefits to Society with this. Mankind have never been so happy, as when the greatest Part of the then known World was under the Dominion of a single Master; and this State of their Felicity continued during the Reigns of five successive Princes. This was the true Æra of the Golden Age, and the only Golden Age which ever had any Existence, unless in the warm Imaginations of the Poets, from the Expulsion from *Eden* down to this Day.

Common sense, however, restores Fielding to the right party by raising a fundamental difficulty:

> In reality, I know but of one solid objection to absolute Monarchy. The only Defect in which excellent Constitution seems to be the Difficulty of finding any Man adequate to the Office of absolute Monarch: For this indispensably requires three Qualities very difficult, as it appears from History, to be found in princely Natures [Moderation, Wisdom, Goodness].
> Now if an absolute Monarch with all these great and rare Qualifications should be allowed capable of conferring the greatest Good on Society, it must surely be granted, on the Contrary, that absolute Power vested in the Hands of one who is deficient in them all, is likely to be attended with no less a Degree of Evil. . . . If . . . the several Tyrannies upon Earth can prove any Title to a divine Authority, it must be derived from this original Grant to the Prince of Darkness . . . .

The forces seem to be drawn: liberty derives from the father-God; oppression, the concomitant of monarchical absolutism, derives from the rebel against the divine Father. Yet the wistful paragraph about the Golden Age which, Fielding says, is 'a Concession, which would not perhaps have been expected from us', reveals a pull towards the Jacobite, if not the Satanic, 'Prince of Darkness'. For the gypsy king is supremely attractive and seducing; and Egyptians, as the founders of absolute monarchy, were associated at the time with the Stuart cause.[30] Specifically, the Copts, to whom the gypsy king alludes, were regarded in post-Revolutionary satire as remote ancestors of the Jacobites. To be drawn to an Egyptian king is to be drawn to the Stuarts, then, and this epiphany reveals what the world could be like if it were governed by a good, wise, generous and hospitable father-king. The tug of common sense is crucial, too, of course, turning this Egyptian chapter into a kind of primal scene, a peeping into the monarchical past to see what was, and how the ghosts of the past still insist on shaping our present. His Egyptian majesty is an archaic form who must be returned to his slumbers. The problem, Fielding suggests, is that he slumbers within each of us even the most hardened Hanoverian propagandist.

The pull of the commitment to the defeated Jacobite patriarch is suggested also by a Virgilian allusion that turns Tom into Aeneas:

> *Æneas* is not described under more Consternation
> in the Temple of *Juno*,
>   *Dum stupet obtutuque; hæret defixus in uno.*
> than was our Heroe at what he saw in this Barn.

The allusion is to *Aeneid*, 1.495, Aeneas 'rapt and intent in concentration' as he gazes at the tableaux of the Trojan war in Carthage's Temple of Juno. Fielding makes a nervous joke (Aeneas is approached by the beautiful Dido, Tom by a gruffer male monarch) which cannot, even if it were intended to, blind us to the emotional depths of the primal paternal scene the line conjures up. For this is what Aeneas sees:

> Agamemnon and Menelaus were there, and Priam; there, too, was Achilles, merciless alike to all three. Aeneas stood still, the tears came, and he said: 'O Achates, where in the world is there a country, or any place in it, unreached by our suffering? Look; there is Priam. Even here high merit has its due; there is pity for a world's distress, and a sympathy for short-lived humanity. Dispel all fear. The knowledge of you shown here will help to save you.' So he spoke. It was only a picture, but sighing deeply he let his thoughts feed on it, and his face was wet with a stream of tears .... Achilles was shown again, this time selling back for gold Hector's lifeless body which he had dragged behind his chariot three times round the walls of Ilium. At that last sight of his

friend, a lifeless body despoiled of arms, and of the chariot, and Priam holding forth weaponless hands in entreaty, Aeneas sighed a deep and terrible sigh . . . .

As Aeneas the Dardan looked in wonder at these pictures of Troy, rapt and intent in concentration, for he had eyes only for them, the queen herself, Dido, . . . walked to the temple in state . . . .[31]

Aeneas confides his thoughts to Achates; Tom keeps his to himself because his Achates, Partridge, has gone off to 'stuff himself with . . . Food', sensing, perhaps, that he has not Latin enough to share this profound moment. For Hanoverian and father-questing Tom now communes with the spirit of old Priam himself in the shape of the 'venerable' gypsy king and in doing so produces an allusive complex that is startling in its ramifications, because if the gypsy king and his people opened up a historical and psychological primal scene, the *Aeneid* line releases a primal historical scene, too, that in turn releases a textual primal scene of immense significance — that of the Player's speech in *Hamlet* recounting the murder of archetypal 'grandsire Priam' by Achilles' son, Pyrrhus:

> Unequal match'd
> Pyrrhus at Priam drives, in rage strikes wide;
> But with the whiff and wind of his fell sword
> Th'unnerv'd father falls. Then senseless Ilium,
> Seeming to feel this blow, with flaming top
> Stoops to his base, and with a hideous crash
> Takes prisoner Pyrrhus' ear. For lo, his sword,
> Which was declining on the milky head
> Of reverend Priam, seemed i'th'air to stick;
> So, as a painted tyrant, Pyrrhus stood,
> And, like a neutral to his will and matter,
> Did nothing.
>
> (*Hamlet*, ii.ii.467–78)

Hamlet silently reproached the parricide Fisher; Partridge will have to have 'the Play, which *Hamlet* introduces before the King', explained to him by Tom (xvi.5); Tom, surely, is, at this moment, only too aware of the labyrinth his Aeneas pose and the Priam allusion have led him into. For he is not merely a weeping Aeneas, nor a stage-managing Hamlet. As the 'venerable' king approaches, embodiment of a benevolent absolutism that belongs irretrievably to the past, he is Priam. And because 'common Sense' dictates that Tom must reject all that this king stands for, Tom has to become Pyrrhus.

The encounter with the gypsy king is central because, among so many other things, it touches on the essential sadness of the battle of the generations — the fact that old men have to die for, or at the hands of, the young. As he pauses in xii.12 with the gypsy king Tom, for that space, does 'nothing', like the Player's Pyrrhus. Then (opening of chapter 13) he rushes from him at great speed, 'travell[ing] Post', Tom's more humane, but equally denying, equivalent of Pyrrhus' descending regicidal sword. He pauses with, and then flees from, this all-too-narcotic paternal shade because in the end he is too close to Tom's imagined father, whose pull, if he yields to it, means his own annihilation. The Virgilian original upon which the Player's speech is based makes this clear:[32]

> [Pyrrhus] dragged Priam, quaking and sliding in a pool of his own son's blood, right up to the altar. He twined his left hand in Priam's hair. With his right hand he raised his flashing sword, and buried it to the hilt in his side. Priam's destiny ended here . . . . His tall body was left lying headless on the shore, and by it the head hacked from his shoulders: a corpse without a name.
> Then for the first time a wild horror gripped me. When I saw King Priam breathing out his life with that ghastly wound, I pictured to myself my own dear father, for both were of an age. . .
> (*Aeneid*, ii.550–62)

This is Aeneas speaking of Priam, whose image at the moment of his horrible death reminds Aeneas of his own aged father, Anchises; and it is the memory of this scene that makes Aeneas weep so profoundly as he stands in the Temple of Juno, 'rapt and intent'. The line from *Aeneid*, i, that heralds the gypsy king's arrival conjures Priam up as a ghost, then, for he is an image of Tom's ideal father. Like that dark father, the Man of the Hill, he is unnamed in the narrative. Both are nameless shadows of the paternal 'corpse [as yet] without a name'.

In *Hamlet*, Priam is linked with Jephthah because a few lines before Hamlet tries to recall, for the Player's benefit, 'Aeneas' tale to Dido — and thereabout of it especially when he speaks of Priam's slaughter', he compares 'that great baby' Polonius to 'Jephthah, judge of Israel' (*Hamlet*, II.ii. 399–400). It probably is not coincidence, therefore, that a few chapters before Tom meets the Priam-like gypsy king he sees a puppet show at an inn, the fracas after which causes the landlady to lament the passing of the moral shows of yesteryear: 'I remember when Puppet-shows were made of good Scripture Stories, as *Jephthah's* Rash Vow' (XII.6). Jephthah's vow was indeed a common subject for contemporary puppet shows; but it is significant that Jephthah springs to Hamlet's mind because he was a loving father whose promise to God unwittingly led him to have to sacrifice his only (female) child. On the primary level it relates to Polonius and Ophelia. On a secondary level it relates to his own sacrifice by Old Hamlet. In *Tom Jones* Jephthah suggests the manic Western, who has just (XII.2) given up chasing Sophia and returned home. More profoundly, he suggests all fathers who have promised or acted rashly or in ignorance: Tom's father in begetting a bastard; Allworthy in expelling Tom; James II in breaking his Coronation Oath.

Thus Jephthah's name, too, must be added to the list of names that have talismanic power in *Tom Jones*. For no sooner has he been invoked than, in the very next paragraph, he seems to appear as another venerable patriarch:

> *Virgil*, I think, tells us, that when the Mob are assembled in a riotous and tumultuous Manner, and all Sorts of missile Weapons fly about, if a Man of Gravity and Authority appears amongst them, the Tumult is presently appeased, and the Mob, which when collected into one Body, may be well compared to an Ass, erect their long Ears at the grave Man's Discourse. XII.6

Jephthah is a remarkably resonant figure. Outcast because he is a bastard, he is called back by the Gileadites to become their 'head and captain' (Judges 11. 11). This early part at least of his story sounds like Tom's expulsion and return ('And Jephthah said unto the elders of Gilead, Did ye not hate me, and expel me out of my father's House?' (Judges 11.7)). It also sounds hauntingly like a version of later Stuart history: James II fled, expelled from his kingdom, in 1688, accompanied by his newly born baby son (the future 'James III', the Old Pretender). Protestant propaganda suggested that the baby was not, could not be, legitimate since the Queen had not appeared to be pregnant. The baby had been smuggled into the lying-in room in a bed warming pan, it was rumoured, and the 'warming pan birth' was still being remembered by Fielding when he wrote *The Jacobite's Journal*.[33]

Jephthah's name, then, would seem to engender within the text this exemplary 'Man of Gravity' who functions exactly like the gypsy king. But the text locates this man in Virgil's epic as well. In fact, he comes from the simile at lines 148–53 of *Aeneid*, I, the book cited in connection with the gypsy king in XII.12. If we follow the allusive trail we once again find Stuarts under the bed.

In *Tom Jones*, the 'Man of Gravity' simile appears as Fielding is explaining how the puppet showman's harangue on the morality of his 'little Drama' was interrupted by the landlady's maid being discovered in sexual liaison with the show's merry andrew and by the landlady's subsequent indignant outburst. In *Aeneid*, I, the simile appears when Juno has persuaded the wind god Aeolus to create a storm that will divert Aeneas from his western journey to Italy. But the storm is a challenge to Neptune's supremacy as king of the oceans, and so he accuses the winds of daring 'without my sovereign consent, to throw sky and earth into confusion'. The storm subsides: 'It had been like a sudden riot in some great assembly, when, as they will, the meaner folk forget themselves and grow violent . . . '. The man of *gravitas* is, in the simile, King Neptune; so that Fielding's apparent reluctance to commit himself to Virgil's authority (*'Virgil*, I think, tells us'), which just for a moment leaves the possibility open that the crowd-quelling leader is Jephthah, can now be seen as one more psychological diversionary (or mock-diversionary) tactic in the battle of the kings and fathers within the novel: of *course* Virgil tells us about the threat to Neptune's authority by a usurper, and he does so in a text which had been reconstructed into an ambiguously pro-Stuart epic by Dryden.[34] Neptune quells the rebels as the gypsy (Stuart) king quells the 'sudden Uproar' in the barn in XII.12, so that the 'Man of Gravity' is apparently a cipher for Stuart absolutism. On the other hand, the 'Man of Gravity's' nearest neighbour in the text is the puppet showman himself — simple-minded and absolute within his own realm but without authority in the realm beyond his own little stage where the real battles erupt. And so the text's emotional pull to the Stuart father-king falters, or at least steadies into some kind of approximation to stasis.

Does it though? The 'Man of Gravity' quells a mob; the puppet showman controls a mob of puppets which, he tells Tom, 'are as big as the Life' (xii.5), a statement which we are to take literally. The show over, their animating principle withdrawn, they collapse into lifelessness, mere corpses. Are they the inanimate bodies of a nation deprived of the paternal nurture of their true (Stuart) king? Or are they the corpses whose very muteness tells us of the arrogance and barbaric stupidity of the Stuart Pretenders in daring to wage unnecessary evil war on British soil once more?

The questions arch over into the adjacent chapter, xii.6, when we are told in yet another simile how swiftly and effectively the showman's harangue was terminated by the irruption of the irate landlady:

> His Mouth was now as effectually stopt, as that of a Quack must be, if in the midst of a Declamation on the great Virtues of his Pills and Powders, the Corpse of one of his Martyrs should be brought forth, and deposited before the Stage, as a Testimony of his Skill.

We have met Fielding's medical jokes before, particularly in connection with Tom's damaged mazard. Here, though, there is a reminiscence of the old notion of the king as *medicus patriae*[35] and the finger is, it seems, being pointed unequivocally at the Stuarts, and particularly Bonnie Prince Charlie, that shadow prince who is quack rather than doctor, killer rather than curer. This interpretation of the simile is supported by the beginning of xii.5, where Partridge hears a drum and sees a banner. The drum is trying to beat us an audience for the puppet show, whose advertising banner it is that Partridge sees. But Partridge, who is masquerading for Tom's benefit as a Hanoverian, thinks it all portends something else:

> [Partridge] followed his Leader, his Heart beating Time, but not after the manner of Heroes, to the Music of the Drum . . . .
> And now *Partridge*, who kept even Pace with *Jones*, discovered something painted flying in the Air, a very few Yards before him, which fancying to be the Colours of the Enemy, he fell a Bellowing, 'O Lord, Sir, here they are, there is the Crown and Coffin. Oh Lord! I never saw any thing so terrible . . .'.

It is as if he has seen one of his ghosts — a crown skull leering over a coffin as a reminder that 'War [is] the Pastime of Monarchs' (v.12); as a *memento mori* for the lost Stuart cause; or as an assertion that the prospect of King Charles (and the other Stuart 'martyrs') is as inviting as that of the King Death of Book II of Milton's *Paradise Lost*.

Contemporaries would have read the emblem less riddlingly, recognising in it a familiar anti-Jacobite *motif* thrust upon the Young Pretender in Hanoverian prints of the '45.[36] Equally, though, those contemporaries would have known that Jacobites were frequently compared to asses, hence the ass frontispiece to the first few numbers of Fielding's *Jacobite's Journal*.[37] Armed with this piece of information we may return to the Virgilian simile of xii.6 with its grave man and its 'Mob, which . . . may well be compared to an Ass' and ask the question, who would have greater 'Authority' over a Jacobite ass of a crowd, Pretender or Hanoverian? The answer is obviously 'either', leaving the problem roughly where it was before, at that point of approximate stasis. After all, at the time of writing (and publication) the 'Man of Gravity and Authority' is likely to be the Hanoverian George II, since he has now wrested all authority from the Stuart claimants and so quelled the Jacobite 'Mob' and persuaded it to lay down its 'missile Weapons'. Yet he could well be one or the other or both Pretenders, true source of regal 'Authority' to the Jacobite ass. And it seems that the text supports the latter through the other simile, quoted above, about the quack and his corpses. The satiric thrust of the simile is directed at the wretched doctor, and all the sympathy at 'the Corpse of one of his Martyrs' which does not, however, merely lie lifeless on the page. Instead, it animates the not very dead controversy over Charles I, king and martyr, so that sympathy for the corpse-martyr revives, as it were, a dead Stuart who becomes the analogue to the 'Man of Gravity' of just a few lines earlier.[38] More than that, does it not supply a head that we can now insert into the blank space under the crown that surmounts the (now empty) coffin?

The tensions evident here as opposite desires tug and strain against each other are present earlier in the book, too, when the Man of the Hill reappears and brings with him, for the first time in that book, King Priam. This is in xii.3, when Tom and Partridge are travelling towards the puppet show. Forbidden by Tom to mention either returning home or Sophia, and having been furiously attacked by Tom for mentioning them once too often already, Partridge searches for another topic and seizes

> upon that which was next uppermost in his Mind, namely, the Man of the Hill. 'Certainly, Sir', says he, 'that could never be a

Man, who dresses himself, and lives after such a strange Manner, and so unlike other Folks.... It runs strangely in my Head, that it must have been some Spirit, who, perhaps, might be sent to forewarn us: And who knows but all that Matter which he told us, of his going to Fight, and of his being taken Prisoner, and of the great Danger he was in of being hanged, might be intended as a Warning to us, considering what we are going about: Besides, I dreamt of nothing all last Night, but of Fighting; and methought the Blood ran out of my Nose, as Liquor out of a Tap. Indeed, Sir, *infandum, Regina, jubes renovare dolorem.*'

Tom and Partridge are off to fight the Young Pretender but the Man intervenes, in Partridge's admittedly biased mind, to inhibit the move and to protect the Stuart cause, thus again acting as the force of reaction his tale revealed him to be. However, it is not so obvious, from the text at least, that, in this instance, it is necessarily good to fight. The clues to this interpretation are Partridge's Latin and haunting allusions in Tom's and Partridge's subsequent dialogue to *I Henry IV*.

The Latin comes from the very opening of *Aeneid*, II, and thus from that emotionally sensitive area examined in the encounter with the king of the gypsies. As Book II opens, Aeneas, having had his memory and tears prompted by the images in the Temple of Juno, is now invited by Dido to supply a text, a narrative underpinning, for these icons of Troy's fall and the horrible murder of Priam. Aeneas replies in the words appropriated by Partridge: 'O Queen, the grief you ask me to revive is too terrible to utter'. Partridge has to appropriate them because at this moment he is horrified at the prospect of fighting the forces of the Stuart king and prince who possess his heart and who, through his Latin, become identified with déd Priam, an archetypal father-king. This is not, however, the first time Partridge has used the phrase. Indeed, it is one of his favourites, and he tends to use it in a pro-Jacobite context as a lament of unutterable pain for things lost and past.[39] But this instance in XII.3 is perhaps the most telling. It floats free of the limitations of its blinkered utterer to evoke the agony of the killing of the father king and to anticipate the emotional and political complexities of the episode of the gypsy king.

The rest of the dialogue between Tom and Partridge in XII.3 abandons Virgil for Shakespeare, the Shakespeare of *I Henry IV*. As they talk over the likelihood of death in battle we begin to hear echoes of v.i, the brief exchange between Falstaff and Hal just before the battle of Shrewsbury.[40] Here is Falstaff refusing to consider dying prematurely for honour:

> *Prince*: Why, thou owest God a death.
> *Falstaff*: 'Tis not due yet, I would be loath to pay him before his day — what need I be so forward with him that calls not on me? Well, 'tis no matter, honour pricks me on. Yea, but how if honour pricks me off when I come on, how then? Can honour set a leg? No. . . . What is that honour? Air. A trim reckoning! Who hath it? He that died a-Wednesday. Doth he feel it? No. Doth he hear it? No. 'Tis insensible, then? Yea, to the dead.

And here is Partridge:

> 'What then!' replied *Partridge*; 'Why then there is an End of us, is there not? When I am gone, all is over with me. What matters the Cause to me, or who gets the Victory, if I am killed? I shall never enjoy any Advantage from it. What are all the ringing of Bells, and Bonfires, to one that is six Foot under Ground?'

Later he says: 'Why I am a middle-aged Man now, and yet I may live a great Number of Years . . . to tempt Death before a Man's Time is come, seems to me downright Wickedness and Presumption'.

Like Falstaff, Partridge is a coward. From that one similarity resound almost infinite echoes, complementing those we also hear from *Hamlet*: Partridge and Falstaff are, like Polonius, buffoon fathers who yet have more than mere buffoonery in them; just as Fortinbras threatens Denmark so in both *Tom Jones* and *I Henry IV* the kingdom is threatened and is preparing for a crucial battle; as Hamlet is doubled by Laertes and Fortinbras so is Hal doubled by Hotspur and Tom by Blifil; in *I Henry IV* as in *Hamlet* and *Tom Jones* the question of 'which king?' is supported by sibling rivalry ('Nor can one England brook a double reign/Of Harry Percy and the Prince of Wales'; v.iv.65–6).[41] Partridge the coward, then, opens up a further perspective of fathers and sons and the death of kings. And yet Partridge is not just a coward. In reply to Tom's paraphrase of the best known part of Horace's *Odes*, III.ii (*Dulce et decorum est pro patria mori*) he says:

> 'That's very certain .... Ay, sure, *Mors omnibus communis*: But there is a great Difference between dying in one's Bed a great many Years hence, like a good Christian, with all our Friends crying about us; and being shot To-Day or Tomorrow, like a Mad-Dog; or, perhaps, hacked in twenty Pieces with a Sword, and that too, before we have repented of all our Sins. O Lord have Mercy upon us! To be sure, the Soldiers are a wicked Kind of People.

With this *kyrie* Partridge speaks a pacifist Christian truth. War is evil, a self-evident proposition so obvious that most ignore it, so that the author himself has had to support it earlier:

> Here we cannot suppress a pious Wish, that all Quarrels were to be decided by those Weapons only, with which Nature, knowing what is proper for us, hath supplied us; and that cold Iron was to be used in digging no Bowels, but those of the Earth. Then would War, the Pastime of Monarchs, be almost inoffensive ....
> v.12

As Partridge sees it, there is little difference between death in battle and murder because both deprive you of your right to repent of your sins, to compose yourself for death.[42] At that point, and with Fielding's sarcasm that war is 'the Pastime of Monarchs' still sounding in our ears, we think of the terrible responsibility of the father-king for his children's souls, and of the agonised cry of the soldier ghost of Old Hamlet, 'armed at point exactly', who was murdered 'even in the blossoms of my sin ... sent to my account/With all my imperfections on my head' (I.ii.200; I.v.76ff.). He is a king who is suffering as he has made many others suffer, and the pity he calls forth is immense and terrible. No one should die like that. If the father king or the elected king will only think, no one will die like that. Then crown and coffin — that complex emblem right at the heart of the novel — will be disjunct. But, as the author despairingly says in v.12, 'such Reformations are rather to be wished than hoped for'.

1.4 THE AUTHORIAL FATHER

> *Hamlet*: ... their writers do them wrong to make them exclaim against their own succession.
> (*Hamlet*, II.ii)

As Sandra Gilbert and Susan Gubar have reminded us, male authors have from time immemorial appropriated the female role of birth-giver.[43] They claim to bear their texts to which, therefore, they are both father and mother. Fielding is no exception, and claims exactly this prerogative of the brotherhood of male authors. Indeed, he revels in the fact of his parenthood, teasing out the ambiguity of his role(s) in relation to the political and psychological preoccupations of his fiction so that from one point of view at least, and not surprisingly, *Tom Jones* emerges as a writhingly complex attempt on Fielding's part to define himself as a writer.

The problem, as we tend to say much too frequently these days, is one of authority. But as Fielding constantly questions his role as author, revealing fundamental paradoxes and inconsistencies, we see that he is as schizophrenic as his text, whose voice is for liberty but whose heart is for the regressive pull of the father. Thus in the opening chapter to Book II Fielding talks of the liberties he will take with time, then continues:

> as I am, in reality, the Founder of a new Province of Writing, so I am at Liberty to make what Laws I please therein. And these Laws, my Readers, whom I consider as my Subjects, are bound to believe in and obey; with which that they may readily and chearfully comply, I do hereby assure them, that I shall principally regard their Ease and Advantage in all such Institutions: For I do not, like a *jure divino* Tyrant, imagine that they are my Slaves or my Commodity. I am, indeed, set over them for their own Good only, and was created for their Use, and not they for mine.

He writes tongue in cheek, but he emerges, if not a tyrant, then an absolutist like the gypsy king, that strange monarch who appears in order to speak to Tom in fractured English of an antiquated monarchical system that somehow, within the greater world, manages to sustain a kingdom of Golden Age purity. As Manuel Schonhorn has noticed, this king intervenes in the narrative as a double for Fielding, embodying and defending an absolutism that Fielding resolutely refused to subscribe to in the constitution of the realm.[44]

Occasionally authorial schizophrenia verges on despair as one or other of the doubles irrupts into the narrative to reveal that he finds life and/or art impossible, or at least difficult, to control. The puppet showman in Book XII is an obvious instance. Even more obviously, there is Dowling, the lawyer who brought the news of Bridget's death (v.7,8) and who possesses the secret of Tom's parentage at this crucial moment when the mother is no more and one of the supposed fathers is supposedly dying. Like an anxious author he does not know what to do with himself or his burden of secrets. When we first hear of him he is 'in a violent Hurry, and protested he had so much Business to do, that if he could cut himself into four Quarters, all would not be sufficient'(v.7). When we hear of him again (vIII.8), shortly before we meet the Man of the Hill, he 'recollected the Face of *Jones*'; but this act of memory, this exercise of one of the mind's traditional stabilising powers, is undone by his even more frenetic subsequent activity: he 'lamented his great Hurry of Business, and wished he could divide himself into twenty Pieces, in order to be at once in twenty Places'. The comedy just about contains the defeatism implicit in the admission that the only way to cope with the multiplicity of ideas and selves as they reflect and overgo the zaniness of the contingent world and, like it, seem to career out of control, is a voluntary suicide by dismemberment. Dismemberment cannot be prevented by remembrance, in this instance, at least. If you are in 'twenty Pieces' you are, after all, in the condition of one of Partridge's dead soldiers, 'hacked in twenty Pieces with a Sword' (xII.3).[45]

The movement of the novel as a whole, however, is towards the recovery of a body or, at least, the name of a body: through Jenny's remembrance of Tom's father and mother in xvIII.7 Tom is, as it were, re-membered. This in itself suggests that the Dowling persona is a momentary one and that there is a strong, albeit qualified, anti-death impetus in the novel which has as part of its purpose at least the guaranteeing, however indirectly, of authorial life and authority. Hence, although *Hamlet* is fundamental to the novel's probing of regressive death wishes and the pull towards the dark father, it can also provide moments of life-affirming comic relief, as when in vII.15 Tom, having been attacked by Northerton, far from being dead and a ghost, 'spoke as heartily as if he was well';

or when the battle in the churchyard (IV.8), with its inevitable echo of Hamlet's fight with Laertes in Ophelia's newly dug grave, becomes simply a decorative mock heroic '*Battle sung by the Muse in the* Homerican *Stile*':

> The whole Army of the Enemy (though near a hundred in Number) seeing the Fate of their General, gave back many Paces, and retired behind a new-dug Grave; for the Church-yard was the Field of Battle, where there was to be a Funeral that very Evening. *Molly* pursued her Victory, and catching up a Skull which lay on the Side of the Grave, discharged it with such Fury, that having hit a Taylor on the Head, the two Skulls sent equally forth a hollow Sound at their Meeting . . . .

The hint of *memento mori* based on contemporary churchyard conditions turns into a joke about mazards, leaving Yorick and Ophelia far behind.[46] And they are left even further behind in IV.9 when Hamlet's graveyard scene is quoted in a context of wife-beating:

> *Black George* was, in the main, a peaceable kind of Fellow, and nothing *choleric, nor rash*, yet did he bear about him something of what the Antients called the *Irascible*, and which his Wife, if she had been endowed with much *Wisdom, would have feared*.

This is a heavy-handed revision of Hamlet's 'I prithee take thy fingers from my throat,/For though I am not splenetive and rash,/Yet have I in me something dangerous,/Which let thy wiseness fear', as he grapples with Laertes in Ophelia's grave. The allusion functions to emphasise *Hamlet* and graves but, surely, more than that. For two lines earlier Hamlet has confronted Laertes with supreme affirmation of his name and identity: 'This is I,/Hamlet the Dane' (v.i.250–1). It is as if Moll's battle in the churchyard has not quite exorcised death's ghost and the awful possibility of annihilation. Fielding has regenerated the graveyard scene ludicrously out of context in the very next chapter in order to protest, however indirectly through the allusion and its immediate context, his sense of 'I'. In revising *Hamlet* he revives himself.

Laertes has, after all, just obliterated distinctions by demanding burial for himself ('Now pile your dust upon the quick and dead'), and it is this loss of self that Fielding's ego is so busily refusing. To be buried is to lose everything including authority, to see the dominance of the coffin over the crown, to have your history reduced to a blank. Fielding anxiously flirts with the possibility, then rejects it, as he does also by setting up the Man of the Hill as narrator and yet another double for himself but only after proleptically demolishing him by the provision of a more acceptable authorial double. The old man is a mysterious stranger with an extraordinary tale to tell, rather like the Hermetic stranger noticed by Frank Kermode in Henry Green's *Party Going* who is somehow unable to communicate at the right time or to the right person what needs to be communicated.[47] As such he is a negation of authorial power, and as a ghostly creature of the night he is a veritable affirmation of authorial death. Fielding demolishes him through the anterior figure of Allworthy, neither mysterious nor a stranger, bereaved of a wife (like Fielding himself),[48] pompous and capable of the most tremendous errors, paternal and explicitly un-ghostlike.

The relationship between the two could not be clearer. The author's negation lives on a hill and has to recount his tale, like Old Hamlet's ghost, at night because ghosts have to flee when they 'scent the morning air' (*Hamlet*, I.v.58). Allworthy also lives on a hill. But he sleeps at night and walks forth at dawn:

> It was now the middle of *May*, and the Morning was remarkably serene, when Mr. *Allworthy* walked forth on the Terrace, where the Dawn opened every Minute that lovely Prospect we have before described to his Eye. And now having sent forth Streams of Light, which ascended the blue Firmament before him, as Harbingers preceding his Pomp, in the full Blaze of his Majesty, up rose the Sun; than which one Object alone in this lower Creation could be more glorious, and that Mr. *Allworthy* himself presented . . . .
>
> Reader, take care, I have unadvisedly led thee to the top of as high a Hill as Mr. *Allworthy's*. . . .   I.4

Moreover, Allworthy's fostering of Tom generates not only *The History of Tom Jones, a Foundling* but also the fantasy of the paternal author, which is particularly strong later in the novel, at XI.1. There we are specifically told 'we consider a Book as the Author's Offspring, and indeed as the Child of his Brain' in a context of child murder and authorial death: the book is vulnerable to the critic and so is the author. As Fielding writes, his vulnerability as an author now fully exposed for the first time, he involves the critic too in the novel's *Hamlet* plot:

> If a Person who prys into the Characters of others, with no other Design but to discover their Faults, and to publish them to the World, deserves the Title of a Slanderer of the Reputations of Men; why should not a Critic, who reads with the same malevolent View, be as properly stiled the Slanderer of the Reputation of Books?

The point is that the slanderer is diabolical, the worst of criminals:

> it is certain that the Thief looks innocent in the Comparison; nay, the Murderer himself can seldom stand in Competition with his Guilt: For Slander is a more cruel Weapon than a Sword, as the Wounds which the former gives are always incurable. One Method, indeed, there is of killing, and that the basest and most execrable of all, which bears an exact Analogy to the Vice here disclaimed against, and that is Poison. A Means of Revenge so base, and yet so horrible, that it was once wisely distinguished by our Laws from all other Murders, in the peculiar Severity of the Punishment.

The critic is a poisoner, operating a kind of sibling rivalry with the author, trying to kill him by blackening his reputation and so denying the validity of his means of living, the book. Thus, although *Othello* and *Macbeth* are actually quoted in this chapter, Fielding's anguish seems to focus on *Hamlet* as he sees himself as a victim of a Satanically Cain-like Claudius, ready with his whisper of poison in the ear.

Not suprisingly the metaphor of the child-book reappears at the beginning of xvi.6, immediately after Tom and Partridge have been to see *Hamlet*, where it is expanded to embrace the novel's characters themselves: 'It is almost impossible for the best Parent to observe an exact Impartiality to his Children . . . As I regard all the Personages of this History in the Light of my Children, so I must confess the same Inclination of Partiality to *Sophia*'. This is the opening to the chapter, which is entitled *In which the History is to look back*. In terms of immediate narrative strategy the history looks back to discover how Blifil persuaded Allworthy that he could win Sophia's affection after all. In terms of that tricky problem of the author and his identities in the novel, it looks back, via the book as child, to the immediately preceding chapter in which, among other things, we encounter the stage Hamlet looking back as he pauses by the newly-dug grave and 'take[s] up the Skull' of Yorick, the friend of his childhood. Hamlet's momentary recollection of Yorick's quasi-paternal love for him ('He hath bore me on his back a thousand times. . . . Here hung those lips that I have kissed I know not how oft') reinforces the author's sense of his protective instincts towards his fictive children.

For Fielding to associate himself, however fleetingly and tangentially, with Yorick is also, of course, to confront in another form the possibility of death and to raise a question intimately connected with that raised in xi.1 about the author as the critic's victim. The question concerns reputation, the name that one bears to posterity. The poisonous critic does not just destroy the writer's contemporary reputation but (perhaps) his name for all time; for if his books are lost to posterity so is the author. In xi.1 Fielding quotes *Othello* on the crime of 'filch[ing] from me my good Name'; but reputation matters to the dying Hamlet too:

> Horatio, I am dead,
> Thou livest. Report me and my cause aright . . . .
> If thou didst ever hold me in thy heart,
> Absent thee from felicity awhile,
> And in this harsh world draw thy breath in pain
> To tell my story.
> (*Hamlet* v.ii.343 ff.)

Reputation means immortality, even if only the kind of immortality enjoyed by Yorick as his skull is affectionately remembered in performance after performance of *Hamlet*, and it is immortality that is guaranteed to the author who is spared by the Claudius–critic. Moreover, with his own immortality assured, the author is enabled to become a kind of necromancer, raising and perpetuating the dead:

> Come, bright love of Fame . . . . Foretel me that some tender Maid, whose Grandmother is yet unborn, hereafter, when, under

the fictitious name of *Sophia*, she reads the real Worth which once existed in my *Charlotte*, shall, from her sympathetic Breast, send forth the heaving Sigh. Do thou teach me not only to foresee, but to enjoy, nay, even to feed on future Praise. Comfort me by a solemn Assurance, that when the little Parlour in which I sit at this Instant, shall be reduced to a worse furnished Box, I shall be read, with Honour, by those who never knew nor saw me, and whom I shall neither know nor see.   xiii.1

In other words, it is only the assurance of reputation and the life it will bestow upon his dead wife that renders the prospect of Fielding's own death, even his own coffin (the prelude to his becoming a Yorick), tolerable. At the same time, however, reputation is a comfort in itself, for the crucial thing that it affords to the individual is a name and the assurance of never being nobody. We have touched on the *nemo* theme earlier. It begins with Captain Blifil's affirmation to Allworthy that 'base-born Children [are] the Children of no body' (ii.2); it is hinted at again in xi.1 as the beleaguered Fielding recalls Captain Blifil's words ("The Slander of a Book is, in Truth, the Slander of the Author: For as no one can call another Bastard, without calling the Mother a Whore, so neither can any one give the Names of sad Stuff, horrid Nonsense, &c. to a Book, without calling the Author a Blockhead'); and it reappears fully fledged in xiii.2 as an even more openly acknowledged fear. The chapter begins:

> The great Happiness of being known to Posterity, with the Hopes of which we so delighted ourselves in the preceding Chapter, is the Portion of few. To have the several Elements which compose our Names, as *Sydenham* expresses it, repeated a thousand Years hence, is a Gift beyond the Power of Title and Wealth.... But to avoid the scandalous Imputation, while we yet live, of being *one whom No-body knows*, (a Scandal, by the by, as old as the Days of *Homer*) will always be the envied Portion of those, who have a legal Title either to Honour or Estate.

Fielding begins to clown again as he considers the decorums of the 'polite' world, but the fear is nonetheless real, as it was in the preceding chapter, that inside his coffin there may be *one whom No-body knows* or even, such is the magical power of words to create and uncreate, no body.[49]

It may be no accident that when Fielding takes leave of us in xviii.1 he begs our goodwill and indulgence in these words: 'If in any Thing I have offended, it was really without any Intention'. For given the pressure exerted by *Hamlet* upon his text, there is possibly an echo of Hamlet's two ghost scenes, i.v (*Horatio*: 'These are but wild and whirling words, my lord'. *Hamlet*: 'I am sorry they offend you . . . ') and iii.iv (*Queen*: 'Hamlet, thou hast thy father much offended'. *Hamlet*: 'Mother, you have my father much offended'). The whirling words defend 'an honest ghost'; the accusations in iii.iv lead to the killing of Polonius and the return of the Ghost, who is invisible to Gertrude but all too visible to Hamlet whose 'bedded hair, like life in excrements,/Start up and stand an end'. Fielding's fear of offending may, then, be intimately bound up with his fear of non-being and his awareness of his coffin. If he offends the living he will not be read; if he offends posterity his 'honest ghost' will fade into impotence and then be heard and seen no more by his Gertrude reader: 'Nothing at all; yet all that is I see' (iii.iv.133).

The idea that *offence* evokes *Hamlet* seems to be supported by the way Partridge comes bursting into the room at the beginning of xviii.2, a very few lines after Fielding has expressed his anxieties about having offended:

Partridge came stumbling into the Room with his Face paler than Ashes, his Eyes fixed in his Head, his Hair standing an End, and every Limb trembling. In short, he looked as he would have done had he seen a Spectre, or had he indeed been a Spectre himself.

Partridge knows all about seeing ghosts, of course, not just because of his story about Frank in viii.11 but because of his attendance at the performance of *Hamlet*. Not only has he heard Gertrude's description of the aghast Hamlet in iii.iv ('your bedded hair'), he has commented on Hamlet's reaction to the return of his father's ghost in horrified detail:

and now when the Ghost made his next Appearance, *Partridge* cried out, 'There, Sir, now; what say you now? Is he frightned now or no? As much frightned as you think me, and, to be sure, no Body can help some Fears, I would not be in so bad a Condition as what's his Name, Squire *Hamlet*, is there, for all the World. Bless me! What's become of the Spirit? As I am a living Soul, I thought I saw him sinking into the Earth'. xvi.5

If Partridge's own aghast appearance in xviii.2 recalls all this and in turn involves itself in Fielding's fears of offending, then the note upon which Fielding leaves us is a very elegiac one indeed. The anti-death gestures, including the recovery of Summer's name if not of his body, offer only incidental solace because the possibility of offending always remains: 'offence' is beyond your control. If the reader take offence he or she will refuse the charitable gesture of memory: the author's ghost will not have a bad reputation but (the fear of xi.1 and xiii.1 and 2) no reputation at all. Partridge, in xvi.5, reminds us – and Fielding – of the absolute gulf that separates the living from the dead: 'As I am a living Soul, I thought I saw him sinking into the Earth'. Fielding's plea for his readers' lenity is a plea above all to the living souls of the future to hear his voice and, in doing so, redeem him and his dead wife Charlotte from 'the Earth'.

1.5 THE GHOSTLY MOTHER

> *Gent*: Her speech is nothing,
> Yet the unshaped use of it doth move
> The hearers to collection.
>
> (*Hamlet* iv.v)

In the first half of the novel the emphasis is almost exclusively on the problem of father and son. The turning point comes with the Man of the Hill's long story of his jealousy of his brother for being the mother's favourite and his consequent general misogyny. 'My Mother, who never loved me' (viii.11) is a perennial male cry and complaint which in the case of the Man of the Hill characterises a misogynist who cannot love and who, in consequence, spends his life regressively with an aged woman who is, we may feel, as much mother substitute as housekeeper, a woman who is always there and ready to look after him.

Despite all the tensions and inhibitions that the novel continues to register in connection with fathers, it is clear that the Man of the Hill's claustrophobically misogynistic tale catapults Tom to the rescue, then into the bed, of Jenny Waters, formerly Jenny Jones, and reputedly Tom's mother, as a prelude to his union with Sophia at the novel's end. But before Tom can actually be united with Sophia he has to encounter another 'mother' in the form of Lady Bellaston. The second half of the novel belongs to the mothers in a way the first does not. And with them, as with the fathers, an elaborate ritual is enacted which appears, again, to possess an extraordinarily Oedipal logic.

Since in any psychoanalytical reading an older woman can be forced into the role of mother figure, it is necessary to show how Fielding establishes Lady Bellaston's maternal credentials. He does so on our second encounter with her, right at the beginning of the London section, when she calls on Mrs Fitzpatrick to look Tom over. Her footman bangs on the door so manically that:

> it may be truly said,
> —*Non acuta*
> *Sic geminant Corybantes Æra.*
> *The Priests of* Cybele *do not so rattle their sounding Brass.*
>
> In short a Footman knocked, or rather thundered at the Door . . . . The Door of the Room now flew open, and, after pushing in her Hoop sideways before her, entered Lady *Bellaston*, who having first made a very low Curtesy to Mrs. *Fitzpatrick*, and as low a one to Mr. *Jones*, was ushered to the upper End of the room.
>
> XIII.4

Beyond the familiar joke about London footmen we hear, through the quotation from Horace's *Odes*, I.16, something more menacing. For Cybele is the Great Earth Mother, usually known simply as *Magna Mater*, and this is our major clue to Lady Bellaston's symbolically maternal relationship with Tom. She was worshipped in winter mysteries (Fielding tells us in this chapter that it was now around mid-December), held at night, which the masquerade in XIII.7, with its jokes about the impresario Heidegger as 'high Priest', votaries, and the absent deity, may in part re-enact.[50] Most significantly, she was the lover of Atys who, for one reason or another (the mythographers give various accounts), was castrated. Read in this light, Lady Bellaston's role as Cybele makes her the dark devouring mother offering an absolute threat to Tom's emergence into manhood and representing the regressive pull to the primal woman to whom the Man of the Hill is committed. Hence her jealousy of Sophia, her encouragement of and complicity in Lord Fellamar's attempted rape of her ('Fie upon it! have more Resolution. Are you frightned by the word *Rape*?'; xv.4), and her cruel lie, told on her behalf to Sophia by another neutered Tom, one Tom Edwards, that Tom is dead: 'I saw the Lad lie dead in a

Coffee-house. — Upon my Soul he is one of the finest Corpses I ever saw in my Life' (xv.3). In the end, the terrible mother does not just consume virility, she kills.⁵¹

Even the versions of the Cybele-Atys myth that suggest that Atys rejected his maternal goddess lover have overtones of male fear of the devouring mother in them and also recall elements in the relationship between Tom and Lady Bellaston:

> *Arnobius* says, *Atys* was a Youth who kept Flocks, and that *Cybele*, even in her old Age, became enamoured of him; and notwithstanding her being a Queen, he still received her with Disdain.

Or, more succinctly, their story 'still . . . appears to turn upon the Amours of an old Queen for a young man who slighted her'.⁵²

The name *Bellaston* might suggest, albeit indirectly, another queen and mother, the vilified Gertrude accused by Hamlet of 'liv[ing]/In the rank sweat of an enseamed bed,/Stew'd in corruption, honeying and making love/Over the nasty sty!' (*Hamlet*, III.iv.91–4), for Latin *belua* means *brute beast*; though *Bellaston* contains additional inextricably entwined overtones of warlike wrath (*bellax*) and beauty (*bella*). So that this beautiful star (*bella-aster*) is extraordinarily attractive to Jones, yet in her authoritarian maternal aspect is repellent and repelling, as easily moved to wrath as to love, and all the time hauntingly brutish.⁵³

The name and behaviour of Lady Bellaston convey, too, the feminist message that she will enjoy herself with as much sexual freedom as a man. In her commitment to freedom of action she complements, somewhat grotesquely, her relation Di Western (mythologically they are the warrior goddess Bellona and virginal Diana). But Fielding was not in any significant sense a feminist, and it is Lady Bellaston's compelling yet forbidden maternal power that dominates most obviously at the masquerade. Here, pursuing Sophia through the woman he is convinced is Mrs Fitzpatrick, but who is really Lady Bellaston, Tom is sucked terribly back into the maternal vortex — how terribly, the depersonalisation of her into a mere talking mask suggests. This is something even more surreal than the life-size puppets of the previous book, a ghostly female shadow, equivalent in many ways to the bizarre and equally nocturnal Man of the Hill who, like the inhabitants of the masquerade world who 'may more properly be said to kill Time in this Place, than in any other' (XIII.7), was accused by Tom of having 'killed so much of your Time' (VIII.15).

This 'Mask [which] walked hastily to the upper End of the innermost Apartment before she spoke' is in fact dressed in a domino, a costume worn merely to convey anonymity. In other words, Lady Bellaston is not pretending to be someone other than herself, she is asserting that she is the nameless (because unnameable) maternal shade, the hooded face of the dead mother herself. For dominos were, historically, veils worn by women in mourning; and when Tom listens to this domino, we have to remember that the eighteenth-century masquerade domino consisted of clock and half-mask which veiled the upper half of the face.[54] Tom is seeing moving eyes and mouth and little more. When we recall her foul breath (XIII.9) we see this unnameable Cybele as a corrupt *memento mori* embodying the full deadness of the lost, absent, mother.

Later, Lady Bellaston is masked in another way, by being twice concealed behind an arras (XIV.2, XV.7). The comic reminiscence of Square deformed to an upper case delta behind the tattered rug in Moll Seagrim's attic bedroom (V.5) is incidental to the primary reminiscence of *Hamlet*, which is soon to be performed (XVI.5). The main arras scene there is, of course, III.iv (Polonius killed behind the arras as he overhears the beginning of Hamlet's crucial confrontation with Gertrude), though it is anticipated at III.i when Claudius and Polonius, 'seeing unseen', listen to Hamlet's verbal lashing of Ophelia. The *Hamlet* scenes say more about the man than the women and the *Tom Jones* chapters (superficially at least) reveal more about the woman than the man, but the allusive point is clear: the inextricability of Gertrude and Ophelia is doubled by the inextricability of Lady Bellaston-as-mother and Sophia.

The level of Oedipal fantasy that is operating in this section of *Tom Jones* is beautifully demonstrated in the first arras episode in XIV.2, where Lady Bellaston is invited to wait behind the bed curtains because Partridge, who has just burst into the room, says that Mrs Honour is on her way upstairs.

> *Partridge* came dancing and capering into the Room, like one drunk with Joy, crying out, 'She's found! she's found! — Here, Sir, here, She's here, — Mrs. *Honour* is upon the Stairs.' 'Stop her a Moment,' cries *Jones*,—'Here, Madam, step behind the Bed, I have no other Room nor Closet, nor Place on Earth to hide you in;

sure never was so damn'd an Accident.' — 'D–n'd indeed!' said the Lady as she went to her Place of Concealment; and presently afterwards in came Mrs. *Honour* . . . .

As Sophia's maid Honour starts to gabble at him about Lady Bellaston, Tom tries to hush her by telling her 'there was a Lady dying in the next Room'. No 'Place on Earth' (but perhaps under it?); 'a Lady dying': the scene corresponds in this respect to the symbolic death enacted by the masquerade. And the *entrelacement* of this in turn with the story of Nightingale merely reveals how acutely attuned the novel is to its preoccupations with maternal death, parent identity, and self-identity. For Tom will not permit Nightingale to abandon the pregnant Nancy, presumably because he senses the scenario of his own conception and birth: 'View the poor, helpless, Orphan-Infant' he says to Nightingale in xiv.7, displaying the 'orphan-infant' self of long ago as he utters the words. The fact that Nightingale is being bullied by an avaricious father who is complemented by a brother of exactly opposite temperament takes us back to the novel's beginning as well, to Captain Blifil and Dr Blifil. Beyond them we sense the fratricide Claudius and his victim, Old Hamlet, the father of one of the novel's other beginnings, the text of *Hamlet*. So that the Nightingale episode plunges down to the novel's deepest core: paternal death and conflict with the father; maternal death (death of the girl-mother, Nancy, and death of the girl's mother, Mrs Miller, are both prospects that Tom invites Nightingale to 'paint to [his] Imagination'); and the fate of the baby.

In view of all this, and in view, too, of Fielding's engagement in the dilemma (provoked and sustained within the novel by *Hamlet*) of the inextricable involvement of one's sense of selfhood in the identity of the parents, there is little need to comment at length on xiii.1, the preliminary chapter of the book that gives birth to Lady Bellaston. The preceding section observed that it contains an image of authorial death and immortality; now the suggestively maternal nature of two muses invoked by Fielding needs to be taken into account. The first is Calliope ('thee, fair, gentle Maid, whom *Mnesis*, happy Nymph, first on the Banks of *Hebrus* did produce'), the benign mother of the poet Orpheus, daughter of Memory. The second is a nameless substantial Grub Street *Frau*, much like the narcotically maternal Dulness of Pope's *Dunciad*, to whom Fielding is attracted with a remarkably overt regressiveness:

And thou, much plumper Dame, whom no airy Forms nor Phantoms of Imagination cloathe . . . . Thee, I call; of whom in a *Treckschuyte* in some *Dutch* Canal the fat Ufrow Gelt, impregnated by a jolly Merchant of *Amsterdam*, was delivered: In *Grubstreet*-School didst thou suck in the Elements of thy Erudition . . . . Come, thou jolly Substance, with thy shining Face, keep back thy Inspiration, but hold forth thy tempting Rewards; thy shining, chinking Heap; thy quickly-convertible Bank-bill, big with unseen Riches; . . . and, lastly, a fair Portion of that bounteous Mother, whose flowing Breasts yield redundant Sustenance for all her numerous Offspring, did not some too greedily and wantonly drive their Brethren from the Teat . . . .

And now this ill-yoked Pair, this lean Shadow and this fat Substance, have prompted me to write, whose Assistance shall I invoke to direct my Pen?

This seems to be an unequivocal recognition that the novel is born in part out of Fielding's anxieties over the mother, the mother whose memory is good (Calliope, daughter of Mnesis: remember me, remember me) but who, nevertheless, could not prevent the dis-membering of her poet son, and the appallingly seductive dark mother who guarantees commitment to her by buying one's affection. The narrative, of course, encodes this double mother in the form of Lady Bellaston, the beautiful star who is also the castrating Queen Cybele, the mother who binds Tom to her (and to whom he wants to be bound) by paying him for his sexual favours (XIII.8).

The astral untouchability of the real mother, as well as the darkness of the terrible mother, are suggested too by Lady Bellaston's pseudonym Queen of Fairies (XIII.6). For the fairy queen is the moon, queen of the night.[55] Her title also points up the darkness of this section of the novel as a whole, which is as bleak and nocturnal as the section devoted to the Man of the Hill. This is the darkest time of the year (XIII.4); there are nocturnal visits; there is the darkly secretive masquerade. In this darkness Tom encounters and sleeps with the deathly image of the maternal shade, Lady Bellaston. In the earlier darkness he encountered the paternal shade of the Man of the Hill and spent one very long night with him. And yet the symmetry is not as exact, nor is it as simple to interpret as this, for we have yet to consider the crucial figure of Mrs Fitzpatrick.

Through her Tom encounters Lady Bellaston and, like that maternal 'mask', she is, as we shall see, ghostly, and thus a reminder of maternal absence. At the same time she is the same age as, and symbolic twin to, Sophia. She mediates between Sophia and Lady Bellaston in other ways, as well. Like Lady Bellaston, she is sexually suspect. But with a history of persecution by the male that in some ways resembles Sophia's own, she doubles as the novel's 'pure' woman as much as its devouring mother. Sophia's encounter with her in Book XI is an essential prelude to Sophia's reunion with Tom, for it seems that she needs contact with a blood relation of the same age group as herself who has been initiated into male sexual 'mysteries' before she can proceed to initiation herself. And in so far as Mrs Fitzpatrick has symbolic affinities with Lady Bellaston, and is the means through whom Tom encounters her, she performs an equivalent function for Tom, beckoning him to the terrible mother, seducing him into Lady Bellaston's bed through her youth and (presumably) greater sexual attractiveness.

Even this does not explain her function satisfactorily, however, for the reader has also to take into account the pairing of Mrs Fitzpatrick's interpolated tale to Sophia of her life's history with that of the Man of the Hill's to Tom.[56] Both answer each other symmetrically, in Books VIII and XI, across the central two books of the novel, IX and X. Why the parallel?

The Man of the Hill offered a case history in his story of sibling rivalry and misogyny. If we add its links with *Hamlet* (see above, pp. 16–18) then we begin to see that Tom is auditor of a history that, although it may have ended as a blank, is, as Freud, Lacan and others would understand it at least, an account of all our (male) yesterdays. What Mrs Fitzpatrick does, in part, to justify her parallelism with the Man of the Hill is to offer to Sophia a way of escape from the masculine aggression and tyranny that he represents. The Man of the Hill's phobias and obsessions are those of Mr Fitzpatrick, Blifil, Squire Western, and so on. Mrs Fitzpatrick is a woman who has fled, as it were, from the Man's misogynistic world in order to redeem a vulnerable sister. The fact that she aids Tom's residual fantasies by introducing him to Lady Bellaston simply suggests that she is authorially permitted to 'know' how residual these fantasies are, how near the psychic health represented by Sophia he really is.

By the time she meets Mrs Fitzpatrick, indeed, Sophia herself has become strangely implicated in her own equivalent of *Hamlet*, the victim, in other words, of obsessive patriarchal conspiracy. Thus, she makes her escape from her tyrannical and imprisoning father at midnight, the time when ghosts walk: 'Twelve Times did the iron Register of Time beat on the sonorous Bell-metal, summoning the Ghosts to rise, and walk their nightly Round' (x.9). The fact that it *is* Sophia who rises, rather than a ghost, is however an indication of the strength of female resistance to the male conspiracy. Then, later, still in the dark, she meets Mrs Fitzpatrick, except that she does not know that it is her cousin, for her encounter is initially with a nameless somebody who has apparently been turned into a ghost. Sophia hears and sees horses 'coming after [her] on full Speed' (xi.2). She fears that it is her pursuing, avenging father, and even when the pursuers turn out to be female the head of the party is perceived as a ghost, albeit a harmless one:

> [Sophia] accosted the strange Lady in a most obliging Tone; and said, 'She was very happy to find they were both travelling the same Way.' The other, who, like a Ghost, only wanted to be spoke to, readily answered . . . .

Both are 'travelling the same Way', away from male tyranny, the blackly Oedipal world that, continuing into an adulthood which recognises nothing but maternal absences, turns women, like fathers, into ghosts. The chronological and spatial proximity of both women to the world of the fathers and the equivalent, tyrannical, husbands, is what is registered by the ghost simile. As they continue travelling, Mrs Fitzpatrick will become more substantial, and when daylight comes (the time for ghosts to disappear) identities can be established and ratified:

> Day-light at length appears in its full Lustre; and now the two Ladies, who were riding over a Common Side by Side, looking stedfastly at each other, at the same Moment both their Eyes became fixed; both their Horses stopt, and both speaking together, with equal Joy pronounced, the one the Name of *Sophia*, the other that of *Harriet*.

While the patriarchal world outside insists that Pretenders are kings, kings pretenders, and that women are whores (for this is the moment when the landlord identifies Sophia as Bonnie Prince Charlie's mistress, Jenny Cameron), Mrs Fitzpatrick unfolds the tale of her prison house. Though she has escaped from her husband and now has both name and physical substance, it is her task to minister to Sophia by offering to her, in her tale, a feminist re-vision of the Man of the Hill's story and a warning of the horrors of marriage to a man as damaged as the Old Man of the Hill himself. The Man's tale begins with a scene of primal hatred implicating father, mother, and two brothers; Mrs Fitzpatrick's opens with the primal bliss of being twinned with another girl, Sophia, 'under the Care of my Aunt *Western*' (xi.4):

> It is natural to the Unhappy to feel a secret Concern in recollecting those Periods of their Lives which have been most delightful to them. The Remembrance of past Pleasures affects us with a kind of tender Grief, like what we suffer for departed Friends; and the Ideas of both may be said to haunt our Imaginations.

Haunted by the shade of her dead adolescent self, she then unfolds the case history of a man who courted her and her aunt, young and old, simultaneously. Whatever the pragmatics of the situation, its psychology is all too obvious, and, after marrying the younger, Fitzpatrick takes his wife to a decaying Irish mansion presided over by that familiar 'old Woman who seemed coeval with the Building, and greatly resembled her whom *Chamont* mentions in the *Orphan*' (xi.5). Fitzpatrick *is*, now, the Man of the Hill, who is similarly tended, since his house and self are cared for by 'an old Woman who . . . answered exactly to that Picture drawn by *Otway* in his Orphan' (viii.10)

Moreover, both Fitzpatrick and the Man of the Hill, by virtue of the *Orphan* allusion, are revealed to be subject to Oedipal fantasies and consequent astygmatic perceptions of women. As Mrs Fitzpatrick unfolds her tale she reveals this to be the supreme male secret, accounting for the surliness discovered in those men closest to a woman, 'a Father, a Brother, or a Husband'. As she speaks we recall the text of *The Orphan* at the very point when the 'old woman' makes her appearance, for the old woman appears out of Monimia's brother's explicitly Oedipal dream which has 'clouded' his brow and persuaded him that his sister is a whore. Remembering the dead father and mother (ii.157ff.), Chamont tells her his dream:

> Three nights ago, as I
> Lay musing in my bed, all darkness round me,

> A sudden damp struck to my heart; cold sweat
> Dewed all my face, and trembling seized my limbs;
> My bed shook under me, the curtains started,
> And to my tortured fancy there appeared
> The form of thee thus beauteous as thou art,
> Thy garments flowing loose, and in each hand
> A wanton lover, which by turns caressed thee
> With all the freedom of unbounded pleasure.
> I snatched my sword, and in the very moment
> Darted it at the phantom — straight it left me;
> Then rose and called for lights, when, oh, dire omen!
> I found my weapon had the arras pierced
> Just where the famous tale was interwoven,
> How th'unhappy Theban slew his father.
>
> *Monimia:*
>   And for this cause my virtue is suspected!
>   Because in dreams your fancy has been ridden,
>   I must be tortured waking.
>
> (*Orphan*, II.220ff.)[57]

Monimia's reply is, in effect, the burden of Mrs Fitzpatrick's tale to Sophia. Just because her husband and his father in fantasy before him inhabit the same world as Chamont and Oedipus, 'th'unhappy Theban', there is no reason why she should acquiesce in their fantasies, or why Sophia should be victimised by them either. And so Mrs Fitzpatrick's voice takes on the warning tones of Mnesis, of Memory herself, as she unravels the awful consequences of living with a man who is the victim of his Oedipal fantasies. The point about the old woman is the subtlest one of all. She belongs to Chamont's waking fantasy world in which, immediately after his dream, he sees himself as Oedipus. He identifies her as his sphinx, which cleverly disguises the fact that she is an image of the dead mother, cold in the ground (cf. II.160). Chamont responds, then, to Monimia's exclamation quoted above:

>   Have a care;
> Labour not to be justified too fast.
> Hear all, and then let justice hold the scale.
> What followed was the riddle that confounds me:
> Through a closed lane, as I pursued my journey

> And meditated on the last night's vision,
> I spied a wrinkled hag, with age grown double.
> Picking dry sticks and mumbling to herself.
> Her eyes with scalding rheum were galled and red;
> Cold palsy shook her head; her hands seemed withered;
> And on her crooked shoulders had she wrapped
> The tattered remnant of an old stripped hanging,
> Which served to keep her carcass from the cold,
> So there was nothing of a piece about her.
> Her lower weeds were all o'er closely patched
> With diff'rent coloured rags black, red, white, yellow,
> And seemed to speak variety of wretchedness.
> I asked of her my way, which she informed me;
> Then craved my charity, and bade me hasten
> To save a sister: at that word I started.
>
> (II.238ff.)

The old woman, together with his dream, empower him to accuse Monimia and require of her a confession of sexual purity. He then warns her against men in general:

> let not marriage bait thee to thy ruin:
> Trust not a man. We are by nature false,
> Dissembling, subtle, cruel, and unconstant.

Beneath the cliché lies a horrifying psychopathological truth about Fitzpatrick, the old Man of the Hill, Western, Blifil, Allworthy and Tom. Mrs Fitzpatrick is an escapee from the Man of the Hill's misogynistic prison camp, but she knows that his fantasies, far from being uniquely his, are rampant in the male world. *Caveat femina* is the message of this part of the novel which, however, simultaneously affirms that in being beware the woman might be able eventually to win. That is why Jenny Jones-Waters echoes and reworks the ghastly tale of Old Hamlet in XVIII.7 (see section 1.1 above), for her revision symbolically identifies and opposes *Hamlet's* Oedipal pressures by disclosing 'the Secret of *Tom's* Birth' (XVIII. 10), thereby clearing the musty air of the male prison house (*Hamlet*, I. v. 14) in which mothers as well as fathers are perpetually incarcerated. Her disclosure should in turn ensure that Sophia's wits will not succumb, as Ophelia's did, to the tyranny of men.

But Fielding reneges on the perception he articulates through Harriet Fitzpatrick's story and Jenny's rejection of *Hamlet* by giving Allworthy the last word. For this magisterial father-as-Law counters Jenny with his own imitation of the demanding voice of Hamlet's ghostly father (xviii. 10) and then, after the marriage, joins forces with Squire Western to haunt Tom and Sophia with the intention of 'correcting' Tom into an image of himself. By letting the shadow of the fathers — however apparently benign — darken the novel's end, Fielding makes impossible Sophia's ultimate escape from male hegemony and ensures that her children, too, will be implicated in the battle between father and son that claims woman as its victim.

2
Dickens: *Great Expectations* and the Ghost of the Father

Dickens was only too well aware of the conceptual similarity between *David Copperfield* and *Great Expectations*: 'To be quite sure I had fallen into no unconscious repetitions, I read *David Copperfield* again the other day, and was affected by it to a degree you would hardly believe'.[1] Both question maternal love, the one through a mother who dies in the course of the novel, the other through a mother who is dead when the novel opens. In both the mother is displaced by a formidably hostile anti-mother (Miss Murdstone, Mrs Joe). Both begin with dead fathers and threateningly murderous images of surrogate fathers. And both try to reconstruct the complex ways in which the child and the adult emerge from the mistily and upsettingly unyielding 'blank of . . . infancy' (*David Copperfield*, chapter 2).

Emotionally and psychologically both novels develop from the same Oedipal matrix;[2] but whereas *David Copperfield* brilliantly proliferates and diversifies, *Great Expectations* compacts its data into a remarkably taut psychography of a mind obsessed with maternal and paternal absence. As in the case of *Tom Jones*, *Hamlet* is implicitly and explicitly present as a governing and defining text.[3] As in *Tom Jones*, too, it is the thanatological aspects of *Hamlet* that are the focus of interest in the performance of the play that the novel describes: the ghost and the graveyard (chapter 31).

Great Expectations's *Hamlet* is, however, more revealing about its fixation on the mother than is *Tom Jones*'s. Gertrude appears as 'a very buxom lady' (*buxom* in the sense of fat rather than pliant or submissive), *ceinte* with brass bands; and Ophelia has a baby:[4]

> Ophelia was a prey to such slow musical madness, that when, in course of time, she had taken off her white muslin scarf, folded it up, and buried it, a sulky man who had been long cooling his impatient nose against an iron bar in the front row of the gallery, growled, 'Now the baby's put to bed, let's have supper!'
>
> (chapter 31)

But *Hamlet* lies a long way ahead. Pip reaches his comic maternal Gertrude-Ophelia only after a dizzying exercise in narrative tautology as doubles repeat and duplicate each other in rapid succession; and as in all Oedipal schemes, the way to the mother is through the father.

2.1 PHOTOGRAPHS AND GHOSTS

Queen: Do not for ever with thy vailed lids
Seek for thy noble father in the dust . . . .

King: But you must know your father lost a father,
That father lost, lost his . . . .

Hamlet: My father – methinks I see my father . . . .

(*Hamlet*, I.ii)

Ghosts are one way in which the dead make the living remember them. A modern equivalent of the ghost for Dickens, when the art was in its monochrome infancy, is the portrait photograph, its gestures frozen and staring intensely yet remotely from a background that is usually dark round the edges but luminously misty where it haloes the central figure.

This is how Dickens understands photography in *Great Expectations*: as the art through which the dead stimulate one's fading memories of them. Except that Pip is the victim of one of history's sad ironies, for his older self is able to obtain photographs at will of the newest baby or most Aged P., but his younger self was born into a world in which photography did not exist and into a social class which could not even have begun to think of the possibility of painted portraits. The reason this matters so much right at the novel's beginning is that Pip has no father or mother. Doubly orphaned, and belaboured by his surviving sister, Mrs Joe, twenty years older than himself and violently punitive and aggrieved ('It's bad enough to be a blacksmith's wife (and him a Gargery) without being your mother . . . . You'll drive *me* to the churchyard betwixt you, one of these days, and oh, a pr-r-recious pair you'd be without me!'), the boy has no means of establishing his identity in relation to his parents. His parents are merely searing absences signified by their tombstones, and his mother's betrayal of him by dying is commemorated in his ogre of a sister who is physically as unmaternal as could possibly be imagined: 'She was tall and bony, and almost always wore a coarse apron, fastened over her figure behind with two loops, and having a square impregnable bib in front, that was stuck full of pins and needles'. *Impregnable*: Pip's young eyes detect in Mrs Joe a mother who does not want, cannot have, babies, and who has sharp metal spikes where her maternal breasts should be, for she could never provide breast milk for him, only a bottle: she 'had established a great reputation with herself and the neighbours because she had brought me up "by hand"'.[5]

The seeds of Pip's elaborate fantasy life are sown in the second paragraph of chapter 1:

I give Pirrip as my father's family name, on the authority of his tombstone and my sister — Mrs Joe Gargery, who married the blacksmith. As I never saw my father or my mother, and never saw any likeness of either of them (for their days were long before the days of photographs), my first fancies regarding what they were like, were unreasonably derived from their tombstones. The shape of the letters on my father's, gave me an odd idea that he was a square, stout, dark man, with curly black hair. From the character and turn of the inscription *'Also Georgiana Wife of the Above'*, I drew a childish conclusion that my mother was freckled and sickly.

Without photographs he has to find traces of his parents somewhere, so he goes to the churchyard. Lacking a framed photograph he searches for a sign in the rectangle of the gravestone, scrutinising the lapidary inscriptions for a parental likeness that will be revealable only through the magic of the still-to-be-invented light writing. The older Pip's mind, as it reaches back to start its narrative, flickers between the art of photography and the craft of stone chiselling, then reveals what his imagination did with the intolerable fact of his parents' deaths: it invented its own images of their characters from the inscribed 'characters' of their epitaphs.

This is where *Hamlet* begins to come in, albeit implicitly, because as he narrates the novel's opening the older Pip knows that many years later he and Herbert, like Tom and Partridge, watched a performance of *Hamlet* (chapter 31). Just as Wopsle's Hamlet's 'greatest trials were in the churchyard', so were the young Pip's. Lacking the static, eternally communicative moment of photographic evidence that his parents existed and were ever involved in his young life, Pip turns to the other extreme, the kinesis of dramatic performance in which, framed on a stage, a son meets his dead father, accuses his mother, and makes the girl he loves unobtainable by causing her to kill herself. In Pip's mind, if not yet in his reader's, the graves of the marsh country churchyard contain the image of the open graves of the Elsinore churchyard and constantly reaffirm the fact that, shut or open, the grave merely frames bones and that the likenesses of the dead in those days before photographs cannot be recaptured.

Another way the dead could be recalled, one particularly in vogue at the time, was through a Medium, something Pip mentions in passing at the end of chapter 4 after he has nearly murdered Uncle Pumblechook with tar-water ('I had filled up the bottle from the tar-water jug. I knew he would be worse by-and-by. I moved the table, like a Medium of the present day, by the vigour of my unseen hold upon it').[6] But just before that *Hamlet* has made its first, apparently innocuous, entry into the novel as 'Mr Wopsle said grace with theatrical declamation — as it now appears to me, something like a religious cross of the Ghost in Hamlet with Richard the Third'. Richard does not reappear; the ghost in *Hamlet* does, and twice: in chapter 31, and when Joe gives an account of an earlier performance by Wopsle on his visit to Pip in London in chapter 27:

'Were you at his performance, Joe?' I inquired.
'I *were*,' said Joe, with emphasis and solemnity.
'Was there a great sensation?'
'Why,' said Joe, 'yes, there certainly were a peck of orange-peel. Partickler, when he see the ghost. Though I put it to yourself, sir, whether it were calc'lated to keep a man up to his work with a good hart, to be continiwally cutting in betwixt him and the Ghost with "Amen!" A man may have had a misfortun' and been in the Church,' said Joe, lowering his voice to an argumentative and feeling tone, 'but that is no reason why you should put him out at such a time. Which I meantersay, if the ghost of a man's own father cannot be allowed to claim his attention, what can, Sir?'

What indeed? And so, sceptical of Mediums, deprived of

photographs, Pip's fancies run free — or as free as the churchyard will let them — and what happens as a result is that the ghost of Old Hamlet suddenly and violently possesses the little Kent churchyard with a demand for silence and succour in the form of the convict Magwitch. He is a convict because it is a role which, albeit invertedly (and it is a novel of inversions from the moment Magwitch holds Pip upside down in chapter 1), allies him with paternal law, Lacan's prohibiting father who guards, in this instance, the mother's grave, forbidding the weeping boy's yearning to return to her through it.[7] He is also a convict because Old Hamlet is one, an escapee like Magwitch from a terrible 'prison-house'. Old Hamlet's bravura display of armour ('Armed at point exactly'; *Hamlet*, I. ii 200) is even mimed by Pip's fancy-become-real in his pathetic way: 'a fearful man, all in coarse grey, with a great iron on his leg'. Yet even as the Magwitch father flickers into life from the rectangular stone frames of the graveyard, demanding to know the whereabouts of Pip's mother and threatening, in brutal opposition to the idea of maternal succour, to devour Pip, cannibalistically assuming him into himself ('what fat cheeks . . . darn Me if I couldn't eat 'em'),[8] Pip imagines him dead again. He has to do this because his quest for his mother is essentially Oedipal, as many of the novel's critics have noticed. Hence, after exacting a sworn promise from Pip as the ghost exacts one from Hamlet, the moment comes for the first parting which re-enacts Pip's death wish for his father:

> 'Goo-good night, sir,' I faltered.
> 'Much of that!' said he, glancing about him over the cold wet flat. 'I wish I was a frog. Or a eel!'
> At the same time, he hugged his shuddering body in both his arms — clasping himself, as if to hold himself together — and limped towards the low church wall. As I saw him go, picking his way among the nettles, and among the brambles that bound the green mounds, he looked in my young eyes as if he were eluding the hands of the dead people, stretching up cautiously out of their graves, to get a twist upon his ankle and pull him in.

With his 'father' back under the ground the green mounds, symbolically maternal, can perhaps emerge from their imprisoning brambles, which means that this evening vision also unwishes the bosomly pins and needles of Mrs Joe to which we are about to be introduced. The consequence of this unwishing will eventually be her death too (chapter 35). But for the moment Pip's childhood magic is not so strong as that of Leo Colston[9] and he has to concentrate still on the convict, who escapes the hands of the dead in order to progress even more deathward to a contemplated suicide by hanging:

> On the edge of the river I could faintly make out . . . a gibbet, with some chains hanging to it which had once held a pirate. The man was limping on towards this latter, as if he were the pirate come to life, and come down, and going back to hook himself up again. It gave me a terrible turn when I thought so . . . But, now I was frightened again, and ran home without stopping.

In order to fulfil the obligation imposed on him by Magwitch, the dark father,[10] Pip has to betray his good father, Joe, becoming racked (like Hamlet) with the burden of secrecy ('I have often thought that few people know what secrecy there is in the young, under terror'; chapter 2), and haunted by 'a ghostly pirate' and by the 'phantom' of the village finger post, as well as by so many other unrecognised 'fancies' that he engenders another 'father' in the shape of the forger Compeyson:[11] the forger-as-fiction, a genuine counterfeit father who turns out to have betrayed the (adoptive) mother, Miss Havisham, and who will, on the lower reaches of the Thames (below Graves-end!), try to fight father Magwitch to the death as Pip finally attempts to rid himself of both dark fathers. As a forger Compeyson also parodies blacksmith Joe, inhabitant of the forge whose redeeming fires can undo shackles and liberate convicts from their prison houses and who is, symbolically, at his most powerful as a blacksmith on Christmas Day as Pip's family try to celebrate a baby whose history was somewhat different from that of the infant Pip's.[12]

Yet Pip's imagination, with Wopsle as 'the Ghost in Hamlet' (chapter 4) no doubt acting as a demonic stimulus, insists on proliferating the most un-Christmaslike fantasies. As Marcellus tells us:

> Some say that ever 'gainst that season comes
> Wherein our Saviour's birth is celebrated,
> This bird of dawning singeth all night long;
> And then, they say, no spirit dare stir abroad . . .

(Hamlet, i.i 163–6)

Pip, however, imagines into existence not just one ghost 'armed at point exactly' but several: 'The apparition of a file of soldiers ringing down the butt-ends of their loaded muskets on our door-step, caused the dinner-party to rise from the table in confusion' (opening of chapter 5). This is in defiance not just of the Christmas superstition about ghosts related by Marcellus but of the blanket obligation upon ghosts to walk only by night. His imagination has also engendered the terrible pseudo-paternal Uncle Pumblechook as a kind of comically grotesque Claudius (chapter 4), a reflection within the forge of the Magwitch-Compeyson father outside, whom he proceeds to try to kill with the tar-water:

> I saw the miserable creature finger his glass playfully, take it up, smile, throw his head back, and drink the brandy off. Instantly afterwards, the company were seized with unspeakable consternation, owing to his springing to his feet, turning round several times in an appalling spasmodic whooping-cough dance, and rushing to the door; he then became visible through the window, violently plunging and expectorating, making the most hideous faces, and apparently out of his mind.
>
> I held on tight, while Mrs Joe and Joe ran to him. I didn't know how I had done it, but I had no doubt I had murdered him somehow.

This version of the father is, however, brought back in from the cold whereas the other two are not. Magwitch and Compeyson are caught fighting in the evening mist in an anticipation of their fight to the death at the end of the novel and in scrambled memory of Hamlet's fight in the grave with Laertes (the latter over Ophelia; the former over Miss Havisham, Estella, and ultimately Pip's long-buried mother), then they are returned by night to their prison: 'cribbed and barred and moored by massive rusty chains, the prison-ship seemed in my young eyes to be ironed like the prisoners'. The parting is, however willed by Pip, nevertheless marked by an act of remembrance: Magwitch 'gave me a look that I did not understand, and it all passed in a moment. But if he had looked at me for an hour or for a day, I could not have remembered his face ever afterwards, as having been more attentive'.

This is Magwitch's 'adieu. Remember me', except that this 'dead' father has now become less a ghost than a photograph indelibly printed on Pip's mind. 'It all passed in a moment', but the image that remains is permanent. From having no likeness and no photograph, Pip has engendered a living likeness (albeit one perceived through the screening and accommodating defence of *Hamlet*) and has retained the image of that likeness. The image now slips below the threshold of vision to join the remains of the real Philip Pirrip as the lights are extinguished: 'We saw the boat go alongside, and we saw him taken up the side and disappear. Then, the ends of the torches were flung hissing into the water, and went out, as if it were all over with him'. Another metaphor, in addition to this one of the torches of the dead, is dangled before us, too. The prison ship, as a 'wicked Noah's ark', receives its prisoners, Magwitch and Compeyson, back two by two into its stiflingly infertile womb, asserting itself not as an emblem of salvation like the ark in Genesis but as yet another image of the destruction Pip metes out to his fathers.

* * * * *

Tomb inscriptions and light-writing prepare us for the moment when, 'a full year after our hunt upon the marshes', Pip inscribes an epistle on his writing slate. With its jumble of characters and numerals it is a silent testament to Pip's psychology as well as to the intense difficulty, and joy, felt by the young child as it begins to make sense of the alphabet:

> 'mI deEr JO i opE Ur krWiTE wEll i opE i shAl soN B haBelL 4 2 teeDge U JO aN theN wE shOrl b sO glOdd aN wEn i M preNgtD 2 U JO woT larX an blEvE ME inF xn PiP.'

This is Pip's first attempt to write his mother tongue, and it turns out to be his equivalent of Hamlet's insisting in his writing tablets as the ghost departs 'that one may smile, and smile, and be a villain' (I.v. 108). As Pip feels more at home with his letters, so is he nearer his mother:

> Much of my unassisted self, and more by the help of Biddy than of Mr Wopsle's great-aunt, I struggled through the alphabet as if it had been a bramble-bush; getting considerably worried and scratched by every letter. After that, I fell among those thieves, the nine figures, who seemed every evening to do something

new to disguise themselves and baffle recognition. But, at last I began, in a purblind groping way, to read, write, and cipher, on the very smallest scale.

(chapter 7)

The metaphor is explicit. Familiarity with the alphabet will liberate Pip from the brambles, the brambles that we have already encountered binding the green mounds in the churchyard in chapter 1, and the punitive briar of Mrs Joe's bosom (chapter 2). In fact, escape from the bramble bush will lead Pip, with mysterious inevitability, into the 'rank' and unweeded garden of Mother Havisham's Satis House. More immediately, however, incipient literacy empowers Pip to express his mind's familial fictions and fantasies with startling accuracy; for the letter is a cryptogram releasing identities and wish-fulfilment with the clarity of a dark yet finely focused photograph.[13]

Thus, the few words that Pip can inscribe in their completeness are (apart from *well* and *then*) JO and ME along with the pronouns I and WE; so that one of the things the epistle is recording is not just Pip's camaraderie with Joe but also his sense of difference from him and, in terms of literacy, his superiority to him, which means that Joe is seen by Pip more and more as the child we have been told he was in the first place ('I always treated him as a larger species of child, and as no more than my equal'; chapter 2). This in turn means that he already senses that Joe is someone whom he can never really imagine himself 'bound' to, as apprentice or in any other way. That, at any rate, is what the misspellings seem to suggest as they raise the phantom of Magwitch in relation to himself and Joe: 'i sHAL soN B HABELL 4 2 TEEDGE U JO'. I shall soon be Abel? I shall son? I shall soon/son be Abel for to teach you, Joe?

Pip's despising of Joe which his command of his mother (tongue) now releases in him generates strange mutterings and hints of villainy: *teaching* Joe is, obviously, killing him off, a threat to do to him what he has already done to Magwitch and, maybe (in Pip's Oedipal fancy at least), to his biological father as well (Jo may even stretch across to embrace *Y*orick, the benevolent childlike paternal *j*oker, firmly dead and for the most part underground, like the unknown Philip Pirrip).[14]

But, of course, as we discover in chapter 40, it is Magwitch who is Abel: 'Magwitch, . . . chrisen'd Abel'. So that the HABELL of the letter means that Pip is proclaiming his identification with Magwitch as guilty convict and, simultaneously, his sense of his

Dickens: Great Expectations

own and Magwitch's Abel-like innocence, benighted as they are in thickets of Pumblechooks, Compeysons, files of soldiers, and so on.

Then the letter promises another threat: I shall soon be Abel for to teach you, Joe, aN theN wE shOrl b sO glOdd. Out of Joe and Abel Magwitch and Pip and Pip's sense that he must avenge himself on the good-natured inferior of a Joe-father, Orl(ick) is, born, Joe's journeyman, who actually appears in the narrative only after Pip's resentment against Joe has been formalised by his being bound apprentice (chapters 13, 15), and whose revenge on Joe on Pip's behalf takes the apparently curiously roundabout form of de-activating Mrs Joe, thus releasing Joe towards Biddy.[15] Orlick is, in a small but crucial detail, characterised in chapter 15 as 'slouch[ing] out, like Cain', an inhabitant of the outer darkness like his imprisoned then transported sibling Abel Magwitch, like the buried Philip Pirrip, and like Georgiana Pirrip and the five little Pirrips.

In effect, then, Pip's slate becomes a kind of memorial tablet, but one that is more like Hamlet's tablets than the Pirrip tombstones since it registers awareness of Cain-like villainy even while not being fully sure how and where to locate it — within or beyond the self. Significantly the slate, with its cryptic signals, elicits from Joe this important message about death and gravestones: that Joe himself was the victim of a tyrannical blacksmith of a father whose tyranny Joe can never bring himself to admit. The significance of this is, first, that it tells us formally that the novel's concern is with the commemoration and reputation of the dead and, second, that Joe validates Pip's own sense of the terror associated with the male.

Joe is really explaining to Pip why he never went to school, and what emerges from his brief narrative is a horribly familiar tale of drunkenness, wife- and child-battering and pathetic, brutal, paternal dependence:

> 'My father, Pip, he were given to drink, and when he were overtook with drink, he hammered away at my mother most onmerciful. It were a'most the only hammering he did, indeed, 'xcepting at myself . . . .
>
> ' 'Consequence, my mother and me we ran away from my father, several times; and then my mother she'd go out to work, and she'd say, "Joe," she'd say, "now, please God, you shall have some schooling, child," and she'd put me to school. But my father were that good in his hart that he couldn't abear to be without us.'
>
> (chapter 7)

What also emerges is the child's need to convince himself of parental goodness, because if parents are not good they could not have loved, and if they could not love they could not have wanted the child in the first place, and if they did not want him he may as well be dead; which is, of course, the main burden of Pip's fears and perceptions at the novel's beginning. Hence Joe's repeated 'my father were that good in his hart' and, after his death, the epitaph he composes for him:[16]

> 'And it were my intentions to have had put upon his tombstone that Whatsume'er the failings on his part, Remember reader he were that good in his hart' . . . .
> 'I made it,' said Joe, 'my own self. I made it in a moment. It was like striking out a horseshoe complete, in a single blow. I never was so much surprised in all my life — couldn't credit my own ed — to tell you the truth, hardly believed it *were* my own ed. As I was saying, Pip, it were my intentions to have had it cut over him; but poetry costs money, cut it how you will, small or large, and it were not done.'

But Pip's slate, with its letters small and large, serves instead, just for a moment, as it brings boy and man together in their dilemma over having had fathers and the complex of guilt, love, and hatred that remembering (or imagining) renews. From one point of view, though, Pip's expectations are this: the equipping of him with the sophisticated tools of remembrance, with a pen instead of a hammer. It is, after all, the emotionally primitive Pip who begets Orlick into the narrative, the journeyman who disables Mrs Joe and who is ever afterwards denoted by her, on her own slate, with the 'mysterious sign' of a hammer (end of chapter 16). As Pip's double he is Pip fossilised at his murderous apprenticeship stage, convinced of his own unloveableness (otherwise his parents would not be dead) and trying to reduce everyone to his own level of spiritual desolation. Pip will be able to accommodate Magwitch, Joe, and the rest of the inhabitants of his mind and memory only when 'poetry' has been bought for him, when he can not only write and speak his mother tongue but the tongues of other motherlands as well:

> When he was not asleep, or playing a complicated kind of Patience . . . he would ask me to read to him — 'Foreign language,

dear boy!' While I complied, he, not comprehending a single word, would stand before the fire surveying me with the air of an Exhibitor, and I would see him, between the fingers of the hand with which I shaded my face, appealing in dumb show to the furniture to take notice of my proficiency. The imaginary student pursued by the misshapen creature he had impiously made, was not more wretched than I, pursued by the creature who had made me, and recoiling from him with a stronger repulsion, the more he admired me and the fonder he was of me.

This is written of, I am sensible, as if it lasted a year. It lasted about five days. (chapter 40)

This is one of the rare occasions when Pip reminds us that his autobiography is actually *written*, that his elaborate, graphic, text is what results from the lack of a parental photograph and from the hieroglyphics of the childhood slate and the lapidary simplicities of the parental tombstone. Magwitch's education of Pip, in other words, which has proceeded apace while he was 'down under' in Australia, enables Pip to recall Magwitch into his life and to discover — along with considerable reluctance to follow through the implications of the discovery — that Magwitch is Abel. Pip 'writes' Magwitch back into Abel, as his slate predicted he might. Simultaneously, Magwitch has been inscribing Pip in fulfilment of his own fantasy. Part of Pip's horror in chapter 40 arises, surely, from the recognition that he really is the product of this 'dead' man's mind, this 'expatriate' back from the netherworld, this 'terrible patron'. For if Pip engendered him way back in boyhood, he has reciprocated by imagining Pip while he was in his Australian grave:

I'm your second father. You're my son — more to me nor any son. I've put away money, only for you to spend. When I was hired-out shepherd in a solitary hut, not seeing no faces but faces of sheep till I half forgot wot men's and women's faces wos like, I see yourn. I drops my knife many a time in that hut when I was a eating my dinner or my supper, and I says, 'Here's the boy again, a looking at me whiles I eats and drinks!' I see you there a many times, as plain as ever I see you on them misty marshes.

'Lord strike me dead!' I says each time — and I goes out in the open air to say it under the open heavens — 'but wot, if I gets liberty and money, I'll make that boy a gentleman!'

(chapter 39)

This Abel, like the first keeper of sheep, his blood, too, crying from the ground (Gen. 4:2, 10), has formed Pip to be his epitaph. What is so shocking is that there appears to be no promised end to the grim infernal circle that we glimpse the full extent of Pip's participation in now, for the first time. For young Abel, even more than the infant Pip, just *was* (chapter 42), and then inevitably became the victim of Compeyson-Cain. There are no reasons, only facts. More terribly and confusingly still, Pip sees him as a murderer ('I had heard that other convict reiterate that he had tried to murder him; . . . I had seen him down in the ditch, tearing and fighting like a wild beast'; chapter 39) and then labels his 'second father' 'uncle' (chapter 40), turning him into Claudius-Cain at the very moment when he perceives him to be a ghost and, in his awful corporeality, not a ghost ('I doubt if a ghost could have been more terrible to me') even as, like Old Hamlet, he grasps his little black book and demands oaths of secrecy from Pip and Herbert (see *Hamlet*, I.v. 157ff.).

Around this point Dickens must mean us to assume that Pip virtually goes mad as his sense of his own and Magwitch's identities utterly fragments into 'wild and whirling' perceptions and words. Pip is to Magwitch as Magwitch is to Pip; alive is to dead; words are to silence; Abel is to Cain; uncle is to father. And that is really only the beginning as the circle whirls at an increasingly sickening speed. For Pip, too, is Orlick-Cain, identified with vertiginous clarity by his familiar emblem at the moment when Magwitch announces himself as his patron:

> 'Could I make a guess, I wonder,' said the Convict, 'at your income since you came of age? As to the first figure now. Five?'
> With my heart beating like a heavy hammer of disordered action, I rose out of my chair, and stood with my hand upon the back of it, looking wildly at him.   (chapter 39)

The hammer emblem brings the numeral zanily into focus as the number of Pip's dead brothers (opening of chapter 1); while the 'guardian' of Pip and the income, Jaggers, seems to become allied to the unlettered Joe, painfully spelling his Js and Os out of Pip's childish slate: ' "Concerning a guardian . . . Some lawyer, maybe. As to the first letter of that lawyer's name now. Would it be J?" '. Most mockingly of all, Compeyson becomes Pip's dead father: ' "what a gentleman Compeyson looked, wi' his curly hair and his black clothes"' (chapter 42); 'the shape of the letters on my father's [tombstone] gave me an odd idea that he was a square, stout, dark man, with curly black hair' (chapter 1). All this confuses Pip so much that he decides that he is fit for nothing now but, like Old Hamlet, to 'go for a soldier' (chapter 41).

Pip's 'repugnance' towards Magwitch (opening of chapter 41) continues to make him feel like Cain, but at this stage in his narrative another text shoulders Genesis and *Hamlet* aside; for the relationship between creator and created, frozen as they are in dependence and opposition, reworks the *Frankenstein* myth,[17] as the quotation from chapter 40 about 'foreign language, dear boy!' makes explicit. Pip, having imagined Magwitch into existence in the first place, and in trying to remake him with disguising clothes on his return, is Frankenstein and Magwitch is his creature re-membered from charnel corpses. But the reverse is also exactly true: Magwitch has remembered Pip and, in showering his money upon him to make him a gentleman, remembered him as well.

2.2 REACHING FOR THE MOTHER

> *Hamlet*: Mother, for love of grace,
> Lay not that flattering unction to your soul,
> That not your trespass but my madness speaks.
> It will but skin and film the ulcerous place,
> Whiles rank corruption, mining all within,
> Infects unseen. Confess yourself to heaven,
> Repent what's past, avoid what is to come;
> And do not spread the compost on the weeds
> To make them ranker.
>
> (*Hamlet*, III.iv)

This chapter began by trying to give some sense of the complexity that the text conveys about Pip's awareness of himself in relation to his dead parents and all the characters who people his life and mind as a result of their deadness. The main thing to emerge is an obsession with the father and variants of the father which, in accordance with Oedipal logic, suggests that the goal of Pip's quest is the mother and images of her. *Great Expectations* is, in fact, a wonderfully imagined exemplification of the phenomenon, described by Strindberg in the preface to *A Dream Play*, whereby 'characters split, double, multiply, evaporate, condense, disperse, assemble. But one consciousness rules over them all, that of the dreamer'.[18] Pip is an Oedipal dreamer, and *Great Expectations* the dream which he is recording for us. It is a mysterious dream that has as its bedrock the sense of loss for dead parents, superimposed on which are strata of hate, betrayal, fear and love. Within these strata lie fossilised fragments of *Hamlet* which, as we begin to piece them together, give one clue at least to the dream's code: it is concerned with fathers and fathers-as-oppressors and with the mother as a strangely combined Gertrude and Ophelia.

The fact that both Pip and Magwitch emerge, half-way through, as having a mutual Frankenstein relationship illuminates rather than confuses the text's logic. Confronted with Magwitch, who has been relegated to the hulk of the prison ship and then transported 'down under', Pip is seeing a zombie, a reanimated corpse ('But I can compare the effect of [the powder he insists on applying to himself], when on, to nothing but the probable effect of rouge upon the dead' (chapter 40)), and he is a corpse reanimated by Pip as that labourer in charnel houses, Frankenstein. The significance of the *Frankenstein* story is that it enables Pip to locate his problem in the mother, for Frankenstein dreams his creature into existence out of his own dead mother:

> I slept, indeed, but I was disturbed by the wildest dreams. I thought I saw Elizabeth, in the bloom of health, walking in the streets of Ingolstadt. Delighted and surprised, I embraced her; but as I imprinted the first kiss on her lips, they became livid with the hue of death; her features appeared to change, and I thought that I held the corpse of my dead mother in my arms; a shroud enveloped her form, and I saw the grave-worms crawling in the folds of the flannel. I started from my sleep with horror . . . .[19]

Frankenstein's dream leads him through his adopted sister to his mother, and he awakens to see the creature he has made from charnel corpses. It is as if he is imagining that he has killed the mother and in gathering together his hocus pocus of corpse fragments he has been trying to retrieve her from the grave and simultaneously give birth to himself again from her dead womb. What Pip does in reanimating Magwitch is, in effect, to use him as a means of getting his mother back. That is why Magwitch almost immediately starts to 'soften', to show female characteristics, and it explains too why Magwitch is now (chapter 42) able to reveal his link, through Compeyson, with the mother whom Pip has also created for himself in the figure of Miss Havisham. The fact that it was Magwitch who made Pip a gentleman, gave him a new birth, re-membered his blacksmith self, also suggests, in terms of the *Frankenstein* myth, his maternal role. Hence his new name, Provis, the provider.[20]

Frankenstein's dream of his dead mother helps us 'place' Miss Havisham as well. Corpse-like, frozen in time, she is a projection into the present of the mother long under the ground. In reminding Pip of this, the reanimated Magwitch's autobiography (chapter 42) enables Pip to approach his centre in the feminine in a way he has not been able to before. Motivated by Magwitch's account of her half brother Arthur's dream (' "She's all in white . . . wi' white flowers in her hair, and she's awful mad, and she's got a shroud hanging over her arm" ') Pip heads for Satis House (chapter 43), approaching Miss Havisham, as at the beginning of the novel (chapter 8), through Estella in the same way that Frankenstein dreams his way back to his mother through the young Elizabeth:

> Estella was knitting, and Miss Havisham was looking on . . . .
> 'And what wind,' said Miss Havisham, 'blows you here, Pip?'
> Though she looked steadily at me, I saw that she was rather confused. Estella, pausing a moment in her knitting with her eyes upon me, and then going on, I fancied that I read in the action of her fingers, as plainly as if she had told me in the dumb alphabet, that she perceived I had discovered my real benefactor.
>
> (chapter 44)

The 'real benefactor' is Magwitch the malefactor perceived by his creature, Pip, as a terrible Frankenstein-like birth-giving father-mother. In coming straight down to Estella and Miss Havisham at Satis, Pip is also registering his sense that his true benefactor has to be feminine, that he locates himself in the female. This is why Estella is knitting; for knitting, along with weaving, has archetypal overtones of the unravelling and patterning of female truth.[21] Even though he is accusing and blaming, Pip is now in a female space, at his maternal centre. Hence the knitting needles transform into a comfortingly hypnotic and rhythmically satisfying dance the wickedly prancing 'pins and needles' that possessed Mrs Joe's bosom. Then, as Pip focuses, trancelike, on the hands — reminder of Mrs Joe and being brought up 'by hand'; reminder of the hand patterned out of the five little graves in the churchyard — he begins to perceive a further maternal image or memory trace which will be clarified some four chapters later when he once more meets Jaggers's housekeeper, Molly:

> The action of her fingers was like the action of knitting. She stood looking at her master, not understanding whether she was free to go . . . .
> He dismissed her and she glided out of the room. But she remained before me, as plainly as if she were still there. I looked at those hands, I looked at those eyes, I looked at that flowing hair; and I compared them with other hands, other eyes, other hair that I knew of, and with what those might be after twenty years of a brutal husband and a stormy life . . . .   (chapter 48)

By the end of this paragraph Pip's perception becomes the 'certain[ty] that this woman was Estella's mother' and it is the hands ('Surely, I had seen . . . such hands on a memorable occasion very lately!') that help him reach it. But 'twenty years' as a round number, as in *Wuthering Heights* the number of years in a generation,[22] takes Pip back to the time when his mother died and to the time when Miss Havisham was betrayed (chapter 42). Molly is both women, as well as Joe's battered mother and the Estella who will be the victim of Drummle. Yet Molly is a criminal, a murderer, for the Pip's-eye view of woman is at one with the flawed Eve view, the Hamlet view. Superimposed on the sentimental memory trace (hands, eyes, flowing hair, the *David Copperfield* image of the mother), then, is its opposite: these hands aren't maternal knitting hands but the hands of a *tricoteuse* bearing the stigmata of their murdering trade, as Wemmick explains in the same chapter. Molly was tried for killing a woman and also suspected of destroying her own child. She was acquitted because 'Jaggers was for her' and did something rather clever with the lacerations on the back of her hands which, on the face of it, were a clear sign that she had struggled with the murder victim:

> Mr Jaggers worked that, in this way. 'We say these are not marks of finger-nails, but marks of brambles, and we show you the brambles. You say they are marks of finger-nails, and you set up

the hypothesis that she destroyed her child. You must accept all consequences of that hypothesis. For anything we know, she may have destroyed her child, and the child in clinging to her may have scratched her hands. What then? You are not trying her for the murder of her child; why don't you? As to this case, if you *will* have scratches, we say that, for anything we know, you may have accounted for them, assuming for sake of argument that you have not invented them?' (chapter 48)

Jaggers is Pip's devil's advocate, exonerating the mother from blame (of murder, of having deliberately betrayed him by dying) while insinuating that she killed her baby, and then he brings brambles back into the text, thus bestowing on this mother prickly, forbidding, hands that fend off instead of comforting, that testify to the impenetrable inhibitions that bar Pip, even in memory, from regaining the mother-as-she-was. Pip overcame brambles in order to learn his mother tongue so that he could, in his autobiography, write the text of his self. What that writing, so promising as an instrument of change in his boyhood, demonstrates as the text begins to close is that the mother is always absent; that brambles remain on Molly, as on the green mounds in the churchyard, as witness to her utter irretrievability and her cruelty in being so irretrievable. The brambles are Pip's version of the 'thorns . . . and thistles' that patriarchy dictates are our inheritance from Eve (Gen. 3:18).[23] The fact that the name Molly is a form of Mary (stainless mother, second Eve) merely confirms Pip's characteristically male confusion over the maternal nature, one that he has already registered in his projection of Miss Havisham as virginal bride and perverter of Estella and that was announced early on, in that first, halting, letter in chapter 7. For it not only names Abel and predicts Orlick but, in its second half, seems to define Pip's problem with motherhood and childbirth: AN wEn i M preNgtD 2 u JO woT larX an bLEvE ME inF xn PiP. Does not this release into the text *wen* (lump, swelling); *impregnated;* Eve *(bleve);* infant *(inf)* and infection *(infxn)*; words which emerge from Pip's sense of himself as Mrs Joe's victim?

* * * * *

Pip's aggrieved sense of injury, together with curiosity and acute anguish, lead immediately after this to the imagining into being of Miss Havisham. The external agents of his meeting with her, however, are Uncle Pumblechook and Mrs Joe who, at the end of this same chapter, ride in out of the cold to tell Pip that he is to go and visit her. With Magwitch, the father as barrier to the mother, relegated to the hulks, slipped below the threshold of consciousness, they pop up like a parody married couple, an 'Uncle' Claudius and Gertrude, as if the disappearance of ghostly Magwitch is too much for Pip to bear because it relieves him of that essential component of his dream life, *Hamlet*. The cold they come riding out of, then, with their good news, is equivalent to the bitter cold on the Elsinore battlements which greets the ghost's return (*Hamlet*, I.i.8; iv.1), which suggests that Miss Havisham's arrival into the novel will complement Magwitch's and parallel that of Old Hamlet.

The parallel is clear and reflects Pip's acute anxiety over his infant loss of his mother, his obsessive sense of her deadness. And so her house is a prison ('a great many iron bars to it. Some of the windows had been walled up; of those that remained, all the lower were rustily barred . . .') and also a ship ('the cold wind . . . made a shrill noise in howling in and out at the open sides of the brewery, like the noise of wind in the rigging of a ship at sea'; chapter 8) to associate it with Magwitch's black and rustily chained hulks and Old Hamlet's purgatorial 'prison-house'. Like Magwitch and Old Hamlet, Miss Havisham too is 'doom'd for a certain term to walk the night' (*Hamlet*, I.v.10) as Pip discovers much later, in chapter 38:

> I was no sooner in the passage than I extinguished my candle; for, I saw Miss Havisham going along it in a ghostly manner, making a low cry. I followed her at a distance, and saw her go up the staircase. She carried a bare candle in her hand, which she had probably taken from one of the sconces in her own room, and was a most unearthly object by its light . . . . During the whole interval, whenever I went to the bottom of the staircase, I heard her footstep, saw her light pass above, and heard her ceaseless low cry.

Even her lingering death by fire is rooted in the torments of Old Hamlet, 'for the day confin'd to fast in fires,/Till the foul crimes done in my days of nature/Are burnt and purged away' (I.v.11–13). In Pip's horrified imagination his mother is not just dead, she is sinful and tormented by the punishments also endured by the Old Hamlet father to whom she is inextricably married.

The bitter winter cold from which Miss Havisham emerges supports an alternative reading of her status as perceived by Pip, however. On this reading the withdrawn Miss Havisham is the mother goddess Ceres grieving over her lost self in the form of her daughter (Proserpina–Estella), and Pumblechook, through whom Pip reaches them, is Pluto, King of Hades, keeper of the dead. Hence his role as 'corn-chandler and seedsman' in whose shop are packeted 'flower-seeds and bulbs' just waiting for 'a fine day to break out of those jails, and bloom', because in the Ceres myth Pluto is the winter guardian of dormant vegetation.[24] The roles are by no means exact: Pluto-Pumblechook has not ravished Proserpina-Estella (symbolically, seed); and the mother grieves even while in the company of her daughter. Yet this very inexactitude of congruence between text and myth is telling: Pip is groping, disoriented. He knows that the mother is prickly Mrs Joe; he hopes that she is her loving opposite. Here, as later with Molly-Eve, he tries to possess the feminine both ways. His *Hamlet* perception operates first: Uncle Pumblechook, hated 'patron' nearly murdered with tar water, is the medium through whom Pip sees Miss Havisham and Estella just as Claudius controls Hamlet's perception of Gertrude and Ophelia. This perception notes the 'rank garden ... overgrown with weeds' that belongs to Satis and equates it with Hamlet's diseased view of the world as 'an unweeded garden/That grows to seed; things rank and gross in nature/Possess it merely' (I.ii.135–7), his response to Gertrude's treachery with Claudius. His Cerealian perspective modifies the data wonderfully but painfully fleetingly. Just for a moment he glimpses that vast interstellar Jungian truth of the *anima* from his Oedipal cavern.[25] This truth says that the rank garden is the world of the grieving mother, the Female, who can return to restore its vegetation when male perceptions of the feminine change; that this Ceres is mourning the effects of male brutality; that this Proserpina, 'scornful [as] a queen' because Proserpina is queen of the underworld, can be restored so that her mother can burgeon into the flower-matron her bridal paraphernalia mockingly suggests she should be; that Estella's candle is the light associated with the questing aspect of the Ceres-Proserpina myth.[26]

The Cerealian perception fragments under the force of Pip's sense of maternal deadness, his conviction that vegetation myths can't be true because, like Donne's lover despairing of St. Lucy's light in the *Nocturnal upon St. Lucy's Day*, he is 're-begot/Of absence, darkness, death; things which are not'. As he describes her the flower girl merely becomes a faded, virginal mummy:

She was dressed in rich materials – satins, and lace, and silks –
all of white. Her shoes were white. And she had a long white veil
dependent from her hair, and she had bridal flowers in her hair,
but her hair was white.... I saw that everything within my view
which ought to be white, had been white long ago, and had lost
its lustre, and was faded and yellow. I saw that the bride within
the bridal dress had withered like the dress, and like the flowers,
and had no brightness left but the brightness of her sunken eyes.
I saw that the dress had been put upon the rounded figure of a
young woman, and that the figure upon which it now hung loose,
had shrunk to skin and bone. Once, I had been taken to see some
ghastly waxwork at the Fair, representing I know not what
impossible personage lying in state. Once, I had been taken to
one of our old marsh churches to see a skeleton in the ashes of a
rich dress, that had been dug out of a vault under the church
pavement. Now, waxwork and skeleton seemed to have dark eyes
that moved and looked at me. I should have cried out, if I could.

By the end of this paragraph she is, like Magwitch, a zombie, the earthbound mother (*Georgiana*) literally excavated from her vault.[27] Like Frankenstein, whose creature rises from the dream of the dead mother, it is her eyes that Pip notices and that terrify him. She is not just ghastly, a skeleton, weird (the word is used of her in this chapter to suggest simultaneously her unearthly, otherwordly, appearance and her matriarchal role in Pip's, as Estella's, life, since *weird*=fate-determining) but somehow dreadfully alive and caught by her pruriently voyeuristic 'son' at that Oedipally sensitive moment when she is about to be married but has no bridegroom. Where Hamlet sees Gertrude recently *re*married, thus living through a fantasy the horror of which Pip will not fully confront even when he goes to watch *Hamlet* itself (chapter 31), Pip stops short at a bride who has been frozen in time at the point when she would have betrayed her son to another man, yet who, in being both bridal and dead-seeming, has, like Gertrude, condensed the two rituals of marriage and funeral so that 'funeral baked meats' seem, terribly, to 'coldly furnish forth the marriage tables' (*Hamlet*, I.ii.180–1). When this ghastly waxwork speaks it confirms Pip's overriding sense of her deadness and his intimate relationship with her: ' "Look at me", said Miss Havisham. "You are not afraid of a woman who has never seen the sun since you were born?" ' Like Mrs Joe recalling the death of Georgiana as she shouts 'You'll drive *me* to the churchyard', Miss Havisham quietly tells Pip that he is her son and that she died the day she gave birth to him, simultaneously announcing her unattainability and bestowing matricidal guilt.

Pip's 'mother' is young and old, accessible through Estella and infinitely, inaccessibly absent; at once Gertrude conflated with Ophelia and Gertrude accompanied by Ophelia; maternal virgin, child burying and child repudiating. These last details, supplied by her imprisoning of Estella in the sepulchral house and her apparently callous signing over of Pip to Joe for his apprenticeship, are reinforced by the way Pip describes Gertrude and Ophelia in the Wopsle production in chapter 31. Gertrude is obviously motherly in being buxom and round like a kettledrum (and bound, incidentally, in the brazen bands of Pip's imprisoning fury), and virginal Ophelia also has motherhood (and infanticide) imposed on her by Pip's crazily monomaniac imagination as he transports himself into the role of imprisoned felon to growl out this amazing *je t'accuse*:

> Ophelia was a prey to such slow musical madness, that when, in course of time, she had taken off her white muslin scarf, folded it up, and buried it, a sulky man who had been long cooling his impatient nose against an iron bar in the front row of the gallery, growled, 'Now the baby's put to bed let's have supper.'
>
> (chapter 31)

As his view of Miss Havisham is focused then refocused, slips then holds, the reader sees her as the dead Ophelia many years on (the Ophelia over whom Gertrude laments she hoped to have decked her bridal bed with flowers, 'and not have strew'd thy grave'; v.i.239), the fertility maiden whose flowers have, as in the Eurydice and Proserpina myths, been transformed suddenly, in a dreadful moment of through-the-looking-glass clarification, into the flowers of death.[28] But Pip's imagination must have her potentially accessible and possessable as well, as she was twenty years earlier in the shape of Ophelia-Estella. The problems of perception, character decomposition and condensation that are constantly going on in Pip's mind are caught with beautiful precision in chapter 8 during his first meeting when Miss Havisham sits in front of her mirror:

> Before she spoke again, she turned her eyes from me, and looked at the dress she wore, and at the dressing-table, and finally at herself in the looking-glass.
> 'So new to him,' she muttered, 'so old to me; so strange to him, so familiar to me; so melancholy to both of us! Call Estella.'
> As she was still looking at the reflection of herself, I thought she was still talking to herself, and kept quiet.
> 'Call Estella,' she repeated, flashing a look at me . . . .

At the beginning, as she gazes into the mirror and names the girl, Miss Havisham is Estella. By the end of the passage she is differentiated from her. Yet as Estella appears with her 'light . . . like a star' the two merge ('flashing a look') and when, slightly later, Pip and Estella settle down in compliance with instructions to play cards, the two merge again. Pip looks from the girl to the dressing table to the youthful bridal dress which is now 'like grave-clothes', the 'long veil so like a shroud', and imagines that he is seeing the buried Ophelia. This, at any rate, is what the next paragraph suggests as its ambiguous *she* hovers in the penumbra of Pip's fantasies:

> So she sat, corpse-like, as we played at cards; the frillings and trimmings on her bridal dress, looking like earthy paper. I knew nothing then, of the discoveries that are occasionally made of bodies buried in ancient times, which fall to powder in the moment of being distinctly seen; but, I have often thought since, that she must have looked as if the admission of the natural light of day would have struck her to dust.
> 'He calls the knaves, Jacks, this boy!' said Estella with disdain . . . .

Is it the mummified bride who plays cards and breaks the silence of that long moment? And as we hear of Pip's 'coarse hands' and 'thick boots' it is as if we are overhearing dead Ophelia complaining of the lumbering grossness of the gravedigger (Hamlet's 'mad knave'; v.i.99). Moreover, it seems certain that it is Pip's morbid conviction that he has actually been in the grave at Satis that compels him, on his next visit, to fight with Herbert, that 'pale young gentleman' of a Laertes, while Estella watches secretly, feeding on the bloodshed like a vampire ('there was a bright flush upon her face, as though something had happened to delight her'; chapter 11).

Hamlet and Laertes struggle as a test of love, and so do Pip and

Herbert. Herbert offers the challenge, as does Laertes, not realising that Pip is fighting for the mother's love, for Estella as Miss Havisham, for Ophelia as Gertrude. (Herbert, after all, has a mother who is alive and all too well and thriving in that suburb, Hammersmith, whose name can sound on his innocent ears without evoking forges, Orlicks, or fathers like Joe's who come home and hammer their wives and children.) Pip knows exactly what he is doing, however. This is why, just before the fight at the end of chapter 11, Jaggers has met him on the stairs, a manifestation of the punitive father-as-Law again, who scrutinises him like one of the lost souls out of Doré's engravings for Dante's *Inferno;* and why the 'mother' has kept on and on about mortality, obsessively showing Pip the table on which she will be laid when she is dead (it is, of course, the table which was laid for, and still contains the rotting remains of, her wedding breakfast, permanent witness to Hamlet's horrified vision of the equation of funeral baked meats and wedding food). The chapter also rings the changes on one of the novel's insistent puns: ' "this house strikes you old and *grave*, boy," said Miss Havisham'; ' "I am not aware," observed the *grave* lady whose voice I had heard but once . . .'.[29]

Pip's experiences at Satis are a kind of pre-view of the *Hamlet* chapter, a menacing involvement of Miss Havisham in his obsessional, psychological plot. She thinks she is *weird*, one who controls her own and Estella's destinies, the one who summons Pip into her and Estella's lives. In fact Pip has somehow summoned her, as he summoned Magwitch, to act out their roles in his own *Hamlet*. This, at least, is what the syntax suggests as it stumbles once more in recording the first visit:

'Mr Pumblechook's boy, ma'am. Come — to play.' . . . 'I am tired,' said Miss Havisham. 'I want diversion, and I have done with men and women. Play.' . . . 'I sometimes have sick fancies,' she went on, 'and I have a sick fancy that I want to see some play. There, there!' with an impatient movement of the fingers of her right hand; 'play, play, play!'

Is the imperative *play* noun or verb? The more it is reiterated the more it insists that it is a noun, and as Pip and Estella act out their roles it is as if Pip is taunting her with the image of her relationship with the husband-father Compeyson as Hamlet taunts Claudius and Gertrude with the play-within-the-play.[30]

More than that, the game of beggar-my-neighbour initiated by the Pip who has bad dreams (as at the end of chapter 2) and chases the bad dream of ambition until he discovers that it is nothing, a mere shadow, and who is surrounded by prisons and prisoners, seems to be located in, and haunted by, another moment in *Hamlet* that occurs just before Rosencrantz and Guildenstern announce the arrival of the players:

Hamlet: What have you, my good friends, deserved at the hands of Fortune that she sends you to prison hither?
Guildenstern: Prison, my lord?
Hamlet: Denmark's a prison.
Rosencrantz: Then is the world one.
Hamlet: A goodly one, in which there are many confines, wards and dungeons, Denmark being one o' th' worst.
Rosencrantz: We think not so, my lord.
Hamlet: Why, then 'tis none to you; for there is nothing either good or bad but thinking makes it so. To me it is a prison.
Rosencrantz: Why, then your ambition makes it one: 'tis too narrow for your mind.
Hamlet: O God, I could be bounded in a nutshell and count myself a king of infinite space — were it not that I have bad dreams.
Guildenstern: Which dreams indeed are ambition; for the very substance of the ambitious is merely the shadow of a dream.
Hamlet: A dream itself is but a shadow.
Rosencrantz: Truly, and I hold ambition of so airy and light a quality that it is but a shadow's shadow.
Hamlet: Then are our beggars bodies, and our monarchs and outstretched heroes the beggars' shadows.

(ii.ii.239ff.)

Hamlet's Platonistic metaphysics are limited and defined by his torment, His obsession with the father-king imprisoned and reduced to the shadow of a beggar ('Remember me'). Pip, too, imprisoned by the same dream, enacts a game through which he will beggar himself and discover that the ghostly shade of the father is a beggarly prisoner. As if to deny what already seems to be perceived as truth, Pip goes home and tells lies, creating out of Miss Havisham's tattered, beggarly substance a visionary queen 'in a black velvet coach' (chapter 9), and forcing Joe, as he broods on his beggarly, earthy, Hamlet self, to transform him into a potential king of infinite space:

> The king upon his throne, with his crown upon his 'ed, can't sit and write his acts of Parliament in print, without having begun, when he were a unpromoted Prince, with the alphabet . . . .

'There was some hope in this piece of wisdom' is Pip's encouraged response, which naïvely ignores the thorns and brambles that guard that very alphabet and turn it into a forbidden and sinful mother who will, at the very moment of his promotion, reduce the Pip-king to a beggar's shadow.

* * * * *

Play means movement, of course, and Pip needs play — *the* play of *Hamlet* — to help him re-enact his Oedipal problem, even though re-enacting will merely entail repetition without resolution.[31] At the same time, though, he needs the static, treasured, memory, the image caught in time, the maternal *gestalt*. Unlike David Copperfield's, his maternal image is, like his paternal image, deathly and terrible, deeply self-destructive. When Pip enters Satis he emerges into the darkness of the grave and he meets his mother as one of the living dead whose essential quality is her stillness. She is unmoving, ghostly. It is not going too far to imagine that Pip visualises her in terms of the maternal photograph he does not possess because his childhood passed in those 'days . . . long before the days of photographs'. Freud was to be fascinated by the possibility of a parallel between the chemistry of photography and the psychology of the memory trace;[32] but Pip's perception belongs less to the laboratory than the studio. As he sees Miss Havisham looming out of the background darkness, stopped in time, he sees and records that very quality of photographic deadness described by Roland Barthes as he elaborates on his idea of the photographer as embalmer:

> Nothing would be funnier . . . than the photographers' contortions to produce effects that are 'lifelike': wretched notions: they make me pose in front of my paintbrushes, they take me outdoors

(more 'alive' than indoors), put me in front of a staircase because a group of children is playing behind me . . . . As if the (terrified) Photographer must exert himself to the utmost to keep the Photograph from becoming Death. But I — already an object, I do not struggle. I foresee that I shall have to wake from this bad dream even more uncomfortably; for what society makes of my photograph, what it reads there, I do not know . . . ; but when I discover myself in the product of this operation, what I see is that I have become Total-Image, which is to say, Death in person.[33]

Pip perceives as a photographer, and Miss Havisham, who is in part living out her own separate fantasy, is as self-conscious as Barthes the sitter. She poses, uncertain which position finally to freeze herself in, relishing that moment of static real Death which will find her finally fixed, framed, within the rectangle of the table and then of the grave. And as she poses she is lit up by candles as the prison ship's blackness was illumined by torches, caught in her continuing lifetime of photographic 'death' as an extraordinary companion portrait to Pip's picture of Magwitch.

Photography pales beside the blinding revelations Pip expects from autobiography, however, because to write is to possess the mother albeit in the rarefied and tricky form of the mother tongue. Hence in the very next chapter (10) he rushes off to Biddy, his more learned fellow orphan, 'to get out of [her] everything she knew'. Eventually she will marry Joe, become Pip's 'mother', and have another little Pip, at which point the Oedipal circle will be completed. As a warning of the taboo about to be broken by even contacting Biddy, a stranger accosts him rather as Jaggers will when he is on his way up to see Miss Havisham in chapter 11. This stranger, too, has something to do with father Magwitch: he is 'a secret-looking man', 'strange', who stirs his rum and water with a file and leaves two one-pound notes with Pip that seem, like Magwitch's grubby testament, 'to have been on terms of the warmest intimacy with all the cattle markets in the county'. The notes haunt Pip and become the substance of bad dreams, yet another consequence of that *Hamlet* scenario where he tried to beggar his neighbour ('there they remained, a nightmare to me, many and many a night and day'). Worse than that, the monarch's beggarly shadow returns as well: 'I was haunted by the file too. A dread possessed me that when I least expected it, the file would reappear' (end of chapter 10); for this is Magwitch's file transformed in the mists of the imagination into the 'apparition of a file of soldiers' that, at the beginning of chapter 5, kaleidoscopically multiplies the paternal ghost of Old Hamlet, fully armed.

The presence of Wopsle while the stranger is catechising Joe and staring at Pip almost guarantees the presence of *Hamlet*:

> as one who knew all about relationships, having professional occasion to bear in mind what female relations a man might not marry; [Wopsle] expounded the ties between me and Joe. Having his hand in, Mr Wopsle finished off with a most terrifically snarling passage from Richard the Third . . . .

For the last time Wopsle put on his Richard the Third act was in chapter 4 when he 'said grace with theatrical declamation — as it now appears to me, something like a religious cross of the Ghost in Hamlet with Richard the Third': Richard is linked inextricably to *Hamlet* in Pip's mind, particularly when it is a question of 'what female relations a man might not marry'.

Shortly after this Pip is placed in Uncle Pumblechook's custody to be bound apprentice to Joe, having been 'sold' to him for twenty-five pounds by Miss Havisham. The violence of Pip's rejection of this attempt of the mother formally to hand him over to the father engenders Cain-like Orlick (chapter 15) and the murderous attack on Mrs Joe, blamed on Pip when Orlick confronts him in the sluice house by the limekilns (chapter 53) and somehow laid at Pip's door in the actual chapter in which it occurs through Pip's collaboration with Wopsle by listening to *George Barnwell*. Perhaps collaboration is the wrong word, for Pip takes on the role of the murdering apprentice who kills his 'uncle [as read by Wopsle] with no extenuating circumstances whatever'. Killing your uncle in a *Hamlet* context is probably all right, except that Wopsle is 'really' Pip's double as the prince, which suggests that *George Barnwell* is a brilliant attempt on Pip's part to opt out of the burdens of his Oedipus complex altogether by killing himself.[34]

Killing yourself and your uncle are not the same as killing your sister-mother, but *George Barnwell* releases Pip back into his autobiography with the guilty knowledge that, on one level at least, as the apprentice in the play he was acting out his own role as apprentice in real life and identifying Joe with the dead uncle. It is a psychologically necessary *non sequitur* that 'With my head full of George Barnwell, I was at first disposed to believe that *I* must have had some hand in the attack upon my sister' because as he sees Mrs Joe lying there he knows he has killed her, that he has imposed on her proleptically the image of Miss Havisham lying on her table after suffering in the flames:

> The unemployed bystanders drew back when they saw me, and so I became aware of my sister — lying without sense or movement on the bare boards where she had been knocked down by a tremendous blow on the back of the head, dealt by some unknown hand when her face was turned towards the fire . . .
> (chapter 15)

A result of the attack is that Mrs Joe, who 'lives' on in the same way that Miss Havisham lives on after her wedding and after the flames because Pip just will not let his mothers go, is relegated to a limbo of pastness: 'Such a fine figure of a woman as she once were, Pip' (chapter 16). Her place in the household is taken by Biddy. As an orphan she is Pip's 'sister', and as a girl on whom Pip is at once dependent and whom he patronizes (chapter 17) she is yet another form of the mother, loving, comforting, sensible: 'She put her hand, which was a comfortable hand though roughened by work, upon my hands, one after another, and gently took them out of my hair . . .' But the emergence of Orlick as her lover in this same chapter ('I — I am afraid he likes me') is an ominous sign that Pip wants Biddy dead, too; that once more he is insisting that his Freudian first and third mothers — the life-giving and succouring mother, the mother earth who receives you in death — are one and the same.[35] Waking into the world and finding his parents dead has totally deformed his perception and his expectations which will not alter when he leaves his fallen paradise for one that is apparently greater (chapter 19):

> We changed, again and yet again, and it was now too late and too far to go back, and I went on. And the mists had all solemnly risen now, and the world lay spread before me.

THIS IS THE END OF THE FIRST STAGE OF
PIP'S EXPECTATIONS.

Pip's journey by stages always ends up on a stage which sees a performance of *Hamlet*. Going back and on are the same process to him, for the world that emerges from the mist narrows to a London that imprisons lawyer Jaggers, extends to Hammersmith and Wemmick's neo-Gothic fantasy of an Elsinore in which his venerable Aged P. of a father is carefully enshrined, and releases ghostly Old Magwitch again.

2.3 EXTENDING THE CIRCUMFERENCE

> *King*: The bark is ready, and the wind at help,
> Th'associates tend, and everything is bent
> For England.
> *Hamlet*: For England?
> *King*: Ay Hamlet.
> *Hamlet*: Good.
> *King*: So is it, if thou knew'st our purposes.
> *Hamlet*: I see a cherub that sees them. But come, for England. Farewell, dear mother.
>
> (*Hamlet*, IV.iii)

Hamlet seems to be saying here that to leave Denmark is to leave his mother. Since this is impossible for him he rapidly returns to encounter mother earth as she surrounds the dead Ophelia. Pip's journey to Little Britain, where Jaggers's office is located, is similarly circular. Sent home to become a gentleman—one who, by definition, keeps his feelings buried—Pip's extended world becomes a burial ground again. Maternal absence breeds death and thoughts of death, including that of the father, and so Jaggers's office in Little Britain is 'just out of Smithfield' (chapter 20), that place of martyrs appallingly tortured and burned to death (an association reinforced by the Bartholomew Close which Pip finds himself strolling through on his tour of Little Britain in the same chapter),[36] and Jaggers's 'own high-backed chair [is] of deadly black horse-hair, with rows of brass nails round it, like a coffin'. Beyond the office lie the law courts outside which Pip is offered a 'full view of the Lord Chief Justice in his wig and robes [as if] that awful personage [were a] waxwork' and a grotesque companion to that other 'ghastly waxwork', Miss Havisham. The exhibitor himself is even more ominous: an 'exceedingly dirty and partially drunk minister of justice' who is dressed in 'mildewed clothes, which had evidently not belonged to him originally, and which, I took it into my head, he had bought cheap of the executioner', he is another on Pip's roll call of the living dead, anticipating the returned corpse of Magwitch, the Frankenstein-like exhibitor of his creature, Pip (chapter 40), and 'the "Jack" of the little causeway' whom Pip, Magwitch, and the others encounter in the pub past Gravesend 'who was sitting in a corner, and who had a bloated pair of shoes on, which he had exhibited while we were eating our eggs and bacon, as interesting relics that he had taken a few days ago from the feet of a drowned seaman washed ashore' (chapter 54). In Pip's imagination everyone either is dead or lives off or with the dead. And so inside Jaggers's office are death masks, 'two dreadful casts on a shelf, of faces peculiarly swollen, and twitchy about the nose' (chapter 20), a wild realisation of those dreadful two one-pound notes that haunted him from their place 'on the top of a press in the state parlour' at the forge (chapter 10) and that had evoked Magwitch and, through him, Compeyson. Or maybe the masks evoke Magwitch and Compeyson directly, bypassing the notes of the mysterious, secret stranger. Is Pip — are we? — looking back at them from beyond their deaths? If so, when did they die – after the text's beginning or before it? What exactly *is* Jaggers's office? For the death masks somehow hint that what Pip encountered in the marshes was a pair of writhing zombies who have left these awful silent testaments to their lives and deaths to be discovered by Pip when he comes to Jaggers.

There is, of course, another possibility: that the masks of these hanged creatures belong to the hanged pirate Magwitch (chapter 1) as the spouse of hanged Mother Havisham (end of chapter 8), so that they are a horribly perverted realisation of the dead father and mother staring out from their tomblike sanctum, their deathly remoteness being reinforced by the fact of Jaggers's absence on the first two occasions Pip visits his office.[37] This idea is less silly than it might at first seem if we take seriously the comparison of the nails on the chair to those on a coffin and imagine the possibility that Jaggers's room is a grave because it is small and lit from above only. In effect, the opening of stage two of *Great Expectations* repeats the beginning of stage one except that there Old Hamlet had leaped out of the grave whereas here young Hamlet climbs into it and, in a grotesque composition of place, imagines the absence of the dead father in the Jaggers–father's absence while the paired death-masks look on. There is the extraordinary detail, too, that the skylight that illuminates the room is 'patched like a broken head', as if the battered mazard of *Hamlet*, v.i (where Hamlet himself scrambles into a grave) had combined with Mrs Joe's sadly battered skull (end of chapter 15) to insist on the parent-ness of this, as of nearly all, images projected into Pip's autobiography:

> Mr Jaggers's room was lighted by a skylight only, and was a most dismal place; the skylight, eccentrically patched like a broken head, and the distorted adjoining houses looking as if they had twisted themselves to peep down at me through it. There were not so many papers about, as I should have expected to see; and there were some odd objects about, that I should not have expected to see – such as an old rusty pistol, a sword in a scabbard, several strange-looking boxes and packages, and two dreadful casts on a shelf, of faces peculiarly swollen, and twitchy about the nose. Mr Jaggers's own high-backed chair was of deadly black horse-hair, with rows of brass nails round it, like a coffin . . . .
>
> I sat down in the cliental chair placed over against Mr Jaggers's chair, and became fascinated by the dismal atmosphere of the place . . . . I wondered whether the two swollen faces were of Mr Jaggers's family, and, if he were so unfortunate as to have had a pair of such ill-looking relations, why he stuck them on that dusty perch for the blacks and flies to settle on, instead of giving them a place at home.

Pip waits in 'Mr Jaggers's close room' for a while (it is 'close' like the bedroom graves of the pub on the river bank in chapter 54, from which 'we found the air as carefully excluded . . . as if air were fatal to life')[38] then moves from his confrontation with the empty coffin, the gazing masks, the peering houses, to the slaughterhouse of Smithfield ('the shameful place, being all asmear with filth and fat and blood and foam, seemed to stick to me'), Newgate prison (outside which the roadway is 'covered with straw to deaden the noise of passing vehicles', in fact because of the trials but suggesting the identical ritual outside a town house in mourning), and the mildewed exhibitor of the waxwork Lord Chief Justice. Into — and out of — all this comes Jaggers, whose name indicates that he is a vagrant dressed in beggarly tatters (the father as 'king of shreds and patches' [*Hamlet*, III.iv.103]), another manifestation of the ' "Jack" of the causeway'. The excitable Jew who greets Jaggers's arrival seems to associate him with death as well, for his frenzied incantation of 'Oh Jaggerth, Jaggerth, Jaggerth! all otherth ith

Cag-Maggerth, give me Jaggerth!' differentiates him from cag-maggers only to assimilate him to it again. And since *cag-mag* is already-slaughtered meat that is sold as fresh meat, *Cag-Maggerth* = *Jaggerth* = *Mag(witch)*, who will return as a corpse from the grave in chapter 39.[39]

It is no wonder that Pip feels oppressed, highly sensitised as he is to what, in the quotation above, he calls 'the dismal atmosphere of the place'. *Dismal* is gloomy; but *dismals* are mourning garments, as Jaggers's clerk Wemmick immediately reminds him:

> I judged him to be a bachelor from the frayed condition of his linen, and he appeared to have sustained a good many bereavements; for, he wore at least four mourning rings, besides a brooch representing a lady and a weeping willow at a tomb with an urn on it. I noticed, too, that several rings and seals hung at his watch chain, as if he were quite laden with remembrances of departed friends. (chapter 21)

From the coffin and the grave and the masks and Jaggers as decaying flesh Pip moves to Wemmick in dismals whose attire tells us what has, really, been apparent all along: that Pip (unlike Wemmick) is in mourning and has never completed the process, has never proceeded beyond the first sense of parental loss and so has never grasped, let alone begun to move beyond, what Freud called the pleasure principle. If we see Pip in terms of Freud's grandson playing with the reel attached to a piece of string, we must understand him as constantly trying to leap over the cotside with the reel-mother:

> What [the grandson] did was to hold the reel by the string and very skilfully throw it over the edge of his curtained cot, so that it disappeared into it, at the same uttering his expressive 'o-o-o-o'. He then pulled the reel out of the cot again by the string and hailed its reappearance with a joyful *'da'* [there]. This, then, was the complete game — disappearance and return. As a rule one only witnessed its first act, which was repeated untiringly as a game in itself, though there is no doubt that the greater pleasure was attached to the second act.
>
> The interruption of the game then became obvious. It was related to the child's great cultural achievement — the instinctual renunciation (that is, the renunciation of instinctual satisfaction)

which he had made in allowing his mother to go away without protesting. He compensated himself for this, as it were, by himself staging the disappearance and return of the objects within his reach.[40]

Pip would follow the reel and thread as a clue to his mother's whereabouts because he never consented to his mother's departure. He is always saying *fort* (gone), always in a state of mourning which Wemmick's 'remembrances' mock because they suggest completed mourning, grief modifying itself into fruitful symbols. The power of mourning successfully completed is suggested in the fact that Wemmick controls (is not controlled by) his Elsinore (which, like the real one [*Hamlet* I.ii.126], comes complete with battlements and cannon), and that he can end up by marrying his Miss Skiffins with no apparent Oedipal trouble at all.

Pip, however, sees him somewhat differently, as an extension of his own continuing grief. To him the lady and the tomb figured on the brooch suggest Estella and the dead parents, and the willow, however familiar in memorial iconography, signifies Ophelia as reported by the grieving Gertrude: 'There is a willow grows askant the brook . . . . When down her weedy trophies and herself/Fell in the weeping brook' (*Hamlet*, IV.vii. 165, 173–4).[41] The brooch doesn't say *da* to Pip, merely *fort*, and then its owner plunges him into the further ruined paradise of Barnard's Inn:

> We entered this haven through a wicket-gate, and were disgorged by an introductory passage into a melancholy little square that looked to me like a flat burying-ground. I thought it had the most dismal trees in it, and the most dismal sparrows, and the most dismal cats, and the most dismal houses (in number half a dozen or so), that I had ever seen. I thought the windows of the sets of chambers into which those houses were divided, were in every stage of dilapidated blind and curtain, crippled flower-pot, cracked glass, dusty decay, and miserable makeshift; while To Let To Let To Let, glared at me from empty rooms, as if no new wretches ever came there, and the vengeance of the soul of Barnard were being slowly appeased by the gradual suicide of the present occupants and their unholy interment under the gravel. A frouzy mourning of soot and smoke attired this forlorn creation of Barnard, and it had strewn ashes on its head, and was undergoing penance and humiliation as a mere dust-hole.
> (chapter 21)

'Dismal'; 'burying ground': the little square contains the churchyard of the beginning and, in its and the Inn's dereliction, Satis's decay and its 'rank garden' (chapter 8) modulated into, merged with, the burial ground of *Hamlet*, v.i. Pip's clue to the modulation is Wemmick's brooch with its willow, lady, and tomb, but in following it he underestimates the tricks his mind plays because of his grief: Barnard's Inn is a grave that is empty of everyone until Herbert-Laertes's arrival towards the end of the chapter (the gap between expectation-of-arrival and arrival evokes the empty space that should be filled by the Ophelia-mother). And when Herbert makes his appearance, he does so like Magwitch from the engraved tombstones, like Old Hamlet to Hamlet, asserting kinship, even identification:

> Mr Pocket, Junior's, idea of Shortly was not mine, for I had nearly maddened myself with looking out for half an hour, and had written my name with my finger several times in the dirt of every pane in the window, before I heard footsteps on the stairs. Gradually there arose before me the hat, head, neckcloth, waistcoat, trousers, boots, of a member of society of about my own standing . . . .

From the name on the window emerges the self as ghost from below, or, in the terminology of *Hamlet*, the ghost from the cellarage. The fact that Pip then (chapter 22) starts talking with him 'with sudden gravity' about being engaged to Estella suggests that for him his problem with the ghost and with his 'pale young gentleman' of a Laertes is, as for Hamlet, really the same: the fight for the mother and for Ophelia is one fight and made all the more appallingly inexplicable by Herbert's simple, decent, open, humanity ('I have never seen any one since, who more strongly expressed to me, in every look and tone, a natural incapacity to do anything secret and mean').

The notion of Pip's swooping back to land on the father again receives support from the name of his new London dwelling. Historically one of the Inns of Chancery, Barnard's Inn had for a century or so ceased to have any connection with the law.[42] In Pip's fantasy world, however, *Barnard* suggests *Barnwell*, murderer of the 'uncle' Hamlet-Wopsle. Moreover, Pip's Barnard is 'a disembodied spirit, or a fiction' in chapter 21. He reappears once more only, to lament Joe's unfortunate visit to London and to *Hamlet* ('an angel could not have concealed the fact that Barnard was shedding sooty tears outside the window'; chapter 27). As the *genius loci* of this decaying house and burial ground, he is related to ghostly Magwitch and Pip's Ophelia-mother of a Miss Havisham and thus also belongs to the *Hamlet* structure. In Pip's perpetual replay of *Hamlet* he is Barnardo, that character so crucial at the beginning of the play, however quickly forgotten after. In fact, he opens *Hamlet* ('Who's there?'), coming on as the ghost will come on later, and has significantly riddling things to say about the ghost and the king: 'Long live the King!'; 'let us once again assail your ears,/That are so fortified against our story,/What we have two nights seen'; and

> Last night of all,
> When yond same star that's westward from the pole,
> Had made his course t'illume that part of heaven
> Where now it burns, Marcellus and myself,
> The bell then beating one —
>
> *Enter* GHOST
>
> *Marcellus*: Peace, break thee off. Look where it comes again.
> *Barnardo*: In the same figure like the King that's dead.

In recounting the previous experience Barnardo engenders its repetition. His words act as an incantation and cause the paternal ghost to reappear 'like the King that's dead' and urge reinterpretation of his earlier *vivat rex*. In Pip's long *Hamlet* Barnard-Barnardo weeps and mourns, suggesting paternal and maternal absence, inviting suicide so that we may share the 'unholy interment' of Old Hamlet's ghost (the phrase comes from the description of the Inn in chapter 21), and through his 'flat burying ground' and Lenten ashes linking the dead father-king with the dead Ophelia ('Do not . . . seek for thy noble father in the dust' (I.ii.70–1); 'Now pile your dust upon the quick and dead' (v.i.244)). Barnard seems also to lament Pip's arrival, as if trying to save him for his Oedipal self, as if to prevent his entry into this stage of his expectations, this beginning-again of the *Hamlet* text; and he does the same in chapter 27 for Joe, grieving that this man should be called from Wopsle's comic *Hamlet* into Pip's darkly repellent reading of the play.

Barnard's Inn, then, condenses all Pip's images of death: the marsh churchyard with its parental graves, Miss Havisham's Satis, the grave from which Old Hamlet comes, the grave into which Ophelia is laid. Herbert rises into this grave world bearing gifts of fruit that come from a healthier, feminine, land, unaware that he is Laertes as potential enemy (until Pip's 'sudden gravity' over Herbert's having once been possibly 'intended for' Estella) and in fact doing all he can to assert himself as friend. In this role he very soon rechristens Pip ('Would you mind Handel for a familiar name? There's a charming piece of music by Handel, called the Harmonius Blacksmith'; chapter 22), attempting through friendship to undo a likely result of Pip's inhabiting Barnard's deathly dust and ashes — that he might, with Barnard's other occupants, feel called suicidally to the grave and, as Hamlet does with Laertes in v.i, not just enter the grave but be conned into thinking that it is only there that you find your true identity ('This is I,/Hamlet the Dane' (250–1)).

Seeing the danger, Herbert offers Pip a change of identity which he happily accepts. Unfortunately, Herbert has been drawn further into Pip's world than he realises. The name cannot transform Pip because it celebrates his blacksmith self, the dark self that bears the burden of the Orlick *persona* and his emblematic hammer (end of chapter 16) and that had reached Little Britain in a hackney cab whose box Pip 'remember[s] to have been decorated with an old weather-stained pea-green hammercloth' (opening of chapter 20). Herbert's magic works for a moment as Pip hears without apparent trauma all that he knows about Miss Havisham and eats his first London dinner rejoicing in the absence of 'old people'; but it has turned to black magic by the end of the chapter when Pip rides to meet the Pocket family in Hammersmith. Mrs Pocket is, clearly, an Inadequate Mother who endangers, deliberately it seems to the critically observing Pip, all her children but particularly Baby; and Mr Pocket seems to be so influenced by the prevailing sense of paternal threat and terror that he feels obliged to introduce himself as being 'not . . . an alarming personage' (chapter 23). In other words, he proclaims himself not-Magwitch, not-ghost, as if he senses that for Pip *Ham*-mersmith doesn't just evoke the forge but *Hamlet* as well, and therefore possesses as its antiphonal companion in Pip's Oedipal darkness Barnard's glaring 'To *Let* To *Let* To *Let*' (chapter 21).

Pip is really building up to Joe's irruption into his autobiography in chapter 27 with his partial account of Wopsle's *Hamlet*. Before that happens he has to define his ominous world a little more, and particularly as it relates to Jaggers, the father-as-Law. Actually it is Wemmick, Pip's psychopomp to the Walworth Elsinore in chapter 25, who functions as hermeneut. Jaggers, says Wemmick to Pip, is ' "Deep . . . as Australia." Pointing with his pen at the office floor, to express that Australia was understood, for the purposes of the figure, to be symmetrically on the opposite spot of the globe' (chapter 24),[43] thus announcing Magwitch's return from down under and simultaneously hazarding the possibilities that Jaggers is Magwitch's London *persona* and a kind of hyperactive equivalent to the Old Hamlet who hops around under the stage (in the underworld yet not completely of it) like a desperate attorney crying out 'swear' (*Hamlet*, i.v.157ff.); which is of course, exactly what Magwitch does with his greasy black testament in chapter 39. Wemmick also reads the death masks for Pip, confirming that one might be Compeyson's since it was bequeathed by 'a gentlemanly Cove' whose crime was forgery, but opening questions about the other, who 'is' Magwitch only in so far as his story involves two women, 'his game' and another (compare chapter 50). As the murderer of his master, though, he sounds like the Pip of *George Barnwell*, the furious avenger of imagined wrongs against the father; and as the giver of the brooch representing the lady and the weeping willow at the tomb with the urn upon it he is Pip, too, toying Hamlet-like with his fantasies of Ophelia and Gertrude, Estella and Miss Havisham. For according to Wemmick 'the lady' is the icon of 'his game' or whore, who thus hangs suspended before us as the text's matrix, the feminine as the object of desire who is also the mother of death and the despised, betraying, harlot.

With these signs activated in his mind, Pip stays the night at Elsinore to see (but not understand) that it can be 'a pretty pleasure-ground' in which male Aged P.s are welcome and celebrated; for Pip, unlike Wemmick, cannot live in two worlds, cannot emotionally negotiate Wemmick's simple chiasmus of a life: 'When I go into the office, I leave the Castle behind me, and when I come into the Castle, I leave the office behind me' (chapter 25). And so he gravitates back to Jaggers, perceiving in his Soho house a dilapidated, grimy, building that evokes Barnard's Inn and, with its decorative swags that look to Pip like gallows nooses ('I know what kind of loops I thought they looked like'; chapter 26), Satis House ('I saw a figure hanging by the neck'; chapter 8). Although *not* Jaggers's office, it is strangely the same as the office, the swag–nooses also evoking the masks of the two hanged men and the potential *homme pendu* who is the real king of the office as of the churchyard and of Pip's new apartment in 'Garden-court' (chapter 39), Magwitch:

> 'By G —, it's Death!' 'What's death?' 'I was sent for life. It's death to come back. There's been overmuch coming back of late years, and I should of a certainty be hanged if took.'
>
> (chapter 39)

So the text riddles on, giving us Jaggers-Maggers as another shady father standing by a 'comfortably laid' table (chapter 26) that is apparently the opposite of Miss Havisham's festal mortuary slab until he elects his favourite son and, as it were, makes it the same. For Jaggers overlooks Pip and Startop to concentrate on Bentley Drummle, 'the blotchy, sprawly, sulky fellow' whom he nicknames 'the Spider', thus identifying him as one of the 'speckle-legged spiders with blotchy bodies' that 'run . . . home' to the decomposed wedding cake on the table where the dead Miss Havisham intends to be laid. Jaggers as father demonstrates to Pip through another double that his Oedipal self wishes to rest in the 'home' of the mother sanctuary. At this point the Soho house is, to all intents and purposes, Satis House, enabling Pip to see in Drummle the realisation of his boyhood's (and manhood's) attraction to Miss Havisham-Estella. She means death to him; he means death to her. That is the meaning of the parallel between Orlick (Pip's murdering blacksmith other self) and Drummle, double for Pip's murderous London self.[44] Orlick slouches and creeps and hammers at Mrs Joe in hatred and also to get at the maternal care that must be in her; Drummle creeps and slouches and marries Estella and beats her up, on Pip's behalf, from the depths of his maimed self to discover the love that must be embedded somewhere within her stony heart; Pip rescues Miss Havisham from the flames only to fight her in a lethal combat:

> I looked round and saw the disturbed beetles and spiders running away over the floor, and the servants coming in with breathless cries at the door. I still held her forcibly down with all my strength, like a prisoner who might escape; and I doubt if I even knew who she was, or why we had struggled, or that she had been in flames, or that the flames were out, until I saw the patches

of tinder that had been her garments, no longer alight but falling in a black shower around us. (chapter 49)

The intensity of the visit to Jaggers's house is such that, out of him and his Drummle self as it engages with the lawyer-father, Pip sees the mother:

[Jaggers] immediately began to talk to Drummle: not at all deterred by his replying in his heavy reticent way, but apparently led on by it to screw discourse out of him. I was looking at the two, when there came between me and them, the housekeeper, with the first dish for the table.

She was a woman of about forty, I supposed — but I may have thought her younger than she was. Rather tall, of a lithe nimble figure, extremely pale, with large faded eyes, and a quantity of streaming hair. I cannot say whether any diseased affection of the heart caused her lips to be parted as if she were panting, and her face to bear a curious expression of suddenness and flutter; but I know that I had been to see Macbeth at the theatre, a night or two before, and that her face looked to me as if it were all disturbed by fiery air, like the faces I had seen rise out of the Witches' caldron.

She set the dish on . . . . She set on every dish; and I always saw in her face, a face rising out of the caldron. Years afterwards, I made a dreadful likeness of that woman, by causing a face that had no other natural resemblance to it than it derived from flowing hair, to pass behind a bowl of flaming spirits in a dark room. (chapter 26)

The hair and large eyes make her a mother archetype. She is Molly who is Miss Havisham who is the apparently bridally attainable yet in the end forbidden Estella–Ophelia. The quest is perpetual ('years afterwards') and always for the same phenomenon: here at last Pip seems to admit that he played *fort-da*. The 'bowl of flaming spirits' hints at souls tortured in purgatory with the face at the centre as some terribly garbled and degraded Dantean Beatrice. But *Macbeth* says something more: that this mother is another manifestation of the mother as witch, the dark mother. (In chapter 11, as Pip watches the spiders, he thinks Miss Havisham 'looked like the Witch of the place'.) She is a killer and in alliance with the father-king against him. As he gazes the more intently at her, her face merges into the black round of the cauldron mouth, filled among other things with

'Finger of birth-strangled babe,/Ditch-deliver'd by a drab' (*Macbeth*, IV.i.30–1) and its apparitions of the bloody child, the crowned babe, and the kings whose line seems to 'stretch out to th' crack of doom'.

This is a variant of Molly-as-Eve above, p.77), the mother as *belle dame sans merci* who, like the Estella vampire (end of chapter 11), combines within herself Macbeth's Scotland and Hamlet's Elsinore in all their admissions of misogyny. To make Pip suffer more, Jaggers now demonstrates Molly's strength of wrist, as if in mocking denial of the possibility that there could ever be such things as loving maternal hands: 'She brought her other hand from behind her, and held the two out side by side. The last wrist was much disfigured — deeply scarred and scarred across and across.' Later these scars will be explained to Pip (chapter 48) but even now, momentarily, their significance glares appallingly as Jaggers caresses her verbally and physically: it was he who made the bramble scars in his role as hostile father. Pip is replaying the primal scene in which father wounds mother and then compels her to wound, deny, murder, abandon the ensuing baby. He suddenly sees the father's hatred of him in his fostering of loathsome Drummle; sees, too, that the father's name sums it all up. For a *jagger* is a prickle, spike, or goad,[45] and Jaggers is the briar who simultaneously prohibits access to the mother and, in wounding her, enacts the burden of all male lust for revenge on the female right back to Eve.

At this crucial point Biddy, the Estella who inhabits the safe side of Pip's grim ravine, writes a letter announcing Joe's intention to visit (chapter 27), and the fears of the father spiral on. Barnard weeps ominous 'sooty tears'; Pip's young servant boy — London equivalent to Trabb's mocking little demon and a miniscule jumped-up Pip (son of a washerwoman, dressed up in 'blue coat, canary waistcoat, white cravat, creamy breeches' and top boots) — appears and is at once christened the Avenger to become a parody Old Hamlet and 'haunt . . . [Pip's] existence'. And into this set-up comes Joe, finding his way laboriously up the stairs, so reluctant to enter that Pip 'distinctly hear[s] him breathing in at the keyhole', as if he were a ghost. When he is brought into the room Pip, wracked on the Oedipal wheel and seeing him through the eyes of his Avenger self as Jaggers, Magwitch, and Old Hamlet, stiffens him into corpselike formality. Incapable of accepting 'his good honest face all glowing and shining' Pip incapacitates him so that he can scarcely eat and is 'afflicted with . . . remarkable coughs'; so that this man who carries news of Wopsle's serio-comic *Hamlet* (which seems, in this account, to preach 'attention [to] the ghost of a man's own father' combined with a happy sense of distance from him, hence Joe's enjoyment of the orange peel that was hurled around) is turned, like Magwitch and Jaggers, into Old Hamlet himself. For in Wopsle's performance the ghost 'not only appeared to have been troubled with a cough at the time of his decease, but to have taken it with him to the tomb, and to have brought it back' (chapter 31) and, like the ghost, Joe will impart his message only when 'us two [are] alone'.

It is, that Pip should visit Miss Havisham, so he immediately travels down, shadowed in the blackness by two convicts (chapter 28), one of whom is the man who gave him the one-pound notes. Their conversation is the jumbled chatter of Pip's own mind ('the very first words I heard them interchange as I became conscious were the words of my own thought, "Two One Pound notes" ') as it names and renames the father. Pip gets off the coach early to distance himself from them but the thoughts remain as, in his 'fancy', he sees 'the boat with its convict crew . . . again [sees] the wicked Noah's Ark lying out on the black water', suffers 'the revival for a few minutes of the terror of childhood', and discovers that 'Uncle' Pumblechook was his 'earliest patron'. This recapitulation of his childhood is preliminary to the discovery that while (like the iceberg and the *Titanic* in Hardy's 'Convergence of the Twain') Drummle was forming in London, Orlick was re-forming down in Kent. The batterer of Mrs Joe is now Miss Havisham's porter; the hatred of the mother for her absence has, during Pip's exile in the city, grown that little bit deeper, and in consequence Miss Havisham has grown more dead, more other-wordly: 'It was like pushing the chair itself back into the past, when we began the old, slow circuit round about the ashes of the bridal feast'.[46]

What is most remarkable about this visit, though, is that with Joe having just mentioned *Hamlet* and Pip being about to see the performance himself, it demonstrates the extent to which Satis and its inhabitants are doomed to be the perpetual performers of Shakespeare's text. Orlick, dressed in grey, with keys like a gaoler, and muttering 'Burn me, if I know!' and 'Burn me twice over, if I can say!', seems to have got involved in the role of imprisoned (and imprisoning) fire-tortured Old Hamlet; Pip makes Miss Havisham into a self-aware Gertrude ('so you kiss my hand as if I were a queen, eh?'); Estella is now a fully-fledged nubile Ophelia; the garden is once again 'overgrown and rank'. Then Soho comes to Satis as, earlier, Satis had gone to Soho: a gesture of Estella's recalls Molly to Pip's mind, though yet only as a 'suggestion', a 'ghost' who beckons from beyond the self she has inherited from Miss Havisham: 'As my eyes followed her white hand, again the dim suggestion that I could not possibly grasp, crossed me. My involuntary start occasioned her to lay her hand upon my arm. Instantly the ghost passed once more, and was gone.'

Accompanying Molly, needless to say, is the ghost of the father, not *seen* at first but, as if to deny the gruesomeness of the Cag-Maggers self while at the same time blatantly announcing his Pilate role as Law and Traitor, *scented* on the air: 'I was conscious of a scent that I knew, and turning, saw my guardian in the room'. In *Hamlet* terms, this appearance of Jaggers is equivalent to that moment in III.iv when, as Hamlet confronts his mother and accuses her, the Ghost enters to remind him of his obligation to her: 'O step between her and her fighting soul'. But the Jaggers father, Pharisee of a lawyer that he is, pretends nothing has happened, even though he has seen Pip holding Miss Havisham and laying her down in her chair after '[rising] up . . . in her shroud of a dress, and [striking] at the air as if she would as soon have struck herself against the wall and fallen dead'. This is a prolepsis of the final struggle after the flames have got her and she can be laid on the table wrapped in cotton wool and winding sheet (chapter 49), and it arises from Pip's 'pushing the chair itself back into the past' so that Miss Havisham's anguish over Compeyson is felt by her to be as new as ever it was ('love is . . . blind devotion, unquestioning self-humiliation . . .') while simultaneously she recognises its pastness and her need to relive it through Estella:

> 'Love her, love her, love her! If she favours you, love her. If she wounds you, love her. If she tears your heart to pieces — and as it gets older and stronger, it will tear deeper — love her, love her, love her!'

Miss Havisham turns herself into Estella and Pip into Compeyson wanting, this time around, a more equal match. But Pip re-enacts a different scenario. As he hears the mother telling him to love her (as Estella) and hears her hatred of 'the smiter', 'he ca[tches] her round the waist', as if in a lover's embrace. At this point Pip the lover and Pip the mother-murderer are absolutely balanced, and at that very moment Pip becomes aware of Jaggers, who calmly takes her chair and propels her forward into her static present again. Hamlet has 'cleft [Gertrude's] heart in twain' (III.iv.158); Compeyson did at least the same for Miss Havisham who, now, sees Pip as Compeyson and therefore as Hamlet. Jaggers as ghost may defuse the situation but, like the ghost of Old Hamlet in III.iv, does not impede the furious impetus of released psychic energy. As a ghost, therefore — what Pip calls a 'cold presence' — he observes as Miss Havisham, 'in a fantastic way', bejewels Estella's hair, bosom and arms into a Bond Street equivalent of the garlanded Ophelia, and then plays cards with the victims of the drama he, as father, has produced:

> Of the manner and extent to which he took our trumps into custody, and came out with mean little cards at the end of hands, before which the glory of our Kings and Queens was utterly abased, I say nothing; nor, of the feeling that I had, respecting his looking upon us personally in the light of three very obvious and poor riddles that he had found out long ago. What I suffered from, was the incompatibility between his cold presence and my feelings towards Estella.

* * * * *

Beyond all this is Joe at the warm heart of the forge, whom Pip's Hamlet self cannot visit ('It was but a day gone, and Joe had brought the tears into my eyes; they had soon dried, God forgive me! soon dried'). Beyond it, too, is Herbert, whose simple loving nature compels him to tell Pip that no good, only 'miserable things', can come from his obsession with Estella (chapter 30) and also to show Pip how easy it is to untangle the Oedipal skein by revealing to him that he is engaged to Clara in defiance of his 'mother's nonsensical family notions' and her father's drunken, gouty, tantrums. Talk of marriage is something Pip will not hear, and so he rushes Herbert off to see *Hamlet* (chapter 31).

This is the moment Pip has been working towards since his beginning, and it is apparently an absurd bathos as the actors do what they will with dress, gesture, and text, and the audience join in with relish. Bathos and absurdity are, however, just what Pip needs to help clear the ghosts and put the mothers into perspective. *Hamlet* in this version, performed in this way, is the text that can release him from his cell, the text that, with the audience's aid, talks with the clear voices of Joe and Herbert speaking of life not death and warmth rather than chill.[47] And it is, of course, not just *Hamlet* that is revised here but Pip's past life too. The 'king and queen elevated in two armchairs on a kitchen-table holding a Court' are a crazy through-the-looking-glass re-run of Joe and Mrs Joe in Pip's childhood by the table in the forge kitchen and, simultaneously, a witty diminution of the Compeyson-Havisham couple as they are commemorated in the decaying bridal cake on the pathetic and sinister table at Satis. The Ghost is a harmless figure of fun and so unsure of his role and lines that no son could feel inhibited by him alive or dead, so the audience receives his 'terrors . . . derisively'. Gertrude, 'a very buxom lady' encircled with brass, is reduced to a figure of pregnant fun ('she was openly mentioned as "the kettledrum" '), and the madness of her partner in Hamlet's and Pip's fantasy, Ophelia, is 'slow', 'musical', and ludicrous. Even coffins are demonstrably empty of corpses: 'The arrival of the body for interment (in an empty black box with the lid tumbling open), was the signal for a general joy which was much enhanced by the discovery, among the bearers, of an individual obnoxious to identification.'

Pip is almost seduced, 'laugh[ing] in spite of myself all the time', but registering enough of the pain, particularly over Ophelia's buried baby of a napkin, to return home to bad dreams: '[I] miserably dreamed that my expectations were all cancelled, and that I had to give my hand in marriage to Herbert's Clara, or play Hamlet to Miss Havisham's Ghost, before twenty thousand people, without knowing twenty words of it'. Hamlet to Mother Havisham's Ghost! It is not surprising that Pip's obsession turns even more, if that were possible, to thoughts of death. Estella arrives to continue her education in Richmond, but for all Pip can see she might as well be at Satis. The 'staid old house' is peopled by be-hooped, be-powdered, and be-patched ghosts, its bell rings 'with an old voice', and even the trees have little sap in them:

> Some ancient trees before the house were still cut into fashions as formal and unnatural as the hoops and wigs and stiff skirts; but their own allotted places in the great procession of the dead were not far off, and they would soon drop into them and go the silent way of the rest. (chapter 33)

From this it is a very little step indeed to an actual death, and so Mrs Joe dies and is buried:

It was the first time that a grave had opened in my road of life, and the gap it made in the smooth ground was wonderful. The figure of my sister in her chair by the kitchen fire, haunted me night and day. That the place could possibly be, without her, was something my mind seemed unable to compass; and whereas she had seldom or never been in my thoughts of late, I had now the strangest ideas that she was coming towards me in the street, or that she would presently knock at the door. In my rooms too, with which she had never been at all associated, there was at once the blankness of death and a perpetual suggestion of the sound of her voice or the turn of her face or figure, as if she were still alive and had been often there. (chapter 35)

He grieves for her as his mother because his road leads nowhere except round in circles: 'as I walked along, the times when I was a little helpless creature . . . vividly returned'. Then, because mother and father, Georgiana and Philip, lie together in the churchyard, the absent father is evoked too as the funeral procession is ' "formed" in the parlour, two and two' and then, at Trabb's command, 'filed out two and two'; for what we see here is the image of the black ark that imprisons Magwitch and Compeyson superimposed on the Old Hamlet of an 'apparition of a file of soldiers' that had appeared in the doorway of that very same house many years earlier.

At this point Pip, almost gratuitously, has his twenty-first birthday and comes of age by reliving his original tombstone fantasy of the churchyard combined with the thanatological fantasy he enjoyed on his first visit to Jaggers's office in chapter 20:

'Take a chair, Mr Pip', said my guardian
As I sat down, and he preserved his attitude and bent his brows at his boots, I felt at a disadvantage, which reminded me of that old time when I had been put upon a tombstone. The two ghostly casts on the shelf were not far from him . . . . (chapter 36)

But that is all, except for the annual income of five hundred pounds (with its hint of the number of sibling graves at the beginning) which is to be his 'until the donor of the whole appears'. That revelation has to wait until he is 'three-and-twenty years of age' (opening of chapter 39). Then, a week after his twenty-third birthday in fact, out of the mud and storm and wind that seem like cannon being discharged (to remind us of prisoners escaped from hulks, of the 'cannon' at Wemmick's castle, of the 'great cannon' of *Hamlet*, I.ii.126), comes the father again, 'a voice from the darkness beneath' but first heard as 'a footstep on the stair' that Pip 'awfully connect[s] . . . with the footstep of [his] dead sister'. Why twenty-three? And why the connection with Mrs Joe?

* * * * *

The answer is that little of what happens in Pip's life is shaped or affected by social custom or ritual. His text is *Hamlet* and, at this stage of his development, his head is buried in the soil of v.i.158–75:

Hamlet:	How long will a man lie i'th'earth ere he rot?
Gravedigger:	Faith, if he be not rotten before a die . . . a will last you some eight year or nine year. A tanner will last you nine year.
Hamlet:	Why he more than another?
Gravedigger:	Why, sir, his hide is so tanned with his trade that a will keep out water a great while, and your water is a sore decayer of your whoreson dead body. Here's a skull now that hath lien you i'th'earth three and twenty years . . . . This same skull, sir, was Yorick's skull, the King's jester.

Yorick and Hamlet loved each other. The most intimate and touching detail revealed in the play is that the man took the boy, paternally, 'on [his] back a thousand times' (v.i.180). He has now been dead twenty-three years and, as Hamlet takes the skull and murmurs 'Alas, poor Yorick', he sees his dead kingly father of the play's beginning ('Alas, poor ghost'; I.v.4). Then just as the dead father becomes a demand who terrifies and maddens, so does the skull become 'abhorred': 'My gorge rises at it'.

It seems that Pip at twenty-three, the man upon whom Magwitch is about to ascend and who has never known his father except by his grave, is being revealed to us as a person who has identified himself with his dead father all his life, who has seen his father only in terms of buried bones and has proceeded to identify him, and himself, as Yorick. And he has done this against all the evidence that there was a loving, kindly man equipped with 'gambols, . . . songs, . . . flashes of merriment' who redeemed paternity and the baby boy with it by instantly filling the dead man's place. In other words, he always refused to see that Joe was an alternative Yorick, perhaps even the real Yorick.

For Pip, then, the father is dead and buried. But at the age of twenty-three, he returns ('I'm your second father. You're my son'; chapter 39). Magwitch is not just the ghost ('Alas, poor ghost') but Yorick identified with the ghost ('Alas, poor Yorick'), come back from the other world. That is why Magwitch is so pleased to see him, why he 'looked about him with the strangest air — an air of wondering pleasure'. He has returned to see the boy he loved; he has come back after a long absence to the mysteriously beautiful world of the living.

Pip's connection of Magwitch's footstep 'with the footstep of my dead sister' has its root, too, in *Hamlet's* graveyard; for Mrs Joe's grave had opened up in response to the *Hamlet* performance of a few chapters earlier: Ophelia then, Yorick now. Pip's confusion over the footsteps thus suggests that he is in a period of complete bafflement over parental identities, that for him the dead are dead and irrevocably one, that in dying with the Yorick father he also died into and with the mother, that his (dead) sister was his (dead) mother (and *vice versa*), and so on. The confusion is, of course, corroborated by *Hamlet's* graveyard, where Ophelia's grave yields up Yorick's skull which is then used, as in the dance of death, to accuse female vanity ('Now get you to my lady's chamber and tell her, let her paint an inch thick, to this favour she must come') which subsequently appears in person as Gertrude accompanied by the king (v.i.210–11). Hamlet has, however, always managed to tell the difference between father and mother whereas Pip, it appears, cannot. After differentiating them at the beginning of his autobiography where, having summoned up the father's likeness he then buried him in order to visit the dead mother in her tomb of a house, Pip now seems to fuse them. Mrs Joe's death opens up a grave that releases Magwitch into the narrative again, this time not to threaten but, after his journey from down under, in which he has been 'sea-tossed and sea-washed, months and months', to undergo a sea change that is a partial sex change.

2.4 COMPLETING THE CIRCLE

King: Thy Loving father, Hamlet.
Hamlet: My mother. Father and mother is man and wife,

man and wife is one flesh; so my mother. Come, for England.

(*Hamlet*, IV.iii)

When he returns to England Magwitch is very much a corpse. This is one reason why Pip's blood runs cold at his touch, why he cannot be disguised, and why when powder is applied to him Pip compares it to 'the probable effect of rouge upon the dead' (chapter 40). Here, then, at the beginning of the third and last stage of Pip's expectations, is the risen father of the beginning of stage one. There is, however, one crucial difference: 'I was softened by the softened aspect of the man' (chapter 39); 'it struck me that he was softened — indefinably, for I could not have said how, and could never afterwards recall how when I tried; but certainly' (chapter 46); 'I felt his hand tremble as it held mine, and he turned his face away as he lay in the bottom of the boat, and I heard that old sound in his throat — softened now, like all the rest of him' (chapter 54).

Softness, in Pip's man-made language, is feminine. Pip softens with the father who suffers the opposite of *rigor mortis* and takes on the essential quality of the mother. The prohibitor now leads him to her through the recognition of the marriage mystery that taunted Hamlet and haunted Pip: 'man and wife is one flesh'.

The immediate clue to what is going on lies in *Hamlet*, v.i, as we have seen, where Ophelia's grave gives us Yorick's skull and then a resurrected Ophelia in the form of Gertrude who scatters flowers into the grave as the presiding maternal spirit of her dead floral maiden self. The mother-maiden archetype hovers within Pip's field of vision as it does within Hamlet's. It defines Estella and Miss Havisham. In slightly grotesque form it heralds Magwitch's arrival back on earth, for at the beginning of chapter 40 we discover that Pip has got rid of his nasty little jumped-up self of an Avenger and replaced him 'by an inflammatory old female, assisted by an animated rag-bag whom she called her niece', who have as significant a part at this stage of the narrative as the Man of the Hill's and Fitzpatrick's old housekeepers in *Tom Jones*. '*Animated* rag-bag' sounds like a motley flower maiden returned from the dead, at once a sort of supererogatory double for Estella and a female 'king of shreds and patches' (*Hamlet*, III.iv.103); '*inflammatory*' suggests that the woman is a regenerated Mrs Joe in her prime, full of pins and ill temper. The softened Magwitch, now Provis the provider, can be favourably compared with her and the daughter. In fact, they empower Pip gradually, as he works his way through the *Frankenstein* terror of chapters 39 and 40, to detect the maternal softness of the man and identify it as a bedrock truth. Beneath parental death and the fictions it engendered lies the truth of paternal and maternal goodness defined as softness — the quality possessed by Joe all along but discoverable by Pip only at the age of twenty-three when Yorick's skull in all its implications displays itself to him and insists, not that he is 'Cain's jawbone, that did the first murder' (as one of Yorick's companion skulls seems to proclaim), but that he is Abel and has endured wrong and 'crieth . . . from the ground' (Gen.4:10). Pip's recognition of the father as a brother, an equal but not a sibling rival, enables him to *care*, to release the feminine (the mother) in himself as he perceives it in Magwitch ('softened by the softened aspect of the man') and regain the mother, albeit in the somewhat indistinct form of Ophelia, as we shall see in a moment.

The 'inflammatory old female' so essential to Pip at this moment is also a prevision of Miss Havisham in the flames of chapter 49, whom Pip can wrestle to the ground and lay to rest now that the father—her husband as the father of Estella and as Pip's patron — has become feminised.

Pip's apprehension of a softened Magwitch is sharpened, finally, by Orlick in the sluice house by the lime kilns (chapter 53). While the 'choking vapour of the kiln [creeps] in a ghostly way' outside, masquerading as Old Hamlet and phantom Magwitch, Pip encounters 'Old Orlick' in a fearsome wrestling match that leads him to confront his own (not his mother's or father's or Ophelia's) grave: ' "You're dead." I felt I had come to the brink of my grave.' Peering into it he discovers who the villain is in the complicated Oedipal game he has been playing:

'It was you as did for your shrew sister.'
Again my mind, with its former inconceivable rapidity, had exhausted the whole subject of the attack upon my sister, her illness, and her death, before his slow and hesitating speech had formed these words.
'It was you, villain,' said I.
'I tell you it was your doing — I tell you it was done through you . . .'.

Orlick is, of course, right. In the struggle between the two he assumes the unlikely role of Pip-Hamlet's Laertes accuser pointing out that he killed Ophelia because he killed (by denying) the father. The *Hamlet* text gives the answer where *Great Expectations*, on behalf of Pip, offers substitutions still (Orlick talks in terms of sibling rivalry: 'You was favoured, and he was bullied and beat'). But we know who 'really' felt 'bullied and beat', who released Orlick into the text, who threatened Joe in that slate letter of chapter 7. All this is being replayed at the apparent hour of Pip's death as Pip confronts the full implications of his Orlick self, is reminded again of '[his] sister's burying', and then focuses on a very simple image of men and women:

> Mill Pond Bank, and Chink's Basin, and the Old Green Copper Rope-Walk, all so clear and plain! Provis in his rooms, the signal whose use was over, pretty Clara, the good motherly woman, old Bill Barley on his back, all drifting by, as on the swift stream of my life fast running out to sea!

Or perhaps not so much men and women as, if we recall that Clara is the name of David Copperfield's dead mother, fathers and mothers.

Pip's rescue by Herbert and Trabb's boy merely enables him to continue his dialogue with Orlick and *Hamlet* (v.i) on an actual stream running towards the sea (chapter 54), and its subject remains Pip's relationship with the feminine in the light of Orlick's revelation of blame. As he guides Magwitch towards Gravesend to his death, they pass the *Ham*burg steamer; an emblem of male frustration in love ('the figure-head of the John of Sunderland making a speech to the winds (as is done my many Johns)'); a minatory (maternal?) female in the shape of 'the Betsey of Yarmouth with a firm formality of bosom and her nobby eyes starting two inches out of her head'; and reminders of the Orlick self in 'hammers going in shipbuilders' yards'. Then, dreamily, Pip's unconscious produces for him the image he has in a way been searching for all along. Magwitch as Ophelia. Not the father united with the feminine but the father *as* feminine. Pip had tried to force the perception earlier, in chapter 46, when parting from Magwitch after commenting on his 'softer condition':

'Good-bye!'
'Dear boy,' he answered, clasping my hands, 'I don't know

when we may meet again, and I don't like Good-bye. Say Good Night!'

'Good Night! Herbert will go regularly between us, and when the time comes you may be certain I shall be ready. Good night, Good night!'

That parting had overlaid Old Hamlet's 'adieu, adieu' (I.v.111) with Ophelia's grief for her dead father: 'I cannot choose but weep to think they would lay him i'th'cold ground. . . . Good night, ladies, good night. Sweet ladies, good night, good night' (IV.v.68ff) and *'He never will come again . . . God a mercy on his soul*. And of all Christian souls. God buy you' (IV.vi.191ff.). Now the forced perception achieves the truth of vision:

'If all goes well,' said I, 'you will be perfectly free and safe again, within a few hours.'

'Well,' he returned, drawing a long breath, 'I hope so.'

'And think so?'

He dipped his hand in the water over the boat's gunwale, and said, smiling with that softened air upon him which was not new to me:

'Ay, I s'pose I think so, dear boy. We'd be puzzled to be more quiet and easy-going than we are at present. But — it's a flowing so soft and pleasant through the water, p'raps, as makes me think it — I was a thinking through my smoke just then, that we can no more see to the bottom of the next few hours, than we can see to the bottom of this river what I catches hold of. Nor yet we can't no more hold their tide than I can hold this. And it's run through my fingers and gone, you see!' holding up his dripping hand.

'But for your face, I should think you were a little despondent,' said I.

'Not a bit on it, dear boy! It comes of flowing on so quiet, and of that there rippling at the boat's head making a sort of a Sunday tune. Maybe I'm growing a trifle old besides.'

He put his pipe back in his mouth with an undisturbed expression of face, and sat as composed and contented as if we were already out of England.   (chapter 54)

Magwitch speaks to Pip through a veil of smoke from the other world, already dead on the water, like Ophelia. Wemmick's memorial brooch with its willow comes to rest here, too, as

Magwitch-Ophelia's watery Sunday tune revives the floating Ophelia's 'snatches of old lauds' which she sings as she, like him, sails on 'As one incapable of her own distress,/Or like a creature native and indued/Unto that [watery] element' (IV.vii.176ff.). As his fingers trail in the water we, with Pip, see Ophelia identifying herself with her dead father as, under the 'willow [that] grows askant the brook', she reaches out her own fingers to wreathe a garland of 'long purples/That liberal shepherds give a grosser name,/But our cold maids do dead men's fingers call' (IV.vii.168-70). Abel Magwitch, the liberal shepherd, would, up till now, have used the 'grosser name'. Here, as Ophelia, he recognises his 'long purples' for the dead fingers they are as they trail in the Thames water on that March day 'when the sun [shone] hot and the wind [blew] cold' (opening of chapter 54).[48]

* * * * *

Seen from this point of view, Magwitch's fight in the water with Compeyson is a re-vision of Miss Havisham's struggle with Compeyson. It is the mother, the feminine, finally seeing off the ghost of the jaunty, gentlemanly, careless dark father. (Significantly, it is accompanied by tyrannical old Bill Barley's death (chapters 55, 58).) But Pip is not, strangely, released from the Oedipal trap. Dead Magwitch-Ophelia could conceivably have led him to a successful erotic (mature) fixation on Estella-Ophelia, but doesn't.

Instead Pip, like the dying Magwitch of chapter 56, 'never justified himself by a hint (that 'he might have been a better man under better circumstances') . . . , or tried to bend the past out of its eternal shape'. When Magwitch dies Pip identifies himself with the self-advertising Pharisee of Luke 18, implicitly pointing the finger at his own unjustness and (mental) adultery: 'Mindful, then, of what we had read together, I thought of the two men who went up into the Temple to pray, and I knew there were no better words that I could say beside his bed, than "O Lord, be merciful to him, a sinner!" ' (end of chapter 56). Magwitch, who, in the sentence quoted from the opening of the chapter, 'never justified himself', is clearly, in Pip's mind, the deeply repentant sinner who says nothing, not even 'God be merciful to me a sinner' (Luke 18:13), but nevertheless goes 'down to his house justified' (v.14). Pip sees this and says what the publican will not say, in a gesture of overwhelming love for Magwitch. But in identifying Magwitch so clearly he casts himself inevitably in the role of the other of the 'two men'. Pip is of course, as we standing outside the narrative perceive him, a redeemed Pharisee, but this is not how he regards himself. Dead softened Magwitch-Ophelia leads, through Pip's illness, to his awakening as a child to gentle, maternal, loving Joe (chapter 57), except that this 'little Pip' is not so much one of the 'little children' of Luke 18:16,17 as the haunted little boy of his autobiography's beginning: 'As I became stronger and better, Joe became a little less easy with me . . . . I soon began to understand that the cause of it was in me, and that the fault of it was all mine.'

The gap opens as Pip wakens from child's to adult awareness and endures again the pain of maternal absence, and it expands spatially as well as chronologically with Pip's long Cain-like exile in the east ('east of Eden', Gen. 4:16), Cain-like because it is born of his knowledge of Joe's and Biddy's marriage and is his response to this re-enactment of the primal union that extruded him into the world only to exclude him in the first place. In the end, then, Pip never breaks out of his self-confining circle and its parental origins. His deepest descent, with Magwitch, simply leads to a further recognition of his pained childhood self and a repetition of the agony that turned the triad mother-father-baby into dead father-dead mother-orphan. His exile is a comment on his acute distress at parental absence, and his 'happy' billet with Herbert and Clara has a self-punishing air about it, as his 'frugal' habits, compelled by his paying off his perpetual debt to Joe, suggest.

When Pip returns to England he conforms exactly to the shape of the past by creeping back to the forge in December and seeing, against all biological possibility, himself again in Joe's and Biddy's son, whom he almost immediately rushes off to the churchyard in an attempt to continue the whole ghastly business in another generation. This is what makes it impossible that Pip could ever marry Estella. There is a positive to emerge from this last chapter, though, and as in the case of *Tom Jones* it lies in the voice of a woman. For the last significant words belong to Biddy who, along with Joe and Herbert, has stood beyond and unsoiled by Pip's problems:

> 'Biddy,' said I, when I had talked with her after dinner, as her little girl lay sleeping in her lap, 'you must give Pip to me, one of these days; or lend him, at all events.'
> 'No, no,' said Biddy, gently. 'You must marry.'

The recommendation is naïvely optimistic but her refusal, her disjunction of the two Pips, shows that she instinctively knows that it is within her power to break the circle that has been circumscribed round the Oedipal triangle. Pip may have placed the little boy on the tombstone and looked with him towards the graves of 'Philip Pirrip, late of this Parish, and Also Georgiana, Wife of the Above' and in doing so become his own Magwitch father, but he cannot transfer his fantasies to the boy. Estella and the whole *Hamlet* fantasy in all its multiply kaleidoscopic implications belong uniquely to the elder Pip. The younger's text will be very different, for it begins with Joe and Biddy, not a parental grave which bursts open to yield an Old Hamlet of a convict and an aged, ghostly, bridal Ophelia.

3
Edmund Gosse's *Father and Son*: Remembering the Mother

Father and Son (1907) is, on the face of it, a straight autobiography, an account of the first twenty years or so of Gosse's life perceived in terms of his temperamental difference from his father. Recognising in it much more than mere fidelity to fact, however, readers have united in praising it as his one great imaginative achievement, an autobiography that is almost a novel. Their reaction is supported by Gosse's most recent biographer, Ann Thwaite, who, explaining that her 'early chapters are designed to be read alongside *Father and Son*', comments:

> Gosse described himself as a 'tainted source' when someone was compiling a bibliography of his work. How much more so can this be said with regard to his own biography. Not only did his memory betray him. He also changed things deliberately very often to make a better story.[1]

But then many theorists of autobiography rightly insist on the genre's fictional nature as the inevitable product of the creative gaps that proliferate between the original experiences (or reports of them), subsequent revisitings by the memory, and the period of writing.[2] In Gosse's case the result is an autobiographical novel with a psychological subtext the richness and complexity of which emerge with startling clarity if *Father and Son* is read alongside Gosse's *The Life of Philip Henry Gosse* of 1890. It appears that Gosse could write his autobiography only after he had performed his filial last rites by presenting to the public an official biography of his father as a formal act of remembrance.

Father and Son is in many ways a generous and loving work. It describes a father who, grief-stricken over his wife's death from breast cancer, had done his best to reach out to his young son. It recognises the tragedy as well as the misguidedness of his single-handed and lonely battle against Lyell, Darwin, and others as he insists on reaffirming the fixity of species and falls into the consequent folly of suggesting that fossils were buried in the earth by God as a test of belief in the authority of the opening chapters of Genesis. While sharing this dispassionate and compassionate voice with *The Life*, though, *Father and Son* also reveals a subtext that is vibrant with the passion of Oedipal confrontation and the need to banish, finally, the paternal ghost.[3] As in *Tom Jones*, this is achieved in part through the prominence given to an external historical moment. The victory of the Hanoverian forces in the '45 marks the death of the father-king in Fielding's novel. The victory of the evolutionists ensures the erasure of the father as geological authority and public figure in *Father and Son*. In both works apparently objective historical forces become metaphors for the relegation and supersession of the father.

But what of *Hamlet*? The play is mentioned once, towards the end, in chapter 9, by the benevolent father figure of James Sheridan Knowles, an aged actor and playwright turned clergyman whom the young Gosse first encounters on his way home from school;[4]

> One day when fortunately I was alone, I was accosted by an old gentleman, dressed as a dissenting minister. He was pleased with my replies, and he presently made it a habit to be taking his constitutional when I was likely to be on the high road .... My friend was the first poet I had ever seen ....
>
> It was from Sheridan Knowles' lips that I first heard fall the name of Shakespeare. He was surprised, I fancy, to find me so curiously advanced in some branches of knowledge and so utterly ignorant of others. He could hardly credit that the names of Hamlet and Falstaff and Prospero meant nothing to a little boy who knew so much theology and geography as I did.
>
> (pp. 117–18)

Voiced as it is by a minister of grace who is a benign double of the father, the list privileges Hamlet who, heading as he does a trio which includes the aged and rejected buffoon-father Falstaff and the old, deposed, exiled and bookish ruler of *The Tempest*, thus takes on an ambiguous status, suggesting simultaneously that the boy is Hamlet to Sheridan Knowles's silvered and marginal Old Hamlet and that Philip Gosse is an even more marginalised Old

Hamlet. 'Hamlet', then, embraces both the father and the son who occupy the stage of the son's autobiography, those 'sole actors' whose confrontations 'within the four walls of a room' the son recalls 'with the minuteness of a photograph' (p. 125) and who were drawn into their claustrophobic closeness by the death of the wife and mother, Emily.

Although considerable space is given over to 'Shakespearean necromancy' (p. 155) in the latter part of *Father and Son*, this is the only place where it names *Hamlet*. It thus differs from the other works discussed in this book with their more generous allusions to the play. It has a central place, however, because it has the characteristic features of a *Hamlet*-based text like *Tom Jones* and *Great Expectations*, even though it is a *Hamlet* fiction in which the nominal source is suppressed to a far greater degree than, say, Golding's *Lord of the Flies* is in Emma Tennant's *Queen of Stones* (1982), or Wilfred Owen's poem in Susan Hill's *Strange Meeting* (1971). In these and similarly allusive fictions, characters manoeuvre only apparently in response to each other. Their 'real' movement occurs in response and relation to the source text. And this is in the end the case with *Father and Son* which has behind it particularly Hamlet, Old Hamlet and Ophelia; so that *Hamlet* is revealed as the fossilised fragment that not only yields clues to the text's evolution and final form but defines the postures adopted by some at least of the main characters within it.[5]

Before starting on *Father and Son* it is useful to glance at a similar autobiography of seventy-five years later, John Mortimer's *Clinging to the Wreckage* (1982).[6] Like many male autobiographies it is obsessed with the father; and like *Father and Son* it gives the father such prominence that the autobiography of the son becomes a part-biography of the father. Mortimer, however, mentions his textual only-begetter at the outset:

> The distant past, when I was acting my solo version of *Hamlet* before the blind eyes of my father, duelling with myself and drinking my own poisoned chalice . . . seems clear as yesterday.

We never do see that moment, yet its potential mythological vastness broods over the text as barrister son conflicts and competes with (Oedipally) blind barrister father, that former warrior clad in khaki rather than complete steel whose photograph heads the illustrations and demonstrates his striking physical similarity to the son whom he overshadows and diminishes with phrases that demand revenge; so that the caption to the photograph of the father as relaxed soldier, 'My father about to avoid doing anything too heroic', ricochets back at the father his *bon mot* on hearing that the son is considering, as World War II looms, being a conscientious objector: "'Do you really think you're brave enough for that?" "What do you mean?" "I think in your case," my father turned his unblinking eyes to where he thought I might be, "I should avoid the temptation to do anything heroic' " (pp. 5–6). Mortimer knowingly conflates punished Oedipus with the dependent ghost of Old Hamlet then teases us, and his memory of his father, by having him doubled as the son's opponent by the grotesque boxing instructor at his Sloane Square school, that pugilistic vegetable of a man who, confronted at the cinema with a horror film in which a ghastly Egyptian 'mummy who was reluctant to remain quietly entombed' disintegrates into gibbering fear and has to be helped out by a St John's Ambulance nurse. The man's fear of the mummy dissolves Mortimer's fear of him. More to the point: 'Many years later I wrote a play about our boxing instructor which caused him to melt, in my memory, into a fictional character' (p. 9); a process that is also applied to the father throughout *Clinging to the Wreckage*.

But there is also a sense in which autobiography forces its author into admitting his own fictionality: 'the writer cannot help exposing himself, however indecently. Every performance he gives, although cloaked in fiction, reveals his secret identity'. This observation is made on a page which compares the hack barrister's sense of himself as an actor with the former yearning of 'the actor who has settled into an unambitious round of voice-overs for breakfast cereals . . . to play Hamlet' (p. 96) and then proceeds to tell how both Mortimer *père* and Mortimer *fils* were impressed by the flamboyantly actorly advocate Sir Edward Marshall Hall, the young Mortimer to the extent that he imitated his mannerisms, voice, and phraseology: 'The tone was unmistakable. The ghost of Sir Edward rode again. How long would it be before I too vanished into oblivion, becoming nothing but a string of improbable anecdotes?' (p.97). The question of identity is bound up with copying a paternal double who vanishes literally like a ghost, and who has been born into the narrative by the naming of Hamlet.

This act of naming in connection with the father and his surrogate is one of several similarities between *Clinging to the Wreckage* and *Father and Son*. Gosse's work, however, is by far the more imaginatively revealing, living up more than anyone could have expected to the demand George Moore appended to his complaint about *The Life of Philip Henry Gosse*: 'I missed the child, I missed your father's life and your life as you lived it together — a great psychological work waits to be written'.[7] Having written *The Life*, Gosse returned almost a generation later to that figure whose anxiety to demonstrate his love for his son ended up alienating him. This time he produced what amounts to an elegy on maternal absence inspired by his father's key contribution to the evolution debate, *Omphalos: An Attempt to Untie the Geological Knot* of 1857. This text, along with *Hamlet*, lurks in the son's unconscious mind as an ultimate image of his distance from his father and his need for his mother. For if to name *Hamlet* is to clarify a fundamental perception about the relationship between father and son, then to name the *omphalos* is to remind the son of his original dismemberment. Philip's *Omphalos*, moreover, reminds the son of that dismemberment without offering any consolation, for it is a totally male-oriented text written by a man convinced that the Creation was perpetrated by a male god and that Adam's navel (in the existence of which Philip was a fervent believer) is the sign and mark of that god's paternity. If we read this text from Edmund's viewpoint we see the complete erasure of the mother and the displacement of the son in favour of Adam. *Father and Son* is a reply to it in the form of a definition of self that offers homage to the father while giving primacy to the continuing pain of the son's separation from the mother and to the absoluteness of his claims upon her.

3.1 THE KNOT SECURED

> Queen: O gentle son,
> Upon the heat and flame of thy distemper
> Sprinkle cool patience. Whereon do you look?
> Hamlet: On him, on him. Look you how pale he glares,
> His form and cause conjoin'd, preaching to stones,
> Would make them capable.
>
> (*Hamlet*, III.iv)

When Moore suggested that 'great psychological work' to Gosse, Gosse paused, thought, reached back into the most scarred recess of his mind, and 'spoke' one memory to him: he is in his cot in his mother's room, he is woken by the sound of the door rustling over the carpet 'and I saw my mother standing in the doorway and as she saw my father she said, "O Philip, it is cancer"'.[8] The incident is recalled in virtually the same words at the opening of chapter 3 of *Father and Son*. Emily Gosse's death when her son was seven and a half haunts the narrative, filling it with images of loss from its beginning in the title page itself. For *Father and Son. A Study of Two Temperaments* is so parodically patrilinear that it registers a yawning blank where the mother should be. Father and son as a yoked pair, like God and Adam in *Omphalos*, run unnaturally counter to the human biological experience which should be expressed in the unity of mother, father, and son; and the son records that Emily herself recognised this by talking of the hiatus her death was about to create and insisting on the family's reunion in heaven:

> My Mother, in her last hours, had dwelt on our unity in God; we were drawn together, she said, elect from the world, in a triplicity of faith and joy. She had constantly repeated the words: 'We shall be one family, one song. One Song! One Family!' My Father, I think, accepted this as a prophecy, he felt no doubt of our triple unity; my Mother had now merely passed before us, through a door, into a world of light, where we should presently join her, where all things would be radiant and blissful, but where we three would in some unknown way, be particularly drawn together in a tie of inexpressible benediction.   (p. 48)

Emily affirms that her absence will be temporary; that *fort!* (to invoke the Freudian pleasure principle game again) will, in the end, become an eternal *da!* for both father and son. But *Father and Son* is concerned with life on earth, not promises for the hereafter, and so, as the title page has already reminded its readers, the 'triple unity' is a pious hope and the precarious dyad the mundane reality. Eventually the father looks for another wife and finds one in Miss Brightwen. She has been preceded by the housekeeper Miss Marks (who always thought she was destined to be Edmund's stepmother), by the teacher Miss Wilks (who, so eagerly but to no avail, stared down the father's microscope and 'learned the Latin names of many of the species' (p.90)), even by mad Miss Flaw. But all they can do in the end is to emphasise

Emily's absence. *Father and Son* repudiates the pretenders and records the son's quest for signs of Emily's abiding presence within, and influence on, him. Its theme is *omphalos*, the sign simultaneously of belonging and of severance.

There is, however, consolation in the possibility of her ghostly presence. The title page's *Father and Son* thus suggests that the reader supply not just the missing person of the *Mother* but, because of the incantatory ring given to it by nearly two millennia of worshipping Christians, the Holy Ghost as well. In other words, the mother is (perhaps) present as ghost or even Ghost, an analogy fostered by her zealous evangelising, by the long tradition which identifies the Holy Ghost as feminine Spirit,[9] and by the extraordinary femaleness that disrupts Edmund's baptism in chapter 8 and which marks the Mother Spirit's reclamation of the son from the religion of the fathers (below, section 3.3).

If the Mother spirit breathes over him here at his rebirth, she also left her imprint on him in more palpable form at his infant naming, for her initials are his initials, and EG signifies at once Emily and Edmund Gosse. If we add to this the fact that Emily was named after a boy, Rousseau's Emile,[10] then the sense of their bonded identity becomes even stronger, suggesting almost a matrilinear coding in the initials equivalent to the patrilinear naming of sons after fathers, as is the case in *Hamlet*. When the parent whose name is borne by the child dies, the child often dies with that parent in a special way, as in *Hamlet*, where the son calls his father back as a ghost and obsessively 'seek[s] for [him] in the dust' (I.ii.71) until he finds his way to a grave in which he will, circularly, discover that he is 'Hamlet the Dane' (v.i.251). Gosse, similarly, in his role of retrospective narrator, sees himself as having died with his mother and seeks to reclaim himself through the exercise of memory and by practising an art that should have been hers had it not been sacrificed to the demanding patriarchate of the Plymouth Brethren, that of writing fiction.

In the depths of the unconscious mind time, or at least a sense of chronology, does not exist. The narrating Gosse of *Father and Son* eases this perception to the surface in order to render his near-death at the moment of birth an image not just of his umbilical severance from her but of what Melanie Klein would recognise as absolute identification with her in her childbirth trauma and her later death:[11]

> my Father told me that my Mother suffered much in giving birth to me, and that, uttering no cry, I appeared to be dead. I was laid, with scant care, on another bed in the room, while all anxiety and attention were concentrated on my Mother.
>
> (p. 8)

The infant silence continues, making a further bond between the two that now speaks not so much of identification through death as of another kind of conspiracy:

> She, however, who had been so much isolated, now made the care of her child an excuse for retiring still further into silence. With those religious persons who met at the Room, as the modest chapel was called, she had little spiritual and no intellectual sympathy. She noted:
>
> I do not think it would increase my happiness to be in the midst of the saints at Hackney. I have made up my mind to give myself up to Baby for the winter, and to accept no invitations. To go when I can to the Sunday morning meetings and to see my own Mother.
>
> The monotony of her existence now became extreme, but she seems to have been happy. (p. 9)

Emily seals the bond by becoming infant too, thereby giving an external sign that she possesses a secret self, one of whose images is the infant son she has brought to birth, another being her locked commonplace book with its 'secret notes', the existence of which is revealed on this same page and which, the narrating son tells us, has been 'seen until now, nearly sixty years later, by no eye save her own'. Baby and locked book are symbolically and inextricably linked from birth, an association that predestinates the son to his literary career, for the book itself is a testament to her suppression of her writing talent in the name of the Father God:

> There seems to have been, in this case, a vocation such as is rarely heard, and still less often wilfully disregarded and silenced. Was my Mother intended by nature to be a novelist? I have often thought so, and her talents and vigour of purpose, directed along the line which was ready to form 'the chief pleasure of her life', could hardly have failed to conduct her to great success.
>
> (p. 16)

It seems, then, that Edmund's subsequent career is a mission; that his literary calling is a redemption of that part of his mother denied in the cause of religion and for which her 'secret notes' were a poor and rather pathetic substitute. As if to insist on the parallel, the son reminds us that he 'was slow in learning to speak', and that his first word was 'book', uttered 'with startling distinctness' (p.14). His infancy ceased, then, with the naming of his future and Emily's lost vocation. Just as the ghost of Old Hamlet penetrates his son's mind, prompting him to erase 'all trivial fond records' in order that he may be remembered and given a voice, so Emily possesses her son and he becomes her instrument. Silent as an infant when she was silent, he survives her death to give her spirit voice.

The father also writes. Indeed, it appears to be he who teaches the son to do so because 'to my Mother . . . it was distasteful to teach, though she was so prompt and skilful to learn' (p.15). But it is the mother who is the creative writer, the one who calls emotionally to the son; so that the father is, merely, the agent offering the means by which the son will approach his mother's suppressed imaginative depths. This is demonstrated neatly by the *abendlied* that is quoted on the same page:

> I cannot recollect a time when a printed page of English was closed to me. But perhaps earlier still my Mother used to repeat to me a poem which I have always taken for granted that she had herself composed, a poem which had a romantic place in my early mental history. It ran thus, I think:
>
> O pretty Moon, you shine so bright!
> I'll go to bid Mamma goodnight,
> And then I'll lie upon my bed
> And watch you move above my head.
>
> Ah! there, a cloud has hidden you!
> But I can see your light shine thro'!
> It tries to hide you — quite in vain,
> For — there you quickly come again!
>
> It's God, I know, that makes you shine
> Upon this little bed of mine;
> But I shall all about you know
> When I can read and older grow.

Long, long after the last line had become an anachronism, I used to shout this poem from my bed before I went to sleep, whether the night happened to be moon-lit or no.   (pp. 14–15)

There could be no clearer statement of the moon-mother as the source of the pleasure principle and centre of the son's life. In context, the knowing 'all about' her reads less like a physico-theologian's attempt to grasp the universe's number, weight, and measure than it does as an attempt to enter into her imaginative mysteries. The poem enshrines the mother as lunar deity who possesses the realms of darkness and mysterious silence which knowledge of his 'letters', the ability to read and write, will empower him to approach. She is a moon whose 'glimpses', or intermittent gleamings (*Hamlet*, I.iv.53), testify to the perpetual succession of *fort!* by *da!*, to a unity of mother and son that cannot be interrupted even by the presence of the father.[12]

The idea of the son as inheritor of his mother's silenced voice and haunting presence is also illuminated by a moment that is mentioned only in passing in *Father and Son* but has now been given its full resonance by Ann Thwaite. This is the 'holiday of nearly ten months in Devonshire' which the family took as a result of the father's physical weakness 'in my third year' (p.11). In 1884 it had recurred to Gosse's mind as his beloved friend Hamo Thorneycroft and his bride Agatha honeymooned in the west country. Thwaite writes:

> The Thorneycrofts were spending some time in the Valley of the Rocks, near Linton in Devon, an area which is the subject of one of the sections of *Seaside Pleasures*, published anonymously in 1853. The family copy I have in front of me as I write bears the pencilled words ' "The Valley of the Rocks" is the sole composition of my mother. E.G.'. He wrote to Hamo of his shadowy memory of Emily 'with her red hair and somewhat white face . . . . You know that I take little interest in Parents as a rule; I think them a mistake, but I make an exception in my unfortunate mother with her morbid intensity and her touch of genius. If you see her ghost in the Valley of the Rocks, you will know her, for I am her image in features.'[13]

Here, thirty years later, Emily is a ghostly Madonna of the Rocks, as mysterious as Leonardo's *Gioconda* when perceived by Walter Pater as an intensely melancholic 'presence that [has risen] so strangely beside the waters'.[14] Edmund bears not just her genetic imprint but her ghostly image too, as the pencilled note resurrected by Thwaite hauntingly confirms, its ambiguous E.G. denoting at once Emily and Edmund, twin authors with but one set of initials.

And yet this ghostly Emily, of whose existence we know from the Thorneycroft letter, is manifestly absent from *Father and Son*'s mention of the stay at Linton, appearing instead in the account of the holiday taken by the family at Tenby in the summer of 1856:

> my seventh birthday was spent in an ecstasy of happiness, on golden sands, under a brilliant sky, and in sight of the glorious azure ocean beating in from an infinitude of melting horizons. Here, too, my Mother, perched in a nook of the high rocks, surveyed the west and forgot for a little while her weakness and the gnawing, grinding pain. (p. 34)

Tenby and their favourite Devon struck the Gosses as being very similar;[15] but it had been to Tenby that Emily had taken the knowledge of her cancer, disclosed to her the previous April. Edmund's Madonna of the Rocks has her origin here, then, at Tenby. It is an image born of pain and the awareness of imminent loss, and it is at Tenby that *Father and Son* enshrines her, preserving the agony of the memory. The Linton Madonna of 1884 is a fantasy, a comforting *revenant* returned to inhabit a place of happiness that she frequented before her illness began, and there is no narrative place for that fiction in *Father and Son* with its uncompromising focus on maternal loss. What the Tenby incident describes, in fact, is the mother confronting the prospect of death, as Philip Gosse's account of the same holiday reminds us:

> It was a lovely evening; and my wife and myself had been taking a walk along Croft Terrace and the edge of the northern cliffs . . . . [We gazed down] on the yellow sands almost literally under our feet, where the people, taking their evening stroll, 'appeared like mice', as Shakespeare says; and the confused sound of their voices, mingling with the whispers of the surf, came faintly up to our ears, telling us how remote we were from the living world.[16]

The *Lear* quotation (from the Dover scene) conceals an appalling degree of grief at a time when Emily was still alive; a grief shared by the son and relived through *Father and Son*'s image of the Tenby Madonna.

* * * * *

At the opening of chapter 2 the son records a very early 'flash of memory' that, in context, again seems to raise all sorts of ambivalent questions about his possession by his mother:

> I am seated alone, in my baby-chair, at a dinner-table set for several people. Somebody brings in a leg of mutton, puts it down close to me, and goes out. I am again alone, gazing at two low windows, wide open upon a garden. Suddenly, noiselessly, a large, long animal (obviously a greyhound) appears at one window-sill, slips into the room, seizes the leg of mutton and slips out again. When this happened I could not yet talk. The accomplishment of speech came to me very late, doubtless because I never heard young voices. Many years later, when I mentioned this recollection, there was a shout of laughter and surprise: —
> 'That, then, was what became of the mutton! It was not you, who, as your Uncle A. pretended, ate it up, in the twinkling of an eye, bone and all!' (p. 13)

It is an extraordinarily suggestive anecdote. For one thing, the silent, mysterious animal, later so 'obviously' a greyhound, seems to be a prevision of the dead mother making her ghostly claim on her son. (Hounds traditionally belong to the hunting moon goddess Diana, and a page or so later we are given the moon poem quoted above.)[17] Support for — indeed, explanation — this interpretation comes from these words of the mother on her deathbed: '"I shall walk with Him in white. Won't you take your lamb and walk with me?" Confused with sorrow and alarm, my Father failed to understand her meaning. She became agitated, and she repeated two or three times, "Take our lamb, and walk with me!" Then my Father comprehended, and pressed me forward' (pp.41–2). To the mother her whiteness is that of a bride of Christ; to the son it is that of a shroud and he is the lamb who is being led to the slaughter, to be reduced to mutton as the mother calls him to her dying, greyhound, self.

On the other hand, if the mother pulls towards death she also, as we have seen, offers 'creative' life, and so another interpretative possibility offers itself: the anecdote recounts a symbolic kidnapping, a wresting by this 'large, long, animal' of the infant to freedom from the prison of male ancestral voices ('the accomplishment of speech came to me very late, doubtless because I never heard young voices'). As such it parallels the kidnapping in chapter 7 when crazed Mary Flaw abducts the son one interminable Sunday evening from beneath the eyes of the preaching patriarch. The two are pursued and, 'a few minutes later, the swiftest of the congregation, with my Father at their head, found us sitting on the doorstep of the butcher's shop' (p.83). Butcher; lamb; mutton. The son is pulled from parent to parent, gravitating from the father's deathly Word to the mother's silenced vocation. The greyhound's act of abduction, like Mary Flaw's, promises life, though, for both acts recall that earlier life-bestowing moment when the Hecate-like crone 'who happened to be' present at the son's birth acted as a midwife, 'awake[ning] in me a spark of vitality' (p. 8) when all attention was focused anxiously elsewhere.[18]

In the light of all this, Uncle A's joke about the disappearance of the mutton reveals, almost, all: ' "It was not you, who, as your Uncle A. pretended, ate it up in the twinkling of an eye . . ."' For the proverbial commonplace has, of course, its origin in St Paul: 'Behold, I shew you a mystery: We shall not all sleep, but we shall all be changed. In a moment, in the twinkling of an eye, at the last trump: for the trumpet shall sound, and the dead shall be raised incorruptible' (I Cor. 15: 51–2). This is the dying Emily's fervent belief and promise to her family of heavenly salvation and reunion. To the narrator of *Father and Son* it is merely teasing, an impish comment on his problem with his mother's 'ethereal memory' (p.10) as she hovers over the narrative and finds her 'image' in her son.

3.2 SEVERING THE FATHER

Hamlet: My father's spirit — in arms! All is not well.

(*Hamlet*, i.ii)

The son's upbringing trained his mind to be sceptical and enquiring, on the paternal model. Had his parents read him stories, 'had they wrapped me in the soft folds of supernatural fancy, my mind might have been longer content to follow their traditions in an unquestioning spirit' (p. 17), But now, sixty years on, his own 'fancy' has been liberated. With the parental God denied, the father dead, and his mother's fiction-creating self resurrected, his autobiography can register its ghosts and even, albeit often indirectly, interrogate them. An example, again from chapter 2, is the skeleton anecdote:

> A lady — when I was just four — rather injudiciously showed me a large print of a human skeleton, saying, 'There! you don't know what that is, do you?' Upon which, immediately and very archly, I replied, 'Isn't it a man with the meat off?' . . . . If I venture to repeat this trifle, it is only to point out that the system on which I was being educated deprived all things, human life among the rest, of their mystery. The 'bare-grinning skeleton of death' was to me merely a prepared specimen of that featherless plantigrade vertebrate, *homo sapiens*. (p. 18)

The anecdote is avowedly repeated because it records 'the only "clever" thing that I said during an otherwise unillustrious childhood', but its introduction of a skeleton at this point in the narrative does rather more than that. It insists, from the perspective of 1907, that a skeleton must be seen not just as a 'prepared specimen' but, like Yorick's skull, an almost ineffably evocative and ponderable mystery. It stands, like the mutton story, at the symbolic threshold of the text, image of the dead mother and of the rejected and now dead father. By observing the father the young son had been enabled to pierce the veiling skin and tissue to the bones beneath: 'I had often watched my Father, while he soaked the flesh off the bones of fishes and small mammals' (p. 18; his explanation for knowing what the skeleton is). Through observation he has come to the Gravedigger's knowledge that 'your water is a sore decayer of your whoreson dead body' (v.i.165–6), and he has done so at precisely the moment when 'my memories . . . now become clear and almost abundant' (p.18). The skeleton, then, is at once the trigger and emblem of memory, the shadowy form that underlies and inhabits the text of *Father and Son* as the stratified fossils underlie the paternal text of *Omphalos* and as Old Hamlet, 'work[ing] i'th'earth so fast' (i.v.70), and Yorick, underlie *Hamlet*.

It is no coincidence that this skeleton inhabits the same,

admittedly rather long, chapter in which the narrator discovers the limits of paternal infallibility, first over a matter of verbal detail then over the punctured garden fountain pipe: 'the theory that my Father was omniscient or infallible was now dead and buried' (p.23). For the death and burial of the 'theory' is the death and burial of the father, a commitment of him to the earth, a willing of him to become 'the bare-grinning skeleton of death' (p.18). And this in turn has the closest of subliminal associations with yet another early memory from chapter 2, where one of the narrator's childhood games seems to come literally to life. The game involves two female dolls and a soldier doll recently added with the outbreak of the Crimean War:

> I used to put the dolls on three chairs, and harangue them aloud, but my sentiment to them was never confidential, until our maidservant one day, intruding on my audience, and misunderstanding the occasion of it, said: 'What? a boy, and playing with a soldier when he's got two lady-dolls to play with?' I had never thought of my dolls as confidants before, but from that time forth I paid special attention to the soldier, in order to make up to him for Lizzie's unwarrantable insult. (p. 20)

Then the soldier doll becomes the real thing in what the narrator calls 'one of my vividest early memories':

> I was playing about the house, and suddenly burst into the breakfast-room, where, close to the door, sat an amazing figure, a very tall young man, as stiff as my doll, in a gorgeous scarlet tunic .... [My Mother] promptly told me to run away and play, but I had seen a great sight. This guardsman was in the act of leaving for the Crimea, and his adventures, — he was converted in consequence of my Mother's instruction, — were afterwards told by her in a tract, called 'The Guardsman of the Alma' .... I see him still in my mind's eye, large, stiff, and unspeakably brilliant, seated, from respect, as near as possible to our parlour door. This apparition gave reality to my subsequent conversations with the soldier doll.

It is memory that turns him into an 'apparition', into the red-coated equivalent of armour-clad Old Hamlet and into something very like the 'apparition of a file of soldiers' that intrudes on Pip's Christmas in its search for his escapee Magwitch of a father. Glimpsed for a moment, he was then killed, and his death adds 'lustre' to the son's dream of him. It is as if the Alma guardsman reveals a truth, shared by mother and son, about the father's tyranny; as if mother and son are complicit in wishing, and achieving, his symbolic death.

At the very least the text demands that we consider the parallel between the death of the soldier and the 'burial' of the father's supposed infallibility a page or so later, while raising the possibility of a pun in *Alma* (Latin *alma* = nourishing, an adjective frequently applied to maternal deities)[19] by following this anecdote with the story of the moth which again suggests the extent of the son's commitment to the mother:

> We had all three been much excited by a report that a certain dark geometer-moth, generated in underground stables, had been met with in Islington. Its name I think, is *Boletobia fuliginaria*, and I believe that it is excessively rare in England. We were sitting at family prayers, on a summer morning, I think in 1855, when through the open window a brown moth came sailing. My Mother immediately interrupted the reading of the Bible by saying to my Father, 'O! Henry, do you think that can be *Boletobia*?' My Father rose up from the sacred book, examined the insect, which had now perched, and replied: 'No! it is only the common Vapourer, *Orgyia antiqua*!', resuming his seat, and the exposition of the Word, without any apology or embarrassment.
> (p. 21)[20]

The anecdote catches the parents touchingly off-guard in one of the most humane vignettes of the whole work. It is also brilliantly evocative of the conflict between the two as the mother cuts across the patriarchal Logos with her excited question about this 'certain dark geometer-moth, generated in underground stables'. The words take on a peculiar resonance in connection with the mother because *geometer*, derived from Greek *gēometrēs* (land-measuring) puns insistently on the etymological possibility that it is also derived from the Greek *gē-mētēr* (earth-mother), so that the moth comes to symbolise the mother's spirit fostered in the 'underground' of her (and the son's) unconscious minds and now liberated for a moment into the oppressive air of Islington as yet another correlate to her 'secret notes'.

Even when paternal authority predictably acts as killjoy by

saying no, the deconstructive play of words continues: *Vapourer*, after all, suggests a hovering and ghostly presence and thus the irresponsibility of the mother's spirit before, and after, her death; while *Orgyia antiqua* ceases merely to denote a genus of moth and resoundingly translates itself into *ancient orgies* and all that they may imply in terms of the cult of the Graeco-Roman mother goddess. At this point the narrator is feeling his emotional way into those mythological areas which had caught the attention of Swinburne, Pater, Hardy's Sue Bridehead, and many more — areas occupied by the mother goddess and which demonstrate once more how bound he is to the 'ethereal' maternal presence.[21]

The symbolic recognition of the moth-mother's free spirit is one thing; her actual assumption of liberty is something threateningly different: 'About this time, my Mother, carried away by the current of her literary and her philanthropic work, left me more and more to my own devices' (p. 23). The son responds by developing night terrors of mother loss involving Oedipal fear of the father:

> The fact was that I was half beside myself with ghostly fears, increased and pointed by the fact that there had been some daring burglaries in our street. Our servant–maid, who slept at the top of the house, had seen, or thought she saw, upon a moonlight night, the figure of a crouching man, silhouetted against the sky, slip down from the roof and leap into her room. She screamed, and he fled away. Moreoever, as if this were not enough for my tender nerves, there had been committed a horrid murder, at a baker's shop just around the corner in the Caledonian Road, to which murder actuality was given to us by the fact that my Mother had been 'just thinking' of getting her bread from this shop. (p. 27)

The maid is the girl who made the son self-conscious about his toy soldier, image of the 'apparition' that was to die at the Alma. Now, from the top of the house, she reinforces his antagonism towards his father by helping to generate 'ghostly fears' of a man breaking in at night that seem to register his terror of the father's depredations (sexual and emotional) on the mother and, also, a wish fulfilment, for as the girl screams the man flees. And then the phrase 'horrid murder' is suspended before us, victim unknown. Perhaps it accuses the man-father; perhaps it designates him a victim of 'murder most foul, as in the best it is' (*Hamlet*, I.v.27), thus turning this figure, silhouetted in the moonlight, into the paternal ghost who 'revisits . . . the glimpses of the moon,/Making night hideous' (I.iv.53–4).

This episode doubles a slightly earlier one in which it is the son this time, and not a silent, nameless, man, who is up in the garret. There he finds 'an ancient hat-box and a still more ancient skin-trunk' (p. 24). He is up there killing time because the mother is at the height of her liberated power as a harvester of souls (p. 23). Occasionally she takes the son with her, but more often she does not: 'when all was done, I had hours and hours of complete solitude, in my Father's study, in the back garden, above all in the garret' (p. 24). Despite denials that he resents her absence, resentment creeps in when he mentions Mrs Jellyby, the careless and abstracted philanthropical mother of Dickens's *Bleak House*, whose presence converts the negatives in this particular sentence into positives: 'I would not for a moment let it be supposed that I regard her as a Mrs Jellyby, or that I think she neglected me' (p. 23). Her daily absences, in other words, are made to anticipate her final absence through death. The skin trunk, in consequence, becomes a particularly dreadful fragmented, dismembered, image of the mother, pushing her back into a dead, remote and misty past and, simultaneously, presenting her as the object of the son's morbidly persistent curiosity. For when probed, this apparently 'absolutely empty' trunk reveals its secret, the secret of the mother's silenced vocation:

> the inside of the lid of it was lined with sheets of what I now know to have been a sensational novel. It was, of course, a fragment, but I read it, kneeling on the bare floor, with indescribable rapture. It will be recollected that the idea of fiction, of a deliberately invented story, had been kept from me with entire success. I therefore implicitly believed the tale in the lid of the trunk to be a true account of the sorrows of a lady of title, who had to flee the country, and who was pursued into foreign lands by enemies bent upon her ruin . . . . This ridiculous fragment filled me with delicious fears; I fancied that my Mother, who was out so much, might be threatened by dangers of the same sort.   (p. 24)

It is as if the son interrogates the mother's dead self only to discover that her novelistic fantasies have produced a lurid fiction of flight that mirrors his own preoccupation with her absence and which, despite his absorbed enjoyment of it, records fear: fear of her disappearances, and fear of the possibility of her murder that parallels the terror voiced over her visit to the baker's shop.[22]

The last anecdote in the sequence immediately follows the 'crouching man' terror:

> But what made me scream o'nights, was that when my Mother had tucked me up in bed, and heard me say my prayer, and had prayed aloud on her knees at my side, and had stolen downstairs, noises immediately began in the room. There was a rustling of clothes, and a clapping of hands, and a gurgling, and a sniffing, and a trotting. These horrible muffled sounds would go on, and die away, and be resumed; and I would pray very fervently to God to save me from my enemies; and sometimes I would go to sleep. But on other occasions, my faith and fortitude alike gave way, and I screamed 'Mama! Mama!' Then would my parents come bounding up the stairs, and comfort me, and kiss me, and assure me it was nothing. And nothing it was while they were there, but no sooner had they gone than the ghostly riot recommenced. (p. 27)

The son's cry for help excludes the father and, predictably, victory over the ghost belongs to the mother as it has to because 'the whole mischief was due to a card of framed texts, fastened by one nail to the wall [that] began to gallop in the draught' from the landing when the door was left ajar; for the text is, evidently, an image of the father as patriarchal Word. By silencing it the mother affirms her closeness to the boy as opposed to the father, banishing his ghost as the intruder was banished in the maid's fantasy as reported by the narrating son.

In grateful recompense the son records a page or so later how, as a result of a caning, 'I went about the house for some days with a murderous hatred of my Father locked within my bosom' (p.29). Murderous? In this particular chapter? From the pen of the Gosse who had planned to collaborate with Robert Louis Stevenson on a murder series for *The Century Magazine* which would consist of 'a retelling of the most picturesque murder cases of the last hundred years'?[23] In the event the project came to nothing, though elements of it surfaced a few years later in *The Strange Case of Dr Jekyll and Mr Hyde* (1886), a fable which, among other things, unites lust-murder with what Karl Miller calls 'the outlines of . . . filial ambivalence'.[24] There is more than the outline of filial ambivalence in *Father and*

Son; and though there is no lust-murder in it, it does record a fascination with the maternal corpse, the paternal ghost, and the ambiance of murder, that not only locates it as a text of its time, but also as the telling psychological study requested by George Moore.

* * * * *

Just before her death the son, by a terrible irony, gets the mother to himself in the most distressing way possible. From October until Christmas Eve 1856 he is her 'sole and ceaseless companion' in Pimlico where she has taken lodgings in order that Dr Fell could start on his process for removing the tumour. When she is not with her doctor the son reads to her, turning himself round so that he may not 'see quite so distinctly that dear patient figure rocking on her sofa, or leaning, like a funeral statue, like a muse upon a monument, with her head on her arms against the mantelpiece' (pp. 34–5). But Emily's 'savage treatment' at the hands of Dr Fell inevitably fails:

> and a day or two before Christmas, while the fruits were piled in the shop-fronts and the butchers were shouting outside their forests of carcases, my Father brought us back in a cab through the streets to Islington. . . . she lingered with us six weeks more, and during this time I again relapsed, very naturally, into solitude. (p. 37)

The carcases impassively anticipate the mother's death and look back to that leg of mutton seized by the mysterious creature some five years earlier. The self-conscious boy victim, the lamb his mother will offer as sacrifice with her dying breath, is mocked by the mute and awful juxtaposition of dying woman and festal carcases which have proliferated to celebrate the motherhood and infancy that are at the root of her faith. It is an even more awful irony that the 'six weeks' she lingers before dying silently duplicate the six weeks she lay in her bedroom after giving birth to her son.[25] Her actual and potential absences from him are appallingly underscored by her physical difference from her former self:

> Now, and for the first time in my life, I no longer slept in her room, no longer sank to sleep under her kiss, no longer saw her mild eyes smile on me with the earliest sunshine . . . . . I felt, as I

Edmund Gosse's Father and Son

stood, awkwardly and shyly, by her high bed, that I had shrunken into a very small and insignificant figure, that she was floating out of my reach. . . . She herself was not herself; her head, that used to be held so erect, now rolled or sank upon the pillow . . . . I could not understand it; I meditated long, long upon it all in my infantile darkness, in the garret, or in the little slip of a cold room where my bed was now placed . . . .

The two retreats which I have mentioned were now all that were left to me . . . .The breakfast room was often haunted by visitors, unknown to me by face or name . . . . In all this time, the agitated, nervous presence of my Father, whose pale face was permanently drawn with anxiety, added to my perturbation, and I became miserable, stupid, as if I had lost my way in a cold fog.

(pp. 40–1)

As the son meditates in the garret on his mother's deathbed he does so, presumably, before those testaments to his earlier sense of her absence, the empty hatbox and the skin trunk. Meantime the house is 'haunted' by faceless anonymous visitors who turn it into a kind of underworld awaiting the maternal shade, and by the father, who looms at him out of his grief-induced fog. The dying mother has generated multiple ghosts. The son's problem after her death is to remember her while accommodating the demands of his alienating and dominant father.

3.3 FATHER ADAM, MOTHER OPHELIA

Hamlet: O God, — I could be bounded in a nutshell and count myself a king of infinite space — were it not that I have bad dreams.

(*Hamlet*, II.ii)

After the mother's death a kind of paternal cousin 'snatch[ed] me from our cold and desolate hearthstone' to her house in Clifton as a physical and emotional assertion of the continuance of maternal warmth (p. 44). It is as if she senses that the mother's burial, mentioned in the preceding paragraph, might draw the boy, like Hamlet in the churchyard, literally to the grave. The son's 'little slip of a cold room' is already rather coffin-like; and the 'cold and desolate hearthstone' registers the transformation of living room into tomb through the absence of the mother as Vesta, mother goddess of the flames of life. The Clifton house responds by offering the compellingly maternal image of a hive (p. 44)[26] and giving the boy a corresponding respite, a period of blissful inactivity which he reports as if it were a kindly haunting dream, a soul-restoring equivalent of the Man of the Hill's erasure of his history to a blank:

> Vague, half-blind remembrances of walks, with my tall cousins waving like trees above me, pleasant noisy evenings in a great room on the ground-floor, faint silver-points of excursions into the country, all this is the very pale and shadowy testimony to a brief interval of healthy, happy child-life, when my hard-driven soul was allowed to have, for a little while, no history. (p. 45)

When his 'history' recommences with the return home, it is remarkable, momentarily at least, for a shift into the comic mode. As father and son become 'great friends' (p. 47) external events make stridently uncensored and exaggerated comments about patricide. For with much of Edmund's time spent pleasurably with his father in his study, the psychological reality can be transferred onto the streets which the son can observe from a distance, his 'pale cheek pressed against the window pane' (p. 45) like the orphaned Jane Eyre, like a ghost himself, or like Hamlet when he sets up the *Mousetrap*: 'At this time, the street was my theatre', and what it stages for him is, among other things, an eccentric Jersey onion seller and Punch and Judy. 'The onion-man was a joy long waited for' because he is a raucous-voiced Protestant who shouts out a rhyme inviting all comers to participate in the killing of the father idol:

> Here's your rope . . .
> To hang the Pope . . .
> And a penn'orth of cheese to choke him.
>
> (p. 46)

While Punch presents the father in two forms — as the irascible and bullying Mr Punch, and as the Devil, the 'figure of shapeless horror' whom the terrified Punch interrogates with ever shriller voice, 'Is it the butcher?'. . . . 'Is it the baker?', thereby recapturing the image of the carcases that faced the mother on her ride home from Pimlico

(p. 37) and the 'horrid murder, at a baker's shop' (p. 27). Shortly after this the father as horrifying yet comic devil becomes the father as buffoon when 'in our lighter moods, we turned to the "Book of Revelation", and chased the phantom of Popery through its fuliginous pages' (p. 52), Philip crazily licensing Edmund's Oedipal need to kill a father: 'Nor could he have desired a pupil more docile or more ardent than I in my flaming denunciations of the Papacy' (p. 52); 'As a little boy, when I thought, with intense vagueness, of the Pope, I used to shut my eyes tight and clench my fists' (p. 53). 'Intense vagueness' is brilliant from the bespectacled narrator who recognises in his 'near sighted' (p. 46) younger self a boy who detected in the distant, amorphous, image of the Pope the spectre of all tyrannical fathers for all time.

These papal phantoms proliferate as the father assumes prominence, first by attempting himself 'to fill as far as might be the gap which the death of my Mother had made in my existence' (p. 47), and then trying to supply it by introducing Miss Marks, who stays as nanny and housekeeper until the advent of the stepmother. The introduction of a substitute is only another way of affirming absence, though, as the comically understated comparison of her to Dickens's Mrs Pipchin reveals in spite of itself: 'I will confess that when, in years to come, I read "Dombey and Son", certain features of Mrs Pipchin did irresistibly remind me of my excellent past governess' (p. 54). For Mrs Pipchin is a fantasy, received by the narrator from Dickens' own haunting by fairy tale, folklore, and *Hamlet*, at once ogress, witch, and a widow who, like a grotesquely chaste Gertrude, inhabits an establishment referred to as the 'Castle' dressed perpetually in widow's weeds.[27] Yet to compare Miss Marks to Mrs Pipchin is, in fact, to produce not so much a parody mother as an equivalent to the crone who presided over his birth. She returned him from death to the mother; Miss Marks's long function as an embodied Mrs Pipchin is to guide him, as a double of Paul Dombey, through a deathlike *rite de passage* that will have as the beginning of its end the arrival of Miss Brightwen, the future stepmother, and his liberation into London and assumption of a career that approximates to that of his dead mother's silenced vocation.

In the meantime, just as Paul Dombey dies into his mother ('Mama is like you, Floy. I know her by the face!') and the sea (chapter 16), young Edmund is immediately taken to live by the sea, at St Marychurch outside Torquay, as if a return to Devon will somehow conjure up the spirit of the Lady of the Rocks with her 'red hair and sorrowful white face'. But what strikes the son about the supposedly maternal Devon landscape — or at least his particular patch of it — is how insistently muddy it is with its 'infinitude of red ploughed fields' (p. 57).[28] What he appears to be registering in this densely written episode is the appropriation of the maternal land- and sea-scape by the father, their erasure by a man committed to the patriarchal Word. For the theme of these pages is *omphalos,* that sign of juncture and severance, and the red mud signifies Adam, whose name means 'earthly man, red, of the colour of blood'.[29]

When father and son arrive in Devon the father is in the thick of the evolution furore. *Omphalos* has just been published and the reviews are uniformly hostile. As winter proceeds, Philip's gloom and bitterness deepen:

> My Father used to tramp in solitude round and round the red ploughed field which was going to be his lawn, or, sheltering himself from the thin Devonian rain, pace up and down the still-naked verandah, where blossoming creepers were to be . . . . It was now that, I fancy, he began, in his depression, to be angry with God. How much devotion had he given, how many sacrifices had he made, only to be left storming round this red morass with no one in all the world to care for him except one pale-faced child with its cheek pressed to the window!
>
> (pp. 62–3)

Edmund watches his father as he had, earlier, watched the patricidal comedy of the street theatre, observing him wrestle in his spirit with the evidence presented by the fossils flung up by the geological gravediggers. Lyell and his colleagues testify to growth, mutability, adaptability; to vanished and evolving forms and species; to reptiles whose fragmentary remains 'with the meat off' (p. 18) are emerging from their prison house, their tale told now by the evolutionists as they ransack the strata of the earth's memory for data and evidence of the truth that lies in bones.

Philip, however, has his own — what he regards as God's — truth, popularly and crudely defined as explaining:

> that God hid the fossils in the rocks in order to tempt geologists into infidelity. In truth, it was the logical and inevitable

conclusion of accepting, literally, the doctrine of a sudden act of creation; it emphasised the fact that any breach in the circular course of nature could be conceived only on the supposition that the object created bore false witness to past processes, which had never taken place. For instance, Adam would certainly possess hair and teeth and bones in a condition which it must have taken many years to accomplish, yet he was created full-grown, yesterday. He would certainly — though Sir Thomas Browne denied it — display an *omphalos*, yet no umbilical cord had ever attached him to a mother. (p. 61)

In defending the Genesis version of creation, the father excludes the maternal female and is observed suffering the consequences of that exclusion by the ghostly boy who seems to represent the mother. From beyond the glass he sees Philip becoming muddier and more patriarchally Adam-like as he prowls round his Eveless mock-paradise of an enclosure.

In this 'dismal winter' (p. 62) Miss Marks is no consolation, and Philip rises from his foray into the fossils' graveyard which is also the burial ground of his hopes like a vituperative Old Hamlet, bitter not so much at his God as at the woman who has betrayed him by dying: father and son go on walks during which 'my Father was so deeply enwoven in the chain of his own thoughts, [that he] would stalk on, without a word, buried in angry reverie' (p. 65). He is buried in his daydream; in the depths of the earth with Adam and the riddle of Genesis; in the grave with Hamlet's father. He is stalking (and wordless) like Old Hamlet's ghost: 'See, it stalks away. Stay, speak, speak' (i.i.53–4). Like Old Hamlet, too, he communicates his infection to his son, who becomes ill. In the meantime the house is damp and chilly, simultaneously affirming the mother's absence and, in a pun that looks back to the moth anecdote of page 21, her ghostly presence: 'The dampness of the house was terrible; indoors and out, the atmosphere seemed soaked in chilly *vapours*' (p. 66; author's italics).

Almost inevitably the murder motif reappears as, in front of the fire, father and son' had long cosy talks together': 'Our favourite subject was murders . . . . We tried other secular subjects, but we were sure to come round at last to "what do you suppose they really did with the body?" ' (p. 64). It is as if the narrating autobiographer of 1907 imagines them as holding perpetual post-mortems on Emily which then take on a bizarre and fantastic life of their own, as in the tale of the gentleman buried in quicklime by a Mrs Manning who was 'hanged in black satin' and which is as ambivalently gynophobic as anything uttered by Old Hamlet about Gertrude or Old Orlick in the lime kilns about Mrs Joe; or the all too recent activities of Burke and Hare, those dealers in bodies 'whose story nearly froze me into stone with horror' ('I could a tale unfold whose lightest word/Would ... freeze thy young blood'; *Hamlet*, I.v.15–16); and 'the Carpet-bag Mystery', which may or may not have been a hoax and which concerned a bag 'found to be full of human remains, dreadful butcher's business of joints and fragments' which, as the autobiographer ponders it in his memory, echoes the skin trunk episode and again becomes a statement about the missing moth-mother: 'Persons were missed, were identified, were again denied — the whole is a *vapour* in my memory which shifts as I try to define it' (p. 65; author's italics).

It is not long before the night terrors return. Now, as earlier, when the mother had solved the riddle of the whispering text and banished the fears generated by the man silhouetted by moonlight on the roof, the father is their centre and origin. They consist in fact of one repeated dream, the substance of which is a 'mad gallop through space [into] a monstrous vortex'. The son is in the grasp, and at the mercy, of an 'undefined force':

> It seemed as if we ... were pushing feverishly on towards a goal which our whole concentrated energies were bent on reaching, but which a frenzied despair in my heart told me we never could reach, yet the attainment of which alone could save us from destruction. Far away, in the pulsation of the great luminous whorls, I could just see that goal, a ruby-coloured point waxing and waning, and it bore, or to be exact consisted of, the letters of the word CARMINE. (p. 84)

Carmine is the most precious of the pigments used by the father in his water-colour drawings, and the son, 'a fervent imitator of his works of art', is 'strictly forbidden' to touch it (p. 86). In represents, then, the father as prohibitor and as Adamically red archetype whom, despite his prohibition, the son has to imitate, assimilate, and supersede. Hence the urgency, the despair, the ominous sense of destruction if that red goal is not attained. And this means in turn that the 'ruby-coloured' point waxing and waning is a hypnotic vision of patricidal guilt, as the narrator himself recognises when he describes the precious carmine as his 'shibboleth of self-indulgence; it was a symbol of all that taste and art and wealth could combine to produce. I imagined, for instance, that at Belshazzar's feast, the loftiest épergne of gold, surrounded by flowers and jewels, carried the monarch's proudest possession, a cake of carmine' (p. 86). The guilt is encoded in the identification of the father with Belshazzar, which makes the son, as scrutineer of 'the letters of the word *carmine*' into Daniel, whose interpretation of the writing on the wall that interrupts Belshazzar's feast leads to the king's death and his own assumption of regal red (Daniel 5).[30]

Unable, however, to solve the riddle of the night-terrors' text as the mother did, the father 'thought to exorcise the demon by prayer':

> On one unhappy night . . . my Father was praying aloud . . . and I was half sitting, half lying on the bed, with the clothes sloping from my chin. Suddenly a rather large insect, dark and flat, with more legs than a self-respecting insect ought to need, appeared at the bottom of the counterpane, and slowly advanced. It walked successfully past my Father's sleek black ball of a head, and climbed straight up at me, nearer, nearer, till it seemed all a twinkle of horns and joints. I bore it in silent fascination till it almost tickled my chin, and then I screamed 'Papa! Papa!'
>
> (p. 85)

The beetle seems to come out of the father's head in a moment of Kafkaesque horror; and the scream is at once a cry for help and a shout of appalled recognition that the beetle *is* Papa, recognition based on the knowledge that carmine is obtained from the cochineal beetle (p. 86). The beetle is the father as king of the prohibited red and as originators of nightmares. Even if he cannot be exorcised he can at least be objectified in the form of yet another symbol.

The carmine dream and its attempted exorcism are preceded by the account of Edmund's kidnapping by Mary Flaw which had ended after the chase led by Philip had discovered Mary and the boy 'sitting on the doorstep of the butcher's shop' (p. 83). Innocent enough in isolation, perhaps, this detail becomes rather menacing in the context of a gentleman buried in quicklime and fragments found in carpet-bags. Not surprisingly Mary brings *Hamlet* into the text, for she derives via Sterne's Maria (*Tristram Shandy* and

Sentimental Journey) from Ophelia: 'She had become crazed, poor thing, in consequence of a disappointment in love'; her conversation 'was a great treat to me. I enjoyed its irregularities, its waywardness; it was like a tune that wandered into several keys' (p. 82). Mary kidnaps Edmund as a gesture of defiance against Philip claiming him for the world of the mothers, and in doing so she becomes a revived Ophelia hitting back at ruthless male tyranny, an unintentionally radical demolisher of the father-as-Word and as Law. This, at least, is how she is reconstructed by the autobiographer's memory of her. For the kidnapping is the climax of one of her splendid and brilliantly destructive parodies of Philip's evening service rituals. Finding the approved form inadequate to her needs, she creates her own para-ritual:

> Mary Flaw went through this ritual, but on a smaller scale. We all knelt down together, but when we rose from our knees, Miss Flaw was already standing up, and was pretending, without a sound, to sing a hymn; in the midst of our hymn, she sat down, opened her Bible, found a text, and then leaned back, her eyes fixed in space, listening to an imaginary sermon, which our own real one soon caught up, and coincided with for about three-quarters of an hour. Then, while our sermon went peacefully on, Miss Flaw would rise, and sing in silence (if I am permitted to use such an expression) her own visionary hymn . . .
> (pp. 82–3)

This mad woman visionary, at once Wordsworthian and Ophelian, is now identified as an image of the dead Emily as she proceeds in defiance of the father with her particular silent vocation, then lifts the boy from his place in the congregation and makes off with him:

> I leaned out across Miss Marks and I caught Miss Flaw's eye. She nodded, I nodded; and the amazing deed was done, I hardly knew how. Miss Flaw, with incredible swiftness, flew along the line, plucked me by the coat-collar from between my paralysed protectresses, darted with me down the chapel and out into the dark, before anyone had time to say 'Jack Robinson'.

The father gets him back, but the kidnapping is apparently the cause of the carmine dream: 'doubtless my nerves were shaken by the escapade and it may have had something to do with the recurrence of the distressing visions from which I had suffered as a very little child' (pp. 83–4). In other words, this momentary escape into the world of the mother has brought all the son's fears of his father to the forefront of his dreaming mind, presenting him in terms of the colour of blood.

Another Ophelia makes an even more dramatic protest some twenty pages later, in chapter 8, at the moment of the son's solemn dedication to the Father God through baptism. The Brethren practise adult baptism, but Philip has managed to persuade the elders that the young Edmund has been visited, despite his youth, by the Holy Ghost, for 'he wished to secure me finally, exhaustively, before the age of puberty could dawn, before my soul was fettered with the love of carnal things' (p. 98). The baptism testifies, as all Christian baptisms do, to 'a new birth and being, a fresh creation in God' (also p. 98). The *omphalos* theme thus begins to sound again: the father is claiming the son for the Father in a ceremony that is to be performed solely by males and which is, it seems, designed to erase the fact of his biological, maternal, birth. And as the baptismal pool is revealed, the son is reduced to the position of a specimen in one of the rock pools he has visited in company with his father, or an exhibit in one of his father's aquaria:

> In the centre of the chapel floor a number of planks had been taken up, and revealed a pool which might have been supposed to be a small swimming-bath. We gazed down into this dark square of mysterious waters, from the tepid surface of which faint swirls of vapour rose .... A sudden sensation of the hymn warned us that the Minister was now ready, and we emerged into the glare of lights and faces to find Mr. S. already standing in the water up to his knees. Feeling as small as one of our microscopical specimens, and infinitesimally tiny as I descended into his Titanic arms, I was handed down the steps to him.
>
> (pp. 104–5)

The males are not allowed to have it all their own way, however, for the baptism is heralded by 'an astounding incident' that occurs where omission marks are supplied in the above quotation. A young woman who has been forbidden baptism by her parents plunges into the pool:

> There was a great splash, and a tall young woman was perceived to be in the baptismal pool, her arms waving above her head, and her figure held upright in the water by the inflation of

the air underneath her crinoline, which was blown out like a
bladder, as in some extravagant old fashion-plate.

The parallel with the drowned Ophelia and her nineteenth-century
sisters as found in the life and works of Rossetti, Dickens,
Tennyson, Jerome K. Jerome and many others,[31] could not be clearer
('Her clothes spread wide,/And mermaid-like awhile they bore her
up' (IV.vii.174–5)), and the relegation of her to the past through the
detail of the 'old fashion-plate' associates her also with the dead
mother.

But this young woman is anything but dead. She has fractured
male ritual with her demand to be heard, positioned herself as icon
at the threshold of the son's baptism and, extraordinarily, proceeds
to take over the subsequent proceedings as the officiating minister
Mr S. assumes, in the son's retrospective portrayal of him, the
Ophelian pose:

> He was dressed in a kind of long surplice, underneath which — as
> I could not, even in that moment, help observing — the air
> gathered in long bubbles which he strove to flatten out.... He
> said, slowly, in a loud, sonorous voice that seemed to enter my
> brain and empty it, 'I baptize thee, my Brother, in the name of the
> Father and of the Son and of the Holy Ghost!' (pp. 105–6)

As Edmund is 'delivered, dripping and spluttering, into the
anxious hands of the women' the analogy with his biological birth
is completed; so that what we have really seen, through the eyes of
the son-as-autobiographer and in absolute defiance of the father, is
a feminine reappropriation of what is her own: the giving of birth,
the bestowing of life. Gosse has created an Ophelia who returns
alive from the water, generates her own baptising minister, and
then implies the feminine identity of the Holy Spirit by suggesting,
as does *Father and Son*'s title page, that she is the Spirit of Emily
claiming Edmund as 'my beloved son' (Matthew 3:17).

* * * * *

The baptism thus answers in a very real way that earlier moving
incident when the father was heard by the son to murmur, in a
momentary reversion to his youthful self, the opening lines of
Virgil's first eclogue:

> Tityre, tu patulae recubans sub tegmine fagi,
>
> he warbled; and I stopped my play, and listened as if to a nightingale, till he reached
>
> > tu, Tityre, lentus in umbra
> > Formosam resonare doces Amaryllida silvas.
>
> 'O Papa, what is that?' I could not prevent myself from asking. He translated the verses, he explained their meaning, but his exposition gave me little interest. What to me was beautiful Amaryllis? She and her love-sick Tityrus awakened no image whatever in my mind. (pp. 92–3)

Virgil's opening paragraph tells of Tityrus filling shady groves with the sound of Amaryllis's name and evokes in the father a correspondingly poignant memory of his lost beloved. Literally translated, even explained, adult sexual love can, of course, 'awaken . . . no image' in young Edmund's mind. Nevertheless the lines haunt him:

> I persuaded my Father, who was a little astonished at my insistence, to repeat the lines over and over again. At last my brain caught them, and as I walked in Benny's garden, or as I hung over the tidal pools at the edge of the sea, all my inner being used to ring out with the sound of
>
> > Formosam resonare doces Amaryllida silvas.

Benny is a companion whom Philip has discovered for his son and whose 'mother — I think he had no father — was a solemn and shadowy lady of means' (p. 88). To teach the trees in his large garden to resound with the name of beautiful Amaryllis is, whether the son admits it or not, to have them echo his loss of his own mother; and to intone it over the tidal pools is to anticipate the maternal Ghost's presence at his baptismal pool.

It seems, indeed, as if the influence of the mother's spirit reaches far beyond the baptism, for once he is a fully baptized Brother, Philip raises 'the embargo laid upon every species of fiction by my Mother's powerful scruple' and gives him a copy of Michael Scott's novel of the early 1830s, *Tom Cringle's Log*, to read. On one level this is a gesture of parental trust now that the son is a formally dedicated member of the sect; on another it is as if the father, like Mr S. in the pool, has been touched by the spirit and been given the maternal ghost's rather sad message that she need not have silenced her vocation for fiction after all, a message also communicated to Miss Brightwen when, as Edmund's stepmother, she positively encourages his reading of novels (p. 129).

3.3 NAMING *HAMLET*

> *Hamlet*: This is I
> Hamlet the Dane.
>
> (*Hamlet*, v.i)

The final phase of *Father and Son* begins as the boy leaves home for school. Travelling there one day he is greeted, in another symbolically Wordsworthian moment, 'by an old gentleman, dressed as a dissenting minister' (p. 117) who confesses that, before his conversion, he was 'on the stage'. This, as we have already seen, is Sheridan Knowles, actor, playwright, and now fervent baptist, an eighty-year-old double for the father who mediates between the worlds of the church and of the liberated imagination and who emancipates the boy by being the first to mention to him 'the name of Shakespeare' and then 'the names of Hamlet and Falstaff and Prospero' (p. 118). This encounter on the road with the ancient man who had (of course) played and who now names Hamlet[32] conjures up, a page later, a parallel meeting on the same road with a 'sympathetic Quakerish lady' whom the son 'little thought ... was to become my stepmother' (p. 120). The naming of *Hamlet* — *Father and Son's* textual ghost — generates Miss Brightwen into the narrative so that she can help reduce the burden of dark paternal dominance and diminish (though not eradicate) the pain still registered by the presence of the maternal shade. She comes as bride and mother at Christmas to soften the memory of the dying mother's last Christmas, and her arrival stimulates the departure of poor Miss Marks, aspiring stepmother and mournful guardian of the home as Pipchin Castle. Told by her relatives that she will have to 'bury' the sickly son as one of her first duties as the second Mrs

Gosse, she denies him his grave by removing the load of blankets with which Miss Marks had oppressed his bed and flinging open his bedroom window, thus exposing him to blasts of the fresh air from which he has been protected 'as if from a pestilence' (p. 123).[33]

As the air blows and he comes out of his grave, the ghosts begin to disappear. By inviting Edmund to read novels the stepmother helps the son release and realise the creative (feminine) self; by marrying, and thereby taking on, the father she helps the son achieve apartness from him. And so the son becomes a kind of blameless Claudius as his precarious faith becomes increasingly hollow, his words flying up while his thoughts remain firmly earthbound: 'It assailed me when I had come alone by my bedside, and had blown out the candle, and had sunken on my knees in my night-gown. Then it was that my deadness made itself felt, in the mechanical address I put up, the emptiness of my language, the absence of all real unction' (p. 124). Becoming a Brother has made him, like Claudius, a fratricide, for he now revels in graveyard poetry, the reading of which enables him to bury his Brother-father once more.

He reads the poems, which he discovers in 'a small, thick volume, bound in black morocco [and which are] of an order as wholly out of date as are the cross-bones and ruffled cherubim on the gravestones in a country churchyard' (p. 174), in order to help while away the tedium of Lord's Days imposed on him with merciless rigour. Young's *The Last Day* gives him the opportunity to curse (or at least question) his birth by aiming symbolically at his father words addressed by a risen soul to God:

> Father of mercies! Why from silent earth
> Didst thou awake, and curse me into birth?
> Tear me from quiet, ravish me from night,
> And make a thankless present of thy light?
> Push into being a reverse of thee,
> And animate a clod with misery?
>
> (p. 135)

Removed from their context and placed in Gosse's narrative in this way, the couplets proclaim the son's sense of his absolute difference from his father and his anguish at ever having been separated from the nocturnal quiet of the moon mother of chapter 2's *abendlied*. A second quotation from the same poem looks back to Uncle A's claim at the opening of chapter 2 that the infant Edmund had eaten up the mutton 'in the twinkling of an eye, bone and all', for it is a grotesquely literalistic vision of the raising of the dead on the last day:

> Now charnels rattle, scattered limbs, and all
> The various bones, obsequious to the call,
> Self-mov'd, advance — the neck perhaps to meet
> The distant head, the distant legs the feet.

Is this the reality underlying my mother's promise of reunion in heaven? is one question posed, only partly tongue-in-cheek, by this pair of couplets which also glance at the father by harking back to the early anecdote of the skeleton as 'a man with the meat off', the 'bare-grinning skeleton of death' of chapter 2. Wicked confirmation for this reading comes later on the same page when father and son kneel down to pray, 'our foreheads pressed upon the horsehair cover of the small, coffin-like sofa' (p. 136). Thinking the father into his coffin does not necessarily solve the problem, though, for the trouble with fathers is that they tend, like Old Hamlet, to return. It is his brooding on this dreadful probability that causes him to recite these lines from Robert Blair's *The Grave* at a children's party, much to the dismay of his hostess:

> If men were nothing, and nought after death, —
> If when men died at once they ceased to be, —
> Returning to the barren Womb of Nothing
> Whence first they sprung, then might the debauchee ....

(p. 137)

* * * * *

Edmund's physical release from his unlikely debauchee of a father comes with his departure for London, called a 'dim wild whirlpool' (p. 161) in order that it may negate and supersede the Devon rockpools, the baptismal pool, and the vortex of the carmine dream. Yet the father still 'torment[s]' him, not by returning as a ghost (for he is not yet, at the time described in the Epilogue, dead) but through the 'grave but gratifying occupation' of pestering him with letters:

The letter, the only too-confidently expected letter, would lie on the table as I descended to breakfast. It would commonly be, of course, my only letter, unless tempered by a cosy and chatty note from my dear and comfortable stepmother, dealing with such perfectly tranquillising subjects as the harvest of roses in the garden or the state of health of various neighbours. But the other, the solitary letter, in its threatening whiteness, with its exquisitely penned address — there it would lie awaiting me, destroying the taste of the bacon . . . . Like all its precursors, like all its followers, it would insist, with every variety of appeal, on a reiterated declaration that I still fully intended, as in the days of my earliest childhood, 'to be on the Lord's side' in everything.
(p. 167)

London marks the beginning of the son's commitment, in terms of career, to the imaginative literature that was the 'silenced vocation' of his mother; but the father calls, tormentor and tormented, from the confinement of his prison-house, announcing his ghostly presence through the 'threatening whiteness' of letters that still retain something of the power of that spectral whispering text that shattered his childhood nights (p. 27).

One final metaphor captures the essence of the conflict between father and son. Arguing about religion, about the state of the son's soul which the father insists on harrowing, the father 'was, indeed most unfairly handicapped, — I was naked, he in a suit of chain armour' (p. 172). This armour of ideological inflexibility assumes a slightly different aspect when the last confrontation between the two takes place in 'the odorous furnace of the conservatory' from which Edmund breaks away to 'bur[y] [his] face in the cold grass of the lawn' (p. 176). Pursued by Philip's letters to London, Edmund has returned to Devon to ask to be left alone:

> I desire not to recall the whimpering sentence in which I begged to be let alone, in which I demanded the right to think for myself, in which I repudiated the idea that my Father was responsible to God for my secret thoughts and my most intimate convictions.
> (p. 176)

The armoured man from whom he tries to protect his secret self is, we now see from the name dropped by James Sheridan Knowles all those pages earlier, Old Hamlet, clad in 'complete steel' (I.iv.52), trying to force on his son the heat of his 'sulph'rous and tormenting flames' (I.v.3), and the metaphor picks up an earlier one in which the father (and the father's house) are compared to the protective carapace of a soldier (or hermit) crab:

> I had great difficulty in persuading myself that I could ever be happy away from home, and again I compared my lot with that of one of the speckled soldier-crabs that roamed about in my Father's aquarium, dragging after them great whorl-shells. They, if by chance they were turned out of their whelk-habitations, trailed about a pale soft body in search of another house, visibly broken-hearted and the victims of every ignominious accident.
> (p. 161)

By leaving the armed father to his 'odorous furnace' this 'pale' youth achieves a separation even more rigorous than those fantasised over by his pale-faced younger self when it had gazed through a window at the Jersey onion seller who shouted — 'in a tone which might wake the dead'! — invitations to murder the Pope, and through another window at his father 'storming round [his] red morass' of a garden like an irascible ghostly Adam.

Philip's last letter, framed tellingly by references to burial (it 'buried itself in my heart' (p. 176); 'If this grace were granted to you, oh! how joyfully should I bury all the past' (p. 178), appeals to the memory of Emily: 'When your sainted Mother died, she not only tenderly committed you to God, but left you also as a solemn charge to me'. Edmund's rejection of his father is, then, a liberation of his mother's ghost from what he now sees as the prison of her religion; and the *Hamlet* subtext of *Father and Son* reveals that when, in its closing words, the son 'took a human being's privilege to fashion his inner life for himself', that inner life meditated on the mysteries of imaginative literature in order that the silenced novelist in Emily might be given a posthumous voice.

4
Iris Murdoch's *The Black Prince:* Overthrowing the Tyrant and Inscribing the Female

> I will arise and go to my father, and will say unto him, Father, I have sinned against heaven, and before thee, and am no more worthy to be called thy son.
>
> Luke 15:18–19

Iris Murdoch's novel *The Good Apprentice* (1985) opens with these verses from the parable of the prodigal son as Edward Baltram, guilt-ridden over the death of his friend Mark, begins his quest for his natural father, Jesse Baltram. The same verses are used in *Henry and Cato* (1976) at the point where Cato has renounced the priesthood, has been apparently abandoned by Beautiful Joe, the youth whom he loves, and has heard of the death of his friend Father Milsom:

> And he thought: I will arise and go to my father, and will say unto him, Father, I have sinned against heaven and before thee, and am no more worthy to be called thy son.[1]

Edward Baltram reaches Jesse, 'that enormous dark figure concealed behind the curtain of the future',[2] after attending a seance at which he is urged 'Come to your father' (p. 62). He meets him at his strange fantasy of a house, Seegard; but Jesse subsequently drowns and is discovered by Edward in the river that runs past Seegard at a spot where there is 'a cluster of willows which seemed to stir his memory' (p. 434). The father, known by Edward throughout his life only by his absence, has now finally departed. Or has he? *The Good Apprentice*, in a way characteristic of Murdoch's novels, invites the reader to make equations that imply theological and philosophical riddles. Jesse, brought home from the river by the tree men, is somehow the Biblical Jesse, celebrated for his sons, the root of Isaiah 11 from whom the branch and flower Jesus will grow; so that he is at once dead and not dead, though the status of his existence is left teasingly open. In the last part, 'Life after Death', Edward relegates him to the province of memory by beginning to read Proust at the end, while the Bloomsbury graffiti writers have inscribed *Jesse Lives* and *Jesse Baltram is King* 'on a wall near the British Museum' (p. 519). *The Good Apprentice* could be a ghost story; it is clearly concerned with the Freudian area of the uncanny. Equally clearly, with its ghostly king of a father, its haunted son, its drowning by a memory-stirring cluster of willows, it is one of Murdoch's *Hamlet* fictions, even though it does not name the play.

The naming of Hamlet is, this late in Murdoch's writing career, scarcely necessary, for *The Good Apprentice* is recognisably the climax to a group of *Hamlet* fictions that began with *The Black Prince* (1973) and includes *Henry and Cato, The Sea, The Sea* (1978) and *Nuns and Soldiers* (1980). Of these last three *Henry and Cato* is closest to *The Good Apprentice*, beginning as it does with Henry, Cato's symbolic twin, about to take possession of his ancestral lands, his father dead and his elder brother just having been killed in a car crash. Henry's story, however, unlike Edward's, contains teasing acknowledgements of *Hamlet*. His mother, Gerda (Gertrude), loved his elder brother more than she loved him, so that in many ways *Henry and Cato* is about Henry's revenge on Gerda, raising questions about his psychological complicity in the death of his father and elder brother, as when he feels 'panic, terror, a kind of nebulous horror as if he were a man destined by dark forces to commit a murder for which he had no will and of which he had no understanding' (p.59). His image of himself fractured by maternal deprivation and indifference, he identifies with the victims of torture and imprisonment that people the Max Beckmann paintings that haunt the novel[3] and, also, with Hamlet:

> He had an instinctive identification with heroes beginning with H. Homer. Hannibal. Hobbes. Hume. Hamlet. Hitler. What a crew. Only his own name seemed empty, a sort of un-name, another cause for resentment, unredeemed by kings.
>
> (pp. 70–1)

A son's quest for, and supplication before, his father is a

fundamental theme in Murdoch's later fiction but, as in *Henry and Cato*, the prodigal son motif is almost invariably shadowed by its Oedipal negative – supplication, in other words, seems to be a penance for entertaining patricidal desires, and the impetus for the paternal quest seems to lie firmly in the patterns of patricide and atonement noticed by Freud in *Moses and Monotheism* and *Totem and Taboo*.

Hamlet is one of many threads in Henry's story, as it is in Charles Arrowby's in *The Sea, The Sea* or in *Nuns and Soldiers*, with its pub called 'The Prince of Denmark' situated near Fitzroy Square.[4] In all of these novels, in fact, *Hamlet* is present yet somehow residual, as if they are texts haunted by a ghost that has been relieved of its burden and is making a rather awkward appearance as a superannuated guest celebrity. This is even true of *Nuns and Soldiers*, which appears to be retelling *Hamlet* from Gertrude's point of view (the central woman is again named Gertrude and within a year of her husband's death she has made an o'er hasty second marriage to a young man half her age) but rapidly turns its (albeit related) centres of interest elsewhere: to the question of vocation and the nature of God, the function and value of art, the question of national identity, and so on.

Hamlet's tameness as an allusive force in these novels can be attributed directly to its centrality in *The Black Prince*, where Murdoch encountered the play head on and almost (but not quite) laid its ghost once and for all as she created in Bradley Pearson, the novel's autobiographical narrator, a writer so involved with *Hamlet* that it takes him some four hundred pages to disclose the extent of his obsession. A main clue to his monomania is the elaborate tutorial on the play given by Bradley to Julian, the daughter of his rival novelist friend Arnold Baffin, which fulfils for *The Black Prince* the function fulfilled by the performance of *Hamlet* in *Tom Jones* and *Great Expectations*, inviting the reader to relate inset text to frame text and elevating *Hamlet* as a mirror of dazzling reflective power.

The essence of the tutorial is Bradley's Oedipal understanding of *Hamlet*, which at once raises questions about the status of the male narrator in relation to the author herself. Murdoch habitually identifies with men and writes from the male viewpoint, but a main argument of this chapter will be that *The Black Prince* is a mimetic text, self-consciously about the tension between male narrator and female author as it is focused by Shakespeare's most Oedipal and (arguably) most misogynistic play.[5] As Bradley erects a Platonic theory of art on the foundations of Ernest Jones's Oedipal *Hamlet* and, of necessity, repudiates the notion of woman as creator and thinker, we hear Murdoch's female self insistently query his interpretation of women and his assumptions about the nature, role, and gender of the artist. Bradley enables Murdoch to enter a paradigmatic male mind and survey the extent to which this phenomenon rejects and dishonours the feminine, while the Oedipal *Hamlet* permits her to overhear the mystery of male encountering male in the form of father and son arguing over woman as both maternal and sexual love object.

In *The Black Prince*, then, Murdoch takes the Oedipus complex as a sadly true working definition – even explanation – of the relationship between the sexes, of Christianity and of Platonist theories of art.[6] In exploring the terrifying depths of Oedipal male myopia it demonstrates a feminist alternative as Julian survives Bradley's obsession to become a poet. In the end, rather like that other radical mid-seventies re-vision of *Hamlet*, Fay Weldon's *Remember Me* (1976), where Madeleine's ghost displaces that of patriarchal Old Hamlet with his cry of 'remember me', *The Black Prince* is a story of woman's revenge on the male for his oppression and suppression of the feminine.

By a neat coincidence *The Black Prince* was published in the same year as Harold Bloom's Oedipally anxious *Anxiety of Influence*. To his astonishing theoretical fiction of 'strong poets, major figures with the persistence to wrestle with their strong percursors, even to the death'[7] Murdoch's theoretical fiction responds by revealing how puny a concept of strength is that is predicated upon the humiliation and misprision of woman.

4.1 APPOLLO, MARSYAS, AND HAMLET

> *Hamlet*: What have you, my good friends, deserved at the hands of Fortune that she sends you to prison hither?
> *Guildenstern*: Prison, my lord?
> *Hamlet*: Denmark's a prison
> *Rosencrantz*: Then is the world one.
> *Hamlet*: A goodly one, in which there are many confines, wards, and dungeons, Denmark being one o' th'worst.
>
> (*Hamlet*, ii.ii)

It is helpful to begin with a plot summary. Bradley is a divorced, fifty-eight year old former tax man who has taken early retirement in order to follow his writing career. As the novel opens he is packed and ready to leave his London flat for a rented seaside house called Patara. There he hopes he will find the solitude and silence he needs to enable him to overcome his writer's block:

> For the first time in my life I wanted silence.
> Of course, as might be pointed out with barbed humour, I had always in a sense been a devotee of silence. Arnold Baffin once said something like this to me, laughing, and hurt me. Three short books in forty years of sustained literary effort is not exactly garrulity. And indeed if I understand anything that is precious, I did understand how important it was to keep one's mouth shut until the right moment even if this meant a totally voiceless life.[8]

Arnold, Bradley's former *protégé*, is in Bradley's view as prodigal and intemperate with words as Bradley is thrifty and chaste.

The narrative begins with the aftermath of a row between Arnold and his wife during which he hits her with the poker and, simultaneously, the irruption into Bradley's life of two figures from his remote past, his divorced, remarried, and subsequently widowed wife Christian, and her brother Francis Marloe. Bradley tries to comfort Rachel and, eventually and momentarily, becomes her awkward and impotent lover while repudiating overtures from Christian and being forced to care for his sister Priscilla, who deposits herself in his flat in a state of nervous breakdown after being left by her husband Roger for a much younger woman. To complicate this characteristically Murdochian plot further, the Baffins' daughter Julian has appeared and requested from Bradley tutorials on *Hamlet* which she is preparing for an examination. The possibility of going to Patara having receded under the pressures of all this contingency, Bradley agrees. While giving her a long tutorial Bradley falls in love with her. Despite parental resistance and imprisonment, Julian escapes to Bradley and drives with him to Patara. Their seaside idyll is interrupted by Arnold, who reveals Bradley's age to Julian and tells her of Priscilla's suicide. The narrative ends with Rachel telephoning Bradley (as Arnold had telephoned him at the beginning) asking for help. She has hit Arnold with the poker and he is dead. Bradley is accused of the murder, tried, and found guilty.

The narrative is framed by two forewords, the editor's and Bradley's, and six postscripts, by Bradley, Christian, Francis, Rachel and Julian, and the editor. Bradley's postscript, the first and longest, tells of his trial and, again, of his love for Julian and his view of the nature of artistic inspiration; those by the *dramatis personae* (to use the novel's own phrase) apportion varying degrees of blame to Bradley. The editor's reveals that Bradley has died in prison of cancer and defends Bradley's story as art: 'Art tells the only truth that ultimately matters. It is the light by which human things can be mended' (p. 416).

At the centre of *The Black Prince*, then, is Bradley's narrative; at its extremities are the contributions of the editor, a certain P. Loxias. Loxias's foreword tells us that he got to know Bradley in prison; that they 'found in each other the blessings of friendship'; that Bradley sensed in him 'his *alter ego*'; and that he, Loxias, is 'in more than one way responsible for the work that follows' (p. 9). *Loxias* is, as many have recognised, an epithet for Phoebus Apollo, god of the sun and of poetry.[9] Does his presence before Bradley in prison suggest that Bradley, at his physical nadir, achieves, like Milton's Samson, his moment of glory, the spiritual possession by the divine that he has been seeking all along? This is a possibility that is reinforced by the appearance of the cave and the sun image ('This morning I had felt like a cave-dweller emerging into the sun. [Julian] was the truth of my life' (p. 285)) that invites a comparison with this passage from *The Sovereignty of Good*:

> Our attachments tend to be selfish and strong, and the transformation of our loves from selfishness to unselfishness is sometimes hard even to conceive of .... One might say that true morality is a sort of unesoteric mysticism, having its source in an austere and unconsoled love of the Good. When Plato wants to explain Good he uses the image of the sun. The moral pilgrim emerges from the cave and begins to see the real world in the light of the sun, and last of all is able to look at the sun itself.[10]

The ideal relationship between the Good and art is explained by Murdoch in *The Fire and the Sun*, her other major Platonic philosophical work: 'the relation of art to truth and goodness must be the fundamental concern of any serious criticism of it'; 'good art thought of as symbolic force rather than statement, provides a stirring image of a pure transcendent value, a steady visible enduring higher good'.[11]

But to see Bradley as an *illuminatus* into the mysteries of Apollo would, in the end, be naive, as most of *The Black Prince*'s critics agree; for the point is that he knows what he is aiming at, does experience illumination of a sort, but is in the end brought up short by his moral blindness. What critics disagree on is where Bradley's failure and blindness lie. The answer to this problem is, though, clearly presented in the *Hamlet* tutorial where Bradley assumes the truth of the Freud-Jones Oedipal reading of the play in order that he may then proceed to his explanation of it as a confession about the nature of creation by Shakespeare the artist. Bradley's procedure neatly demonstrates the dependence of his male-oriented theory of artistic inspiration on the Oedipus complex, and Murdoch achieves through it the more general exposure — demolition, even — of the woman-repudiating aspect of the Plato who is, in so many other ways, fundamental to her thinking. For the most that the feminine can ever be to Bradley, as to all mainstream Platonists, is a stepping stone to the male god. Here is the revealing crux of the *Hamlet* tutorial which is placed, literally and symbolically, *en abysme*, in the middle of the novel:[12]

> 'Did Shakespeare hate his father? Of course. Was he in love with his mother? Of course. But that is only the beginning of what he is telling us about himself . . . He has performed a supreme creative feat, a work endlessly reflecting upon itself, not discursively but in its very substance, a Chinese box of words as high as the tower of Babel . . . .*Hamlet* is words and so is Hamlet. He is as witty as Jesus Christ, but whereas Christ speaks Hamlet is speech. He is the tormented empty sinful consciousness of man seared by the bright light of art, the god's flayed victim dancing the dance of creation . . . . How veiled that deity, how dangerous to approach, how almost impossible with impunity to address, Shakespeare knew better than any man. *Hamlet* is a wild act of audacity, a self-purging, a complete self-castigation in the presence of god . . .'. (pp. 199-200)

This is apparently inspired, and after uttering it Bradley reports himself 'exhausted, almost dazed, damp with sweat from head to foot as if I were outlined with warm quicksilver', thus perceiving himself momentarily as Mercury, messenger of the gods, patron of language and music, symbol of both substance and goal of the alchemists' work, guide of and communer with the souls of the dead.[13] Yet, gifted by his nascent love for Julian with such Hermetic eloquence and perception, what does Bradley see after all but an Oedipal Shakespeare performing a masochistic and exhibitionistic ritual of self-abasement before a sadistic god who is the 'great ... and ... terrible godhead' of his prison confession (p. 390) and in effect nothing more than a projection of the feared terrible father, product of Oedipal fantasy? Bradley's Shakespeare is, of course, Bradley himself, whose name partly anagrammatises into Bard Spear. (As B.P. he is also Hamlet, the Bard's son, one of the Black Princes of the novel's title.)

The myth that underlies Bradley's vision in the tutorial and beyond it is a favourite with Murdoch, that of Apollo and Marsyas. Male orthodoxy as exemplified by the Neoplatonists construed Apollo's flaying of Marsyas the flautist as, to quote Axel in *A Fairly Honourable Defeat* (1970), an image of 'the inevitable agony of the human soul in its desire to achieve God'. For them the violation of the body revealed the beauty of the soul. To Dante, the myth offered validation of his artistic self.[14]

Bradley's use of the myth is in this tradition, but his Oedipal preface brilliantly deconstructs the Neoplatonist orthodoxy to suggest the myth's historical origin in one of the ancient battles between patriarchy and matriarchy. The Apollo who emerges now is the destroyer and woman hater, equivalent of the Hamlet who, identifying Gertrude with Ophelia (p. 195), vilifies and destroys them. This reading recalls that Marsyas was playing the flute, Pallas's instrument, when he challenged Apollo to the contest which he lost: recalls, in other words, that Apollo's lyre vanquished the voice of the goddess of wisdom and that the victory was greeted with almost universal grief: 'the country people, the sylvan deities, fauns ... the nymphs, all wept'.[15] Bradley reveals a view of the flayed victim and the god that is absolutely homoerotic and attributable, as Francis Marloe insists, to his Oedipal relationship with his parents. Francis may be bumptious, self-advertising and intolerable, but his perception of Bradley is truer than many critics have been prepared to allow. Bradley's suspicion of his Freudianism ('My mother filled me with exasperation and shame but I loved her. (Be quiet Francis Marloe.)' (p. 15)) is itself suspect.

The deconstructive process continues after the tutorial:

> I opened the window and a breath of slightly cooler air entered the room, polluted and dusty, yet also somehow bearing the half-obliterated ghosts of flowers from distant parks. A massed-

up buzz of various noise filled the room, cars, voices, the endless hum of London's being. I opened the front of my shirt all the way down to the waist and scratched in my curly mat of grey hair.

(p. 201)

A couple of pages earlier Bradley has described his chest hair as 'copious but grizzled. (Or, if you prefer, a sable silvered)' (p. 197), thereby identifying himself as Old Hamlet (I.ii.240–2). This, together with the Mercury-quicksilver description that he applies to himself just before he opens the window in the above quotation, suggests that, as he now faces Julian, he has summoned up and combined several of the souls of the mythological and fictional dead. Bradley confronting Julian recalls Apollo confronting Marsyas but transformed now into a tableau in which Bradley is Old Hamlet and simultaneously his own dead father confronting himself-as-son in the shape of Julian as Hamlet. The feminine is totally excluded as Bradley continues: 'So you played Hamlet. Describe your costume', and the issues raised by this multiple image are resolved, or at least clarified, by the phrase that Bradley now quotes at Julian: 'She was dreamy, combing her layers of greeny-golden hair with long fingers, seeing herself as Hamlet, sword in hand. "Here thou incestuous murderous damned Dane —" ' (p. 202). For if quotations and allusions are to mean anything in this riddle of a novel, this one says that Bradley's ecstatic tutorial vision has merely stimulated, brought right into the foreground, the preoccupation with Oedipal incest from which he began. His words are, of course, Hamlet's last, death-dealing, words to Claudius as he gives him the poison. Following Ernest Jones's lead (as Bradley himself does) in applying principles of doubling and inversion to the text, we must infer that what we have here, at the centre of this particular Chinese box, is Bradley as his own (Old Hamlet) of a father accusing his Julian-Claudius-Hamlet of a self of incest guilt.[16]

The fact that Julian is a girl and therefore, in the pantheon of Bradley's subconscious, 'really' Ophelia, as Bradley has already acknowledged (p. 196), merely reinforces the Oedipal inference. Oedipally father and son are identified; so that Bradley as Old Hamlet accusing himself in the form of Julian-Hamlet by using words directed by Hamlet at the dying Claudius is also Bradley as lover of his mother confronting her as Ophelia. As Bradley remarks to Julian's baffled commonsense after she has said that she cannot 'see why [Hamlet] should think Ophelia is Gertrude, they're not a bit alike': 'The unconscious mind delights in identifying people with each other. It has only a few characters to play with' (p. 195).

Bradley opens the window onto his claustrophobic hothouse of a tutorial about the agonies of the male creator exultant before the father god, and what enters is 'cooler air... bearing the half-obliterated ghosts of flowers from distant parks'. The language is beautifully, hauntingly, metaphorical: parks are female spaces 'down among the women';[17] and the air, suffused with the dust of death (as in the church near Patara later) bears the ghostly memory of the Ophelia flower maiden infinitely multiplied to embrace all mothers, muses, and *animae* that the Apollonian artist has erased through the exercise of his rampant and excluding male ego.

If Apollo silenced the feminine when he vanquished Pallas's reed flute, he also humiliated and denied her at Patara. Bradley's seaside retreat borrows its name from the Lycian town which was celebrated for its temple of Apollo,[18] and the point of the name is not to compound riddles, though it might on the face of it seem as though it is, but rather to clarify in yet another way the relationship between Bradley's Apollo-based theory of art and the sexual humiliation and denial of the feminine.

It is at Patara that Bradley rapes Julian, an act born out of his knowledge of his sister, Priscilla's, suicide and his decision to do nothing about it for the moment, not even tell Julian: ' "Oh Bradley, please, don't be so rough, please, Bradley, you're hurting me." Later on she was crying. There had been no doubt about this love-making. I lay exhausted and let her cry' (p. 328).

By any criterion this has been the 'love-making' of an egotistical sadist and fantasist. Startled by Julian's metamorphosis into Hamlet he has grabbed at her and pushed her into the bedroom and onto the bed. Afterwards, she has been monosyllabic and numb, aware of the ominous presence of demons, those Murdochian symbols of malignant fantasy: ' "Let's draw the curtains. I feel bad spirits are looking in at us" ' (p. 330). When they start to talk, Julian confesses to feeling 'quite impersonal', Bradley to having 'come through [his] ordeal'. In terms of the Platonist ideology to which Bradley subscribes, he has been possessed by 'the god, the black Eros' (p. 331), has enjoyed a *raptus* that has taken him significantly nearer the 'greater and more terrible godhead', Apollo (p. 390), and has communicated his power to Julian. But if we see him as one of Iris Murdoch's courtly lovers, like Montague Small in *The Sacred and*

Profane Love Machine (1974) and, above all, like Charles Arrowby in *The Sea, The Sea*, then his possession ceases to be the gift of a god which he has passed on to another and becomes instead merely the willed projection of what Murdoch has called 'fantasy-myth',[19] the freedom-denying reduction of another to the myopia of one's own perceptions.

As we know, the symptom of Bradley's myopia is his preoccupation with Hamlet and Ophelia. And so, just as the *Hamlet* tutorial's ecstasy had collapsed into the revelation of Bradley's Oedipal obsession, the Patara ecstasy is undermined, too. He has violated Hamlet in order to produce Ophelia:

> She was [now] wearing the blue dress with the white willow-spray pattern which she had been wearing when she fled.... There had been a lot of tears but none now. She looked so much, and beautifully, older, not the child I had known at all, but some wonderful holy woman, a prophetess, a temple prostitute. (pp. 330–1)

The willow is Ophelia's emblem, sign that Bradley, like Hamlet, has drowned the girl in the flow of his outrageous egotism. When he proceeds to equate holy woman with *hetaira*, as if there could be no difference between holiness and prostitution, the relevance of the Patara allusion becomes clear, for at the centre of the cult of the Pataran Apollo was a prostitute.

Our authority here is Herodotus, whose comment is embedded, significantly, in his description of the shrine of Baal (Zeus Belus) in Babylon:

> But no image has been set up in the shrine, nor does any human creature lie therein for the night, except one native woman, chosen from all women by the god, as say the Chaldaeans, who are priests of this god.
> These same Chaldaeans say (but I do not believe them) that god himself is wont to visit the shrine and rest upon the couch, even as in Thebes of Egypt, as the Egyptians say (for there too a woman sleeps in the temple of Theban Zeus, and neither the Egyptian nor the Babylonian woman, it is said, has intercourse with men), and as it is likewise with the prophetess of the god at Patara in Lycia, whenever she be appointed; for there is not always a place

of divination there; but when she is appointed she is shut up in the temple during the night.[20]

The more one's mind plays on this passage, the more shabby Bradley becomes. He is a sham Apollo who has brought his own concubine to his Pataran temple, and the god he admires so much is after all no better than a Soho punter, dangerously akin to Baal, the most-named and ill-reputed pagan god of the Old Testament. Israel goes whoring after him and his para-deities (Judges 8:33), serves him (II Kings 17:16), and her prophets prophesy by him (Jeremiah 2:8). To follow him is to abandon the path of goodness and of truth. Herodotus's linking of Apollo Patareus with Baal is crucial to this novel which names Julian after one of the great medieval visionaries of the mystery of divine love (p. 55) and calls Bradley's divorced wife Christian, though she is partly Jewish (' "Our mother was a Christian convert" ', Francis tells Bradley, who had courted, married, lived with, and divorced Christian without ever discovering the Jewish connection (p. 148). The link suggests that Bradley's Apollo is a false god whose need for a temple harlot testifies less to his godhead, his power to bestow the divine *raptus*, than it does to his subjection to the goads and tugs of the flesh and the fantasies of his own depraved mind; it suggests that he needs this specially selected woman for much the same reasons that Hamlet needs to vilify and sexually humiliate Ophelia.

Herodotus indicates that Apollo was not present at Patara all the time. He was there, as Servius informs us in his brief but crucial note on *Aeneid*, IV.143, for the six winter months of the year, spending the six summer months at Delos. The line that prompts Servius's note describes Aeneas as 'like Apollo when in winter he leaves Lycia and the river Xanthus and visits maternal Delos' when he appears in order to go hunting with Dido.[21] Once the hunt has started, a severe rainstorm leads the two to shelter in a cave and make love: 'on that day were sown the seeds of [Dido's] suffering and death'. Rumour reports 'how they were now spending all the long winter together in comfort and self-indulgence, caught in the trap of shameful passion'. Later, Jove's messenger, Mercury, will tell Aeneas to abandon Dido so that he may fulfil his 'great destiny', the founding of his Latian kingdom. Patriarchy and the heroic code mass all their might against what the outraged Iarbas calls *a mere woman, a vagrant (femina . . . errans;* 1.211), and Dido, cursing Aeneas's faithlessness, kills herself.

Servius's explanation of the simile at line 143 makes Aeneas into

Apollo Pataraeus hibernating with his temple prostitute until the call to his greater duty forces him to leave her. And clues in Murdoch's text nudge us into connecting *Aeneid*, IV with Bradley's Patara. For one thing, Patara is recorded on the name plate in 'Italian lettering' (p. 311); for another, a piece of driftwood picked up by Julian has had etched on it by the sea 'a sort of delicate sketch of an old face, a sketch such as some Italian artist, Leonardo perhaps, might make in a rather abstract way in his notebook' (p. 313). *Italian* in both instances invites the speculation that we are pondering fragments of Roman history, that as Bradley makes his way with Julian to Patara he is treading a path into an archaic past in which he will assume the role not just of Apollo but of Aeneas-Apollo, and that Julian will be forced into the role of Dido-like *hetaira*.

Then, fifty pages later, after his trial and sentence for Arnold's murder, Bradley meets his double, P. Loxias, Apollo Loxias, Apollo the oblique, Apollo the crooked one, reputedly so named from his riddling and ambiguous oracles.[22] As Loxias, matching narrative mode to name, tells us in his foreword, 'What follows is ambiguous and sometimes tortuously told. Man's searchings and his strugglings are ambiguous and vowed to hidden ways' (p.9). But in the end they are perhaps not quite so hidden. For if Apollo Pataraeus permits Bradley to fulfil his Hamlet fantasy and use Julian as a whore, then Apollo Loxias reveals the reason why he needed to do so in the first place: 'I own no lord but Loxias; him I serve', declares Tiresias to Oedipus in Sophocles's *Oedipus Tyrannus*. The blind seer, who knows what the god knows, names him at this point in the play as the arch-riddler and master of the Oedipal secret. The name will be used later by Jocasta when Oedipus begins to suspect that he may have killed his father, and, later still, Oedipus will name him: 'Loxias once foretold that I should mate with mine own mother, and shed with my own hands my own father's blood'.[23] The mystery encoded in the epithet Loxias is thus the Oedipal mystery, and in finding his way to Loxias at the end of his life Bradley confronts this fact in its stark and horrifying simplicity.

4.2 OPHELIA'S SISTERS

> *Hamlet·* Now get you to my lady's chamber and tell her, let her
> paint an inch thick, to this favour she must come.
> (*Hamlet*, v.i)

Despite his difficulty in deciding how to open his narrative, Bradley knows that it ought to begin with an image of hurt womanhood, either 'with Rachel's tears, or Priscilla's. There is much shedding of tears in this story' (p. 21). He knows, too, that the origins of this image lie in his parents' papershop and his relationship with his dead parents and with Priscilla (pp. 14–15). In the event, however, he decides to begin with Francis Marloe, who stands on his front doorstep 'with copious greyish longish frizzy hair' emanating 'something significantly ill-omened' and riddlingly mutters '"She's back . . . . He's dead. She's back"' (pp. 23–4). Old Hamlet returns from the dead to tell of murder; Francis irrupts, ghostlike, into Bradley's life to tell of the apparent return from the dead of Christian, the divorced wife whom Bradley has erased from his memory: 'I . . . was able to feel that she had died' (p. 25). Christian returns as a *revenant* ('Francis had certainly raised ghosts himself of a particularly nasty kind' (p. 52)), but before we see her Bradley focuses his narrative attentions on Rachel. Arnold has 'killed' her as Bradley 'killed' Christian and invites Bradley round to view the result. As Bradley describes her we discover a middle-aged Ophelia who is a double for Christian and also for Bradley's dead mother:

> There was a darkening reddish bruise under one eye and the eye was narrowed, though this was hard to see because the eyelids of both eyes were so grossly red and swollen with weeping. Her upper lip was also swollen on one side. There were traces of blood on her neck and on her dress. Her hair was tangled and looked darker as if wet . . . . (p. 34)

It is as if Bradley is a sadistic voyeur at the aftermath of some orgiastic primal scene, already relishing his attack on Julian at Patara. The assault itself has been perpetrated by Arnold, of course. But the act of describing and recreating it makes it Bradley's, and in any case the two are paired like Henry and Cato, Cain and Abel, Claudius and Old Hamlet. Arnold's killing of Rachel because 'she was yelling like a fury and saying awful things about my work' (p. 37) parallels Bradley's infinitely earlier banishing of Christian because 'I say her as a death-bringer. Some women are like that' (p. 25). To both, woman is threat and destroyer, and both, in this opening scene at least, express the need to turn the totem woman into Ophelia: Arnold by battering her with a poker and then pouring a jug of water over her; Bradley by reliving the scene in such minute detail.

This Ophelia-vision of Rachel will soon empower Bradley to become her (rather ineffectual) lover. In the meantime Murdoch gives Bradley a moment of perception that locates his Ophelia syndrome in the fundamental human and animal need for a scapegoat:

> She sighed very deeply and flopped her hand back on to the bed, lying now with both hands symmetrically by her side, palms upward, like a limp disentombed Christ-figure, still bearing the marks of ill-treatment. Tufts of cut hair adhered to the dried blood on the bosom of her blue dress. (p. 39)

This is, symbolically at least, 'the blue dress with the white willow-spray pattern' which Julian wears for her escape to Patara and puts on after her rape (p. 330); but here it drapes an Ophelia perceived as the ultimate masochist's victim, Christ. As Beautiful Joe will say of the crucified Christ in *Henry and Cato*, 'If a gang done that, they'd get ten years even if the bugger survived' (p. 69). This particular bugger in the form of Rachel survives to have her revenge by killing one of the gang (Arnold) and giving the other (Bradley) his ten years. Furthermore, Rachel as Christ gives her name to Christian, another of the survivors at the end of this novel which teases us, particularly at the beginning of Part 3, with the question of evolutionary success and failure. These, then, are the basic elements from which Murdoch creates in *The Black Prince* her feminist attack on the Oedipus complex as it parades itself under the mask of male sentimentality over the 'Hamlet vocation'.[24]

Bradley's description of Rachel's bedroom, too, is paradigmatic. The room is shared by Rachel and Arnold, though we would never suspect this from his hard-eyed Juvenalian (and Hamlet-like) concentration on cosmetics and the frailties of the female body:[25]

> A dressing-table can be a terrible thing. . . . The plate glass 'table' surface was dusty and covered with cosmetic tubes and bottles and balls of hair. The chest of drawers had all its drawers gaping, spewing pink underwear and shoulder straps. The bed was chaotic, violent, the green artificial silk coverlet swooping down on one side and the sheets and blankets creased up into a messy mass, like an old face . . . . The whole room breathed the flat horror of genuine mortality, dull and spiritless and final.
> (p. 38)

This is Rachel's deepest private self mercilessly exposed, yet there is hurt here as well as Bradley catalogues these images of female vulnerability and the grave of a bed; for the sheets and blankets, creased 'like an old face', anticipate sobbing, desperate, and ugly Priscilla who is herself a transfigured hieroglyph of their dead mother, whose death bed Bradley is recreating here ('My mother lived to see my first book published. She was proud of me' (p. 15); 'Priscilla's woebegone tearful face was crumpled and old. Had she every really resembled my mother?' (p. 85)).[26] And it is out of this vision of the Rachel-mother and Bradley's speculation as he walks back to his 'cosy womb' of a flat (p. 22) that she might still be 'lying like a disfigured corpse staring at the ceiling' (p. 53) that Julian enters the narrative. The moment is brilliantly achieved, for 'she' is at first a 'he' as Bradley's dreamlike perception insists that this strangely posturing figure can exist only as an adjunct of his obsessed self intoning a funeral liturgy over the dead Ophelias who inhabit the burial chambers of his mind:

> He was standing upon the kerb and strewing flowers upon the roadway, as if casting them into a river . . . . [He] appeared to be chanting some form of repetitive litany. I now saw that what he was strewing was not so much flowers as white petals. Where had I seen just such petals lately? The fragments of white paint which the violence of Arnold's chisel had dislodged from the bedroom door . . . . I had paused and had been watching him for some time and was about to set off again towards the station when, with one of those switches of *gestalt* which can be so unnerving, I realized that the light had deceived me and that this . . . was a girl whom I knew. It was Julian Baffin, Arnold and Rachel's teenage daughter and only child. (So named, I need hardly explain, after Julian of Norwich.) (pp. 54–5)

Julian, then, emerges out of Bradley's fixation on Rachel as corpse and simultaneously out of his image of himself as Rachel's attacker: s/he is strewing the petals of white paint he (as Arnold) had created by chiselling at the door in his attempt to view the woman he had battered and 'drowned' with the jug of water. (The white paint-petals probably derive, in Bradley's fevered mind, from white violets and thus complicate the issue further by meshing with Ophelia's 'violets [which] withered all when my father died' (IV.v.182–3) and punning homophonically on *violets* and *violence*.)

Iris Murdoch's The Black Prince

This moving icon is also wonderfully proleptic in her refusal to remain bound within Bradley's Hamlet-engineered prison, however: she opposes his sick fantasy with the totemic power of her name and as her Julian self scatters, as Ophelia never quite managed to, the remembrances of an unwelcome lover to the winds.

If Julian is at once within and beyond Bradley's fantasies then Priscilla is completely inside them, constantly threatening and finally achieving suicide, another middle-aged Ophelia who now presents herself at Bradley's front door, pushes her way into the bedroom, and lies there, 'pitiful and ugly.... Her swollen face, the scene in the dim light, reminded me of Rachel' (p. 74). Bradley has literally become the hero of his own novel, that 'nebulous work' he has described slightly earlier as 'now a *nouvelle*, now a vast novel, wherein a hero not unlike myself pursued, amid ghostly incidents, a series of reflections about life and art' (p. 62). The 'ghostly incidents' continue as Bradley leaves his flat with its enshrined Priscilla to visit Christian in the time capsule of their old flat, the lease of which she has retained. In fact, the journey from Priscilla to Christian is no journey at all, for his unconscious with its limited number of characters to play with (p. 195) perceives them as aspects of one figure. Inevitably, therefore, Priscilla moves in with Christian, and Bradley discovers in them the twinned obverse and converse of a maternal Ophelia, dead yet alive, ugly yet with a haunting mermaid-like beauty, Priscilla dressed in a black *negligée* and looking ancient juxtaposed against Christian dressed in green, combing at her reddish-brown hair with her fingers (p. 110).

Bradley replays the scene later when Julian returns to Priscilla the Chinese bronze of a lady riding on a water buffalo that Bradley has given her but which really belongs to Priscilla:

> [Julian] pushed the water buffalo lady along the coverlet, as if she was amusing a child....
>
> Julian had retreated to the bottom of the bed.... [She] looked as if she were begging Priscilla's pardon for being young and good-looking and innocent and unspoilt and having a future, while Priscilla was old and ugly and sinful and wrecked and had none. (pp. 134–5)

The bronze itself merely reiterates Bradley's obsession. The buffalo keeps its rider out of the water but gets so damaged during the course of the novel that we get the feeling that she, like Ophelia, is in danger of death by water. She ghosts Priscilla, so that both become witnesses to the sterile negative imposed on women's history by the Oedipal male. For Bradley's corpselike sister, apparently the victim of self-loathing after being rejected by her husband Roger in favour of his young mistress, Marigold, is really bearing the burden of Bradley's separation anxiety, that moment, constantly replayed in his mind, when he first discovered that *fort* need never necessarily be followed by *da*.

The point emerges with appalling clarity when Bradley goes down to Bristol to confront Roger, misses his train home and rings his flat to speak to Priscilla but gets no reply:

> Ships are compartmental and hollow, ships are like women. The steel vibrated and sang, sang of the predatory women, Christian, Marigold, my mother: the destroyers. I saw the masts and sails of great clippers against a dark sky. Later I sat in Temple Meads station and howled inside myself, suffering the torments of the wicked under those pitiless vaults. Why had no one answered the telephone? (pp. 109–10)

The phone wires, like the string on the balloon he chases after a few pages later (pp. 123–4), are his umbilical link with the maternal feminine, the fact of whose perpetual absence his mind recreates obsessively by flinging up corpse after corpse as if it were a superhuman gravedigger. And so: 'Priscilla, do try to relax, you're as rigid as a corpse' (p. 133); and (when Bradley and Rachel are holding hands on the verandah, sitting awkwardly in deck chairs): 'So two corpses might ineptly greet each other on resurrection day' (p. 118); and '[Rachel] led me by the hand, and in a moment we were in the bedroom where I had seen Rachel lying like a dead woman with the sheet over her face' (p. 155).

Indeed, Bradley's unconscious mind flickers from Priscilla to Rachel and back again so rapidly that it is not all that clear which of them he is seeing in bed at any given time. It is, therefore, no surprise that after Priscilla's funeral Rachel should appear at the door of Bradley's flat, as Priscilla had first appeared there, bearing a message from the deepest recess of his memory:

> Seeing Rachel there in the flat was like a bad trip in a time machine. There was a memory-odour like a smell of decay. I felt distressed, physically repelled, frightened. Her wide round pale

face was terribly familiar, but with the ambiguous veiled familiarity of a dream. It was as if my mother had visited me in her cerements. (p. 354)

In his first discussion of *Hamlet* with Julian, Bradley had asserted that 'the ghost was a real ghost' (p.160), but it is not until this appearance of Rachel that we know how he can be so certain. He is, simply, possessed by the ghost of his mother, a terrifying fictional counterpart to the Edmund Gosse of *Father and Son*. His life is one long attempt to repair the damage of severance and umbilical dismemberment by acts of remembrance which betray him by refusing to remember anything except corpses.

Death and, more importantly, the fear of death inform Bradley's view of women. Unlike the Neoplatonist, for whom death is the welcome and necessary prelude to union with the divine, and unlike Freud's ideal old man who embraces the goddess of death as the final mother of his life,[27] Bradley repudiates death while living it constantly. It is out of his repudiation and fear that his tutorial on *Hamlet* springs, with its attempt to transcend the stuff of Oedipal conflict ('Did Shakespeare hate his father? Of course. Was he in love with his mother? Of course.' (p. 199)) that is baffled by the pressing presence of 'the half obliterated ghosts of flowers from distant parks'. And it is his horror of maternal absence and death that defines his feelings for Julian, turning his hexaemeron of love — that 'new world' which he creates at the beginning of Part 2 — into yet another fantasy of destruction. Despite his present from the shoe shop, Bradley can only leave Julian as, in the sagely choric words of Francis, he left Priscilla, 'fruitless and bootless. Fruitless and bootless' (p. 133).

4.3 ARRIVAL AT THE PAST

Hamlet: What man dost thou dig it for?
Gravedigger: For no man, sir.
Hamlet: For what woman, then?
Gravedigger: For none neither.
Hamlet: Who is to be buried in't?
Gravedigger: One that was a woman, sir; but rest her soul, she's dead.

(*Hamlet*, v.i)

If Bradley's vision of his 'mother... in her cerements' sounds rather gothic, even reminiscent of Frankenstein's dream of his mother in her shroud, then that is predictable too; for *The Black Prince* is, like *Frankenstein*, a text written by a woman to disclose, through the image of a male creator, the mystery of woman as artist.[28]

In Victor Frankenstein's dream his kiss kills, turning Elizabeth into 'the corpse of my dead mother' at the moment his grotesque giant of a baby leaps into life. Bradley, similarly, has the doubtful gift of being able to link birth and the charnel, most obviously when, on the third day of his new world of love, he becomes tormented by the memory of kissing Julian: 'I felt her flesh upon my lips. Phantoms were bred from this touch. I felt like a grotesque condemned excluded monster' (p. 246). This makes him the creature rather than the creator, a reversal that has to be understood as a consequence of his earlier speculation about the moment when he actually fell in love with Julian: 'I had known this child since her birth. I had seen her in her cradle. I had held her in my arms when she was twenty inches long' (p. 205).

Through this moment of memory which signals the birth of love Bradley literally re-creates Julian. But what Murdoch is concerned with charting is not so much the degree of his unselfing here, his loss of his obsessional centre, as the continuing reflexiveness of his experiences, his refusal, even when irradiated by love, to take his eyes off Julian's copy of *Hamlet*, his inability to escape from the self-created demon of Priscilla: 'Priscilla got up and walked stiffly towards the bed. She got into it. It was like a corpse climbing into its coffin. She pulled up the bedclothes' (p. 224). Priscilla is the Rachel of the beginning and his dead mother. The *volte face* which registers Bradley's change from creator, as he recalls baby Julian, to excluded creature, as he feels her flesh upon his lips, is, then, explained by the intervening image of Priscilla. This woman who constantly proclaims that she is going mad and that she will kill herself is Bradley's archetypal Ophelia and his absent mother. When he turns the eye of love on Julian he, like Frankenstein, can do nothing but replicate images of death which present and re-present his exclusion from the maternal presence. In Bradley's memory his kiss has transformed the flesh of his Julian baby into that of his dead mother which means that he, in turn, becomes the baby, repudiated and rejected. The quotation continues: 'How could it be that I had actually kissed her cheek without enveloping her, without becoming her? How could I at that moment have refrained from kneeling at her feet and howling?'

Bradley's death-dealing myopia dominates his view of Julian for the rest of the novel:[29] When she is kept by her parents from seeing him he imagines her 'locked . . . in her room. I pictured her lying there and crying, a tumbled figure of despair with her shoes off and her hair all tangled. (The vision filled me with pain, but it was rather beautiful too.)' (pp. 289–90): a clear enough example, if we still needed one, of the way his aesthetic perceptions are dictated by his Oedipal needs as the imprisoned Julian becomes 'beautiful' in direct proportion to her approximation to her battered shoeless mother of the beginning and the desperate and equally shoeless Priscilla.[30] When he actually sees her at St Cuthbert's, Philbeach Gardens, he reiterates the identification, recognizing what she will look like at fifty and comparing her with the Rachel of the beginning (p. 294) in a setting which symbolically juxtaposes the Ophelia vision against the strengths of the archetypal feminine:

Pale green angelica-coloured light entering through Victorian stained glass failed to dissipate the magnificent and soothing gloom of the place. Framing an elaborate reredos apparently made of milk chocolate, a huge melancholy rood screen which looked as if it had been rescued from a fire at the last moment announced that *Verbum caro factum est et habitavit in nobis*. Behind a sturdy iron railing at the west end a murky dove-pinnacled shrine protected the font, or perhaps the cave of some doom-obsessed sibyl or one of the more terrible forms of Aphrodite. Powers older than Christ seemed to have entered and made the place their own. High above us a black-clad figure paced along a gallery and disappeared. (p. 294)

If Rachel's appearance at the flat after Priscilla's funeral is a trip in a time machine for Bradley, presenting him with a Miss Havisham-like image of his dead mother, then in this scene at St Cuthbert's it is Murdoch as narrator who discloses further and more dizzyingly archaic vistas into the realm not just of the mother but of the Mother. For it reveals the primal powers of the Goddess herself, the ancient one whose representative Julian is simply by virtue of being a woman: the powers, in other words, that Apollo perceived in the richly reedy register of Marsyas's pipe and that Bradley is perpetually having to suppress, for they speak of female freedom and creativity, the death of male hegemony.

In this superb *tour de force* Murdoch presents the Goddess both as she was and as she is, filtered through the distorting lens of male perception and appropriation, at once Ophelia and Aphrodite. The font, now the preserve of the male Christian Trinity, expands to suggest that it contains the water from which Aphrodite was born, and its dove of the Holy Spirit reverts momentarily to its ancient meanings as Aphrodite's bird and, simultaneously, because of the naming of 'some doom-obsessed sibyl', sybilline dove of Dodona.[31] The 'black-clad figure', similarly, is at once a priest, dedicated by his vocation to suppressing and denying the powers of the Goddess and exalting in their place the creative powers of a male deity ('The Word was made flesh': John 1:14), and primordial Eros, born, according to the ancients, in close conjunction with Mother Earth.[32]

Meanwhile the whole scene is suffused with aqueous light from the stained glass which catches and defines Julian as she sits beside Bradley 'with her weary lucid face and her blue dress with white willow leaves on it' (p. 295). She has escaped from her parental prison into this more insidious one, created by Bradley in collusion with the powers of Western Christendom with their preference for women in the form of dead martyrs.

It is, then, with a Saint Ophelia wrested from the shrine of the archaic goddess of love that Bradley proceeds to Patara, home of the woman-denying god. Before he does so, however, he returns to his flat and is subject to one more visionary moment in which the powers of the feminine are evoked, too late to be seized by Bradley, perhaps, but nonetheless insistently and urgently there, registering their refusal to be suppressed and silenced. Entering the flat he hears 'a curious noise such as some bird might make, a sort of descending "woo-oo" ' (p. 298). It is Priscilla, voluntarily discharged from her electric shock treatment (that last resort of medical males confronted with mad Ophelias), uttering her womb cry that encodes her sense of loss at having had no babies (compare p. 149) and her sense of unity nevertheless with the creative feminine. The cry also makes her a dove of Aphrodite and a Dodonian dove, archaic and strong, a female voice that overrides the voice of the male god, a memory trace from way beyond the strait-jacket of Bradley's reductive unconscious mind. When Bradley peeps in to view the source of the sound she is, of course, just Priscilla again, reeking of formaldehyde and thus a preserved corpse of an Ophelia who announces, at the threshold to Part 3, that the journey Bradley is finally to make is a retreat into a historical past that images his psychological regression. It stops short at Patara, home of Apollo the woman-destroyer, because Bradley's Apollo fixation renders him incapable of breaking through to the shrine of the Goddess in whichever of her 'terrible' manifestations.

Patara signifies the possession and humiliation of woman in the name of the god. It is an ancient temple exposed, as through the opening up of a vast fissure in the earth's crust, to Bradley's view, and as he travels towards it with Julian he begins to talk in terms of geological time, posing momentarily in his backward flight as a mid-nineteenth-century evolutionist:

> 'There isn't any future. We shall go on and on driving this car forever. That's all there is.'
> 'You mustn't speak like that, it's false. Look, I've brought brown bread and toothpaste and a dustpan.'
> 'Yes. That's a miracle. But it's like fossils which religious men used to think God put there when He created the world in 4000 BC so that we could develop an illusion of the past.'
> 'I don't understand.'
> 'We have an illusion of the future.'
> 'That's wicked talk and a betrayal of love'. (p. 307)

Julian holds up her pathetically ordinary and tangible domestic purchases as an act of faith in her and Bradley's love for each other, as an assertion of her belief in the powers of Aphrodite. Bradley counters by identifying her as a Philip Gosse vainly adhering to a divine law that is denied by the evidence. But Bradley's progressive evolutionary stance is itself regressive. In refusing Julian's offer of absolute love (p. 309) he doubts the redemptive power of Aphrodite, forcing Julian back into the Ophelia mould just as, in St Cuthbert's, he had viewed her as Ophelia in denial of the ancient feminine powers that were resonating there in response to her. Now, to prove her love, she jumps out of the moving car in a gesture of symbolic suicide. And what Bradley discovers when he runs back to her is an image that would have delighted Rossetti, Millais, and all those other connoisseurs of Hamlet's bedraggled beloved:

> The creamy moon had become smaller and paler and more metallic. Darkness began to thicken about us in the dense air as we held each other in silence.

'Bradley, I'm getting cold, I've lost my sandals.'
I let go and swivelled my body round and began kissing her cold wet feet as they lay dinting a cushion of damp spongy moss. Her feet tasted of dew and earth and the little green frond-flowers of the moss, which smelt of celery. I clasped her pale wet feet in my arm and groaned with bliss and longing. (p. 310)

By refusing Julian's offer of love Bradley ensures the perpetuation of the Ophelia icon, and the archetypal planet of the feminine registers her protest by becoming 'smaller and paler and more metallic'. When they reach Patara Bradley's necrophilia reaches even more astonishingly Iachimo-like proportions:[33]

I went into the bedroom. Julian, in a mauve and white flowered petticoat with a white fringe was lying on the bed deeply asleep.... She lay on her back with her throat exposed as if to the knife. Her shoulders, pale in colour, were as creamy as the moon at dusk.... (p. 311)

Maybe this overgoes even Iachimo: maybe this is Hamlet lusting after Ophelia when she has just been dragged dead from the river.

* * * * *

Just for a moment, though, and by an accident (to use one of Murdoch's favourite words) the gods are kind. Bradley and Julian sleep side by side in total unawareness of each other and waken to a piscatory idyll of Elizabethan intensity which offers Bradley yet another chance of redemption from the Oedipal bind. It is a visionary transmutation of *Hamlet's* graveyard scene in which earth's buried bones and decomposed corpses become, as in a Shakespearean romance or the third book of Spenser's *Faerie Queene*,[34] the sea's washed treasures: a sheep's skull, stones and shells, and a piece of driftwood. All are beautiful, speaking of a world that is totally opposite to the underworld of ghosts and demons in which Bradley habitually walks. Here, outside Patara itself, Ophelia can be erased after all. The sheep's skull parodies the skulls of *Hamlet's* Act v and ponders Hamlet's 'is not parchment made of sheepskins' (v.i.112) by presenting the substantial reality that underlies parchment's impermanence, a reality born of transformation through the power of the sea that echoes the magic performed in *The Tempest*'s 'Full fathom five'.[35] The stones and shells, less obviously worked on by the sea, are simply its gifts, beautiful in themselves. But the driftwood has been fashioned even more so than the skull into a supreme art work for its cracks and wrinkles have all been:

> Smoothed and joined by the sea water until it looked like a sort of delicate sketch of an old face, a sketch such as some Italian artist, Leonardo perhaps, might make in a rather abstract way in his notebook. I took the sheep's skull . . . . It had been smoothed and caressed and polished until it seemed more like a work of art, some exquisite fabrication in ivory, rather than one of nature's remnants. (p. 313)

These art works are pure, born from the sea like dreams from the unconscious mind, fully formed and healing.[36] The external signals which have pointed to a journey into the past — the geological debate; Patara's name; the fact that it is written in 'bold Italian lettering' — are now confirmed as having heralded for Bradley a potentially benevolent night journey. He has gone to sleep with drowned Ophelia; he has awakened after that 'precious, precious night' to the sea's solution to that image: the fact of metamorphosis. The sea's message is that the art work is the product of process, a process that is in part analogous to that of dream work. Julian places the wood in the centre of the chimney-piece where we might expect to find a clock. It is an emblem of Bradley's escape from the time capsule which he shares with the corpses of his parents, the Priscilla corpse, wet and shoeless Rachel, and Ophelian Julian. In the wood's 'delicate sketch of an old face' lies the answer to Bradley's earlier obsessive comments on Priscilla's and Rachel's aged faces. Bradley knows, as he picnics by the sea with Julian, that he has entered a magically redemptive space:

> It was just perfect communion and rest and the kind of joy which comes when the beloved and one's own soul become so mingled with the external world that there is a *place* made for once upon the planet where stones and tufts of grass and transparent water and the quiet sound of the wind can really *be*. It was perhaps the other side of the diptych from last night's moment of seeing Julian in the twilight lying motionless beside the road. But it was not really connected, as moments of pure joy are not really

connected with anything. And human life which has such moments has surely put a trembling finger upon nature's most transcendent aim. (p. 314)

It *is*, of course, connected, as dead Catherine beyond the window is connected to living Heathcliff, and as Alice's daily life is connected to looking-glass land. If Bradley could retain the joy and make the connection he would be well on his way towards the Good. But he cannot, and the image of his failure is a church which he and Julian visit in the evening of that same day:

> After tea we drove over to the big church and walked about inside its bony emptiness . . . . There was no stained glass, only huge perpendicular windows through which the cool sun shone on to the pale rather powdery stone of the floor, casting a little shadow into worn *requiescats* many centuries old. The church in the flat land was like a great ruined ship or ark, or perhaps like the skeleton of some enormous animal, under whose gaunt ribs one moved with care and pity. We trod in silence with soft feet, padding and prowling, separated from one another and yet connected, pausing and gazing at each other across slanting shafts of powdery air, leaning back against the pillars or against the thick wall where the cold damp stone was like the touch of death or truth. (pp. 315–16)

The connection which Bradley describes here is false, the contaminated product of his anxiety-ridden self, for it is perceived through the powdery dust that speaks of death and separation. Where St Cuthbert's had revealed a possibility of redemption rooted in the ancient cults of matriarchy, this church exposes Bradley's deathly regressiveness in all its bleakness. It is a ship and therefore, to him at least, like the ship at Bristol (p. 109), image of the womb and of the mother as traitor who has to be destroyed for her treachery. And so Bradley relishes the powdery stone with its reminders of death and then imagines the church into a re-membered dinosaur skeleton, ultimate reminder, despite the human ingenuity expended on its articulation, of death and extinction, and exact opposite of the sheep's skull and the transfigured piece of wood.

Bradley's wish to kill, to punish every woman because of his mother's betrayal of him with his father and her abandonment of him through dying, now reaches Priscilla, who kills herself, thus finally completing her enactment of Ophelia's history and fulfilling Bradley's fantasy of humiliation and domination: 'I wanted to take Priscilla in my arms and make her live again . . . I was stricken with guilt and horror at my unforgivable failure to keep my dear sister alive' (pp. 324–5). He decides, of course, not to tell Julian about the suicide until he has made love 'properly' to her which means, simply, that he now performs the necrophiliac act he has promised earlier. With Priscilla, image of his mother (p. 82), dead on his own terms, Bradley revives her in Julian, rapes her, then turns her afterwards into Pataran temple prostitute.

The sea, earlier on the vehicle of the unconscious mind with its storehouse of treasures, now turns hostile, releasing malevolent demons, one of which will take the form of Arnold Baffin, who will come that night and batter away at the front door like the sheriff at the 'Boar's Head', Eastcheap, when he comes to call another old man from his fantasies to a cold world based in the realities of decay and mutability (*I Henry IV*, II.iv). Arnold ends the saturnalia by telling Julian the Oedipal truth of Bradley's love for her. It is, of course, as Murdoch's dazzling narrative complexities insist, only one aspect of the truth, but it convinces Bradley, who falls asleep with Julian still at Patara, dreams of Priscilla, and wakens to a 'ghastly' room and house from which Julian is obviously absent. She has fled 'in her blue willow pattern dress', an Ophelia created by Bradley to help him re-enact once more that perpetual drama of maternal deprivation by which he lives.

Bradley goes to Priscilla's cremation and then to his flat, where he is tortured by Julian's absence. It is then that Rachel comes, bringing the 'memory-odour like a smell of decay': 'it was as if my mother had visited me in her cerements' (p. 354). Bradley insists on seeing his mother but the 'real' Rachel is intent on bringing him 'back to reality' (p. 357), though she does it in terms guaranteed to aggravate his obsession:

> 'You are the sort of person who goes around in a dream smashing things, No wonder you can't write. You aren't really here at all. Julian looked at you and made you real for a moment. I made you real for a moment because I was sorry for you. Now that's all over and all that's left of you is a sort of crazy spiteful vampire, a vindictive ghost.' (p. 363)

For what happens next (after Bradley has, with Francis's help, ripped up Arnold's complete works and flung 'the white cascading sheaves of print' so that they rise around him like Ophelia's river (p. 364)) is that Bradley tells Francis how much he loved his mother and recalls the names of other women he claims to have loved: 'Annie. Catherine. Louise. It's odd how names remain, like skeletons with the flesh fallen away. They designate something that happened. They give an illusion of memory. But the people are gone as if they were dead. Perhaps they are dead. Dead as Priscilla . . .' (p. 367). Rachel has, in effect, uttered a curse that turns Bradley's mind sufficiently to make him actually suffer, for a moment at least, the fate of Ophelia; for he speaks at the end of this section in the words of Ophelia herself maddened by a parent's death: ' "But oh if she would come back in the morning! What was it you said? A concentration camp. I'll meditate on that. Good night. Thank you, thank you. Good night" ' (p. 368). The 'she' whose return he hopes for is Julian. But by now Julian is merely a sign for Bradley's mother, 'dead and gone' and laid 'i'th'cold ground' (*Hamlet*, iv.v.29–30, 70).

Rachel's psychological revenge for having been an Ophelia for so long rapidly becomes physical revenge when she summons Bradley by phone: 'I hardly recognized her. Or rather, I recognized her as a portentous *revenant*, the weeping distraught figure of the beginning of the story' (p. 375). She has killed Arnold, Bradley is accused of the murder, and Rachel does nothing to exculpate him. Ophelia — the Ophelia engendered by Bradley at the opening of his narrative — has returned like Weldon's Madeleine[37] and had her revenge, relegating her only begetter to a prison cell in which, as in his flat, he looks out onto an 'old brick wall' (p. 391; p. 22) and muses on his mad water maiden:

> What we [Bradley and Loxias] have seen together is a beauty and a glory beyond words, the world transfigured, found. It was this, which in the bliss of quietness I now enjoy, which I glimpsed prefigured in madness in the watercolour-blue eyes of Julian Baffin. She images it for me still in my dreams.
>
> (p. 391)

* * * * *

The point of ending with a trial is, as in Fryniwyd Tennyson Jesse's *A Pin to See the Peepshow* (1934) or Beryl Bainbridge's *Watson's Apology* (1981), to remind us how impossible the uttering of truth is and therefore how fragile the verdict born of that impossibility. And beyond the trial in *The Black Prince* lie further reminders of the hermeneutic nightmare spawned by the fall of the tower of Babel in the form of the postscripts. What this structural detail conveys unequivocally, though, is that the females have survived; or, at least, those outside Bradley's family circle have. The voice that was silenced when Apollo claimed victory over Marsyas is now liberated in the survivors Christian, Rachel, and the poet Julian. They speak partially, egotistically, embarrassingly, but they are alive and, in Julian's case at least, acutely perceptive; for it is she who finds her way through the hiccupping syntax of her postscript to a statement, in defiance of Apollo Loxias, about the feminine nature of language: 'the highest art is poetry because words are spirit at its most refined: its ultimate matrix' (p. 410).

Matrix shimmers here, registering *pregnancy* and *womb* among its meanings.[38] Julians 'words are spirit . . .: its ultimate matrix' answers Bradley's '*Hamlet* is words and so is Hamlet' (p. 199) by proposing the possibility of a completely feminine discourse, the liberation of language from the neo-Freudians' phallogocentric Babel and its relocation in *ruah*, feminine spirit.[39]

This is the root meaning of *The Black Prince*, a text in which Murdoch writes as a man and yet from which 'something about the female predicament' emerges. Actually it is rather more than 'something'. It is a text which releases its fictional narrator into his own novel of ghostly pursuit (a fiction 'wherein a hero not unlike myself pursued, amid ghostly incidents, a series of reflections about life and art' (p. 62)) and makes him the scapegoat for several thousand years of Oedipal patriarchy. The assertiveness of Loxias's voice at the end is an irrelevant mythological fossil except insofar as it confirms Rachel's identification of Apollo as 'a notorious rapist and murderer, a well-known musical virtuoso, whose murder, by a peculiarly horrible method, of a successful fellow-musician made the headlines some considerable time ago' (p. 407) and narrates the survival of 'the little bronze of the buffalo lady' (p. 415). The males in this novel speak for the death-instinct; the female voice, fractured and shell-shocked though it is at the end, speaks for life, prophesying that spirit as matrix will dispel the ghostly presence of the fathers and their anxiety-ridden sons. This most brilliantly and elaborately sustained *Hamlet* fiction, in other words, turns its source text on its head, dismissing its accrued male mythology of kings, usurpers, sibling rivals, tormented fathers and avenging sons and offering in its place a countertext of feminine revenge that, playing with the Freudian oppositions *thanatos* and *eros*, implicitly subverts any text produced under the anxiety of influence, and especially those devoted to perpetrating *Hamlet's* patriarchal fictions.

Notes

Introduction

1. Sigmund Freud, *The 'Uncanny'* (*SE*, xvii).
2. On repression, see Freud, *Remembering, Repeating and Working-Through* (*SE*, xii). Works by other theorists mentioned in this paragraph that are specifically relevant to this study, though often implicitly rather than explicitly present, are: Jacques Lacan, *Ecrits* (Paris: Seuil, 1966) and *Ecrits: A Selection*, tr. Alan Sheridan (London: Tavistock Publications, 1980); Jacques Derrida, *Writing and Difference*, tr. Alan Bass (London, Melbourne and Henley: Routledge and Kegan Paul, 1981) and *Of Grammatology*, tr. G. C. Spivak (Baltimore: Johns Hopkins U. P., 1976); Luce Irigaray, *Speculum of the Other Woman*, tr. G. C. Gill (Ithaca: Cornel U.P., 1985) and *This Sex Which Is Not One*, tr. Catherine Porter (Ithaca: Cornell U.P., 1985); Hélène Cixous, 'The Laugh of the Medusa', tr. Keith Cohen and Paula Cohen, *Signs*, I (1976), repr. in Elaine Marks and Isabelle de Courtivron (eds), *New French Feminisms* (Amherst: Univ. of Massachusetts Press, 1980), pp. 245–64, and her 'Fiction and Its Phantoms: A Reading of Freud's *Das Unheimliche* (The 'Uncanny')', tr. Robert Dennom, *NLH*, vii (1975–6) 525–48. In addition, see Julia Kristeva, *Desire in Language: A Semiotic Approach to Literature and Art* (New York; Columbia U.P., 1980), Robert Young's valuable anthology *Untying The Text: A Post-Structuralist Reader* (Boston, London, Henley: Routledge and Kegan Paul, 1981), Norman O. Brown, *Life Against Death: The Psychoanalytical Meaning of History* (Middletown, Conn: Wesleyan U.P., 1959) and R. C. Davis, (ed.) *The Fictional Father: Lacanian Readings of the Text* (Amherst: Univ. of Massachusetts Press, 1981).
3. For other attitudes to and appropriations of *Hamlet*, see Martin Scofield, *The Ghosts of Hamlet: The Play and Modern Writers* (Cambridge: Cambridge U.P., 1980), W. H. Quillian, *Hamlet and the New Poetic: James Joyce and T. S. Eliot* (Ann Arbor: UMI Research Press, 1983), and David Gervais, 'Delacroix' "Hamlet"', *Cambridge Quarterly*, xiii (1984), 40–70. The Oedipal *Hamlet* emerges from Freud's *Interpretation of Dreams*, ch. 5 where it is discussed in connection with *Oedipus Tyrannus* and Shakespeare's grief for his dead father and dead son Hamnet (*SE*, iv). Freud's idea was expanded by Ernest Jones, *Hamlet and Oedipus* (London: Gollancz, 1949). On Freud and the Oedipus complex see Peter Rudnytsky, *Freud and Oedipus* (New York: Columbia U.P., 1987), esp. pp. 82–5.
4. Karl Miller, *Doubles: Studies in Literary History* (Oxford: Oxford U.P., 1985), ch. 3.
5. The origins of the Roman festival of *parentalia* (honouring of the

dead, particularly the fathers) are attributed to Aeneas and his anniversary ritual for his dead father Anchises in Virgil, *Aeneid*, v and Ovid, *Fasti*, II.533–70.

6. First quotation from Keith Thomas, *Religion and the Decline of Magic* (Harmondsworth: Penguin, 1978), p. 719; second from C. G. Jung, *Psychology and Alchemy*, tr. R. F. C. Hull (London: Routledge and Kegan Paul, 1980), p. 333 and note.

7. I use the word 'pornographic' here to denote the male sense of the right to appropriate (colonise) the female body and its consequent parcelling-up of the body into discrete, sexually consumable and exploitable, areas: see Andrea Dworkin, *Pornography: Men Possessing Women* (London: The Women's Press, 1981).

8. Deborah Johnson, *Iris Murdoch* (Brighton: Harvester 1987). For Irigaray, see *This Sex Which Is Not One* (n. 2 above).

9. Iris Murdoch, *The Fire and The Sun: Why Plato Banished the Artists* (Oxford: Clarendon Press, 1977), p. 88.

10. For her claim, see ch. 4 below.

11. Harold Bloom, *The Anxiety of Influence: A Theory of Poetry* (New York: Oxford U.P., 1973); Wendell Johnson, *Sons and Fathers: The Generation Link in Literature 1780–1980*, p. 5n. Johnson's study is underpinned by the gender assumptions imposed by 'orthodox' Christian definitions of Father and Son.

Chapter 1

1. Many critics have noticed in passing that *Hamlet* is crucial to the novel: e.g. Ronald Paulson, 'Life as Journey and as Theater: Two Eighteenth-Century Narrative Structures', *NLH*, VIII (1976–7), 45–58. Among those who have commented in greater detail the following should be mentioned: Maurice Johnson, *Fielding's Art of Fiction* (Philadelphia: Univ. of Pennsylvania Press, 1961), ch. 6; Manuel Schonhorn, 'Heroic Allusion in *Tom Jones*: Hamlet and the Temptation of Jesus', *SNNTS* (*Studies in the Novel*; Denton, Texas), VI (1974), 218–27, and B. R. Lindboe, ' "O Shakespear, Had I Thy Pen!": Fielding's Use of Shakespeare in *Tom Jones*', *SNNTS*, XIV (1982), 303–15. On Garrick's Hamlet, see G. W. Stone, Jr. and G. M. Kahrl, *David Garrick: A Critical Biography* (Carbondale and Edwardsville, Ill.: Southern Illinois U.P., 1979), pp. 540–48.

2. Quotations from *The History of Tom Jones, a Foundling*, Ed. M. C. Battestin and Fredson Bowers, 2 vols (Oxford: Clarendon Press, 1974).

3. Fielding had already poked fun at the supposed superstitiousness of Jacobites in *The Jacobite's Journal*, which ran for forty-nine issues between 5 December 1747 and 5 November 1748. See especially numbers 1–7 (5 December 1747–16 January 1748): *The Jacobite's Journal and Related Writings*, ed. W. B. Coley (Oxford: Clarendon Press, 1974).

4. Fielding's apparently sceptical attitude to ghosts is discussed by L. F.

Sells, 'Tom Jones and The Secrets of the Invisible World', N and Q, CCXXVI (1981), 231–3. On the Derby murder, see n. 24 below.

5. These comments are illuminated by Eve Tavor's reading of the novel in the light of Hume's Treatise of Human Nature: Scepticism, Society and the Eighteenth-Century Novel (London and Basingstoke: Macmillan, 1987), ch. 3, esp. pp. 138–49.

6. William Empson, 'Tom Jones', Kenyon Review, xx (1958), 217–49.

7. The Orphan; or, The Unhappy Marriage (1680), ed. A. M. Taylor, Regents Restoration Drama Series (London: Edward Arnold 1977), Act II, 11. 232–5. It is worth noting that Garrick played Chamont regularly during the 1740s: Stone and Kahrl, David Garrick, pp. 524–5.

8. On Tom Jones and Oedipus Tyrannus, the plots of which were linked in Coleridge's mind ('Upon my word, I think Oedipus Tyrannus, the Alchemist, and Tom Jones, the three most perfect plots ever planned': Table Talk, 5 July 1834; cit. F. T. Blanchard, Fielding the Novelist: A Study in Historical Criticism (New Haven and London: Yale U.P., O.U.P., 1927), pp. 320–1), see Northrop Frye, Anatomy of Criticism (Princeton, N.J.: Princeton U.P., 1957), page 181; H. K. Miller, Henry Fielding's 'Tom Jones' and the Romance Tradition, English Literary Studies Monographs, VI (1976) (British Columbia: Univ. of Victoria), pp. 37–8; William Park, 'Tom and Oedipus', Hartford Studies in Literature, VII (1975), 207–15; and Bernard Tabbs, Fielding's Oedipal Fantasy: a Psychoanalytic Study of the Double in 'Tom Jones', Ph.D., The American University 1976 (synopsis in DAI XXXVII (1976), 1524A). Plot similarities include: the foundling motif; Oedipus's flight from Corinth to prevent him killing his father and mother (compare Tom's expulsion from Paradise Hall after Allworthy's near death and the death of Tom's mother, Bridget); the killing of Oedipus's actual father, Laius, while on a journey (reversed in Tom's rescue of the Old Man of the Hill); and the affinity between the Old Man in his nocturnal darkness, speaking as the voice of history and contemplation of the divine, and blind Tiresias, knower of divine truths.

9. For the bare facts, see W. L. Cross, The History of Henry Fielding, 3 vols (New Haven: Yale U.P., 1918), I.26–40. M. C. Battestin's 'Henry Fielding, Sarah Fielding, and "the dreadful Sin of Incest"', Novel, XIII (1979–80), 6–18, is fascinating, though it ignores the Catholicism, as does Morris Golden's perceptive 'Public Context and Imagining Self in Tom Jones', PLL, xx (1984), 273–92. A conventionally moral (as opposed to psychological) view of Tom Jones's incest motif is taken by Michael Hall, 'Incest and Morality in Tom Jones', The South Central Bulletin, XLI (1981), 101–4.

10. Lewis and Short, Latin Dictionary, s.v. secerno. Insofar as the revelation of the secret unites Tom with his parents (or, at least, the idea of them), secret in Tom Jones functions as an analogue to Derrida's brisure (cleaving understood simultaneously as splitting and embracing) as explored by Maud Ellmann's 'Disremembering Dedalus: "A Portrait of the Artist as a Young Man"', in Robert Young (ed.), Untying the Text: A Post-Structuralist Reader (Boston, London and Henley: Routledge and Kegan Paul, 1981), pp. 190–206.

11. Quoted from New Arden edition. However, Fielding probably heard Horatio and Marcellus say something rather different in response to Hamlet's question. In the 1676 quarto of *Hamlet* and texts derived from it (e.g. the 1718 *Hamlet* published by Wellington), they reply 'As death, my Lord'; which reinforces wonderfully the dark ambiguities I detect in *Tom Jones*.
12. For further insights, see Eve Tavor, *op. cit.*, (n. 5), ch. 3, *passim*.
13. For the Calvinism, see Battestin's note, *ed. cit.* (n. 2), I.79. Allworthy will turn Tom into 'an abandoned Reprobate' upon his expulsion in VI.11 as a result of young Blifil's misrepresentations, thereby identifying himself with Captain Blifil as paternal prohibitor, the Freudian-Lacanian father-as-Law who divides the boy from Oedipal union with the mother. As a Justice of the Peace (embodiment of Law) Allworthy busily banishes Tom's supposed mother in I.8.
14. *Odyssey*, IX. 366–7 ('No man is my name').
15. H. K. Miller however, sees the 'old' Tom of the end as a laudable example of the *puer senex*: 'The "Digressive" Tales in Fielding's *Tom Jones* and the Perspective of Romance', *PQ*, LIV (1975), 258–74, p. 264.
16. Sophocles, *Oedipus Tyrannus*, ll. 122–3: 'His story was that robbers — not one but many — /Fell in with the King's party and put them to death': tr. E. F. Watling in *Sophocles: The Theban Plays* (Harmondsworth: Penguin, 1974), p. 29.
17. Edward Dudley and M. E. Novak (eds), *The Wild Man Within: An Image in Western Thought from the Renaissance to Romanticism* (Pittsburgh: Univ. of Pittsburgh Press, 1972), pp. 183–221. H. K. Miller, *art. cit.* (n. 15 above), pp. 261–3, adds the romance hermit and Spenserian Despair.
18. Douglas Brooks, *Number and Pattern in the Eighteenth-Century Novel: Defoe, Fielding, Smollett and Sterne* (London and Boston: Routledge and Kegan Paul, 1973), pp. 103–4.
19. For valuable comments on the Man's psychological 'self-enclosure', see Morris Golden, *Fielding's Moral Psychology* (Amherst: Univ. of Massachusetts Press, 1966). See especially his citation on p. 19 of Fielding's *The True Patriot*, n. 23: 'I have heard of a man who believed there was no real existence in the world but himself; and that whatever he saw without him was mere phantom and illusion.'
20. *OED*, *Frank*, a^2: medieval latin *Francus* = *free* in the sense of *liberated from obligation, not bound*. There is a complex interplay in the novel between this notion and the *habeas corpus* act's guarantee of personal liberty against the Crown: see D. Oswald Dykes, *Source Book of Constitutional History from 1660* (London: Longmans, Green and Co., 1930), pp. 55–8.
21. *OED*, *Recognizance*, 1: recorded before a magistrate (image of the father-as-Law!). Battestin's edition, I. 458–9, quotes a slightly more pointed definition from Wood's *Institutes* (1745 edn): 'A *Recognizance* is a Bond of Record acknowledged to the King, upon condition to pay a certain Sum of Money if the Condition is not performed'. Bonds to kings — living, dead, exiled — appear almost everywhere in *Tom Jones*.
22. According to Milton, who inherited a long exegetical tradition,

	Nimrod was a tyrannical hunter of his fellow men: *Paradise Lost*, XII.24–62. Cf. the huntsman in *Joseph Andrews*, III.6.
23.	Edward Hyde, first Earl of Clarendon, *The History of the Rebellion and Civil Wars in England*, 7 vols (Oxford, 1849) I.57–61 (Book I, Para. 89–93), where the ghost of the father, Sir George Villiers, appears three times to 'an officer in the king's wardrobe in Windsor Castle' in an attempt to get him to warn his son (George Villiers, first Duke of Buckingham) that 'if he did not do somewhat to ingratiate himself to the people . . . he would be suffered to live [only] a short time' (p. 58).
24.	Battestin's edn, I.402–3n and 458n.
25.	Battestin's edn, I.402–3n.
26.	Useful background to my comments here is to be found in Coley's edn of *The Jacobite's Journal* (n. 3 above), and Brian McCrea, *Henry Fielding and the Politics of Mid-Eighteenth-Century England* (Athens, Ga: Univ. of Georgia Press, 1981).
27.	*The Jacobite's Journal*, no. 16, 19 March 1748 (ed. Coley, p. 204) Cf. no. 3, 19 December 1747.
28.	John Milton, *A Defence of the People of England* (*Pro Populo Anglicano Defensio*, 1651), In D. M. Wolfe (gen. ed.), *Complete Prose Works of John Milton*, 8 vols (New Haven and London: Yale U.P., 1953–82), IV.i (1966), 327.
29.	Manuel Schonhorn, 'Fielding's Ecphrastic Moment: Tom Jones and his Egyptian Majesty', *SP* LXXVIII (1981), 305–23.
30.	See Douglas Brooks-Davies, *Pope's 'Dunciad' and the Queen of Night; A Study in Emotional Jacobitism* (Manchester and Dover, N.H.: Manchester U.P., 1985), pp. 127–35, and M. C. Battestin, 'Tom Jones and "his Egyptian Majesty": Fielding's Parable of Government', *PMLA*, LXXXII (1967), 68–77.
31.	Virgil, *The Aeneid*, tr. W. F. Jackson Knight (Harmondsworth: Penguin, 1974), pp. 41–2.
32.	*Ibid.*, p. 67.
33.	*The Jacobite's Journal* no. 6, 9 January 1748 (ed. Coley, p. 125).
34.	Steven Zwicker, *Politics and Language in Dryden's Poetry: The Arts of Disguise* (Princeton, N.J.: Princeton U.P., 1984), ch. 6, and Douglas Brooks-Davies, *Pope's 'Dunciad'* (n. 30, above), pp. 46–66 and notes.
35.	E.g. Henry Peacham, *Minerva Britanna* (1612), plate 30; C. G. Jung, *Psychology and Alchemy*, tr. R. F. C. Hull, second edn (London: Routledge and Kegan Paul, 1980), pp. 327–39.
36.	E.g. 'The Rebellion Displayed. Most humbly Inscribed to his Sacred Majesty King George' (1745), with crowns and coffin in the foreground: H.M. Atherton, *Political Prints in the Age of Hogarth: A Study of the Ideographic Representation of Politics* (Oxford: Clarendon Press, 1974), plate 58.
37.	For documentation, see Brooks-Davies, *Pope's 'Dunciad'*, pp. 122–3, 134, 139n, 155–7, and 165n; Fielding, *Jacobite's Journal*, no. 13, 27 February 1748.
38.	H. W. Randall, 'The Rise and Fall of a Martyrology: Sermons on Charles I', *HLQ*, X (1947), 135–67. The 'Form of Prayer with Fasting, to be used yearly on the 30th of *January*, being the day of the Martyrdom

of the Blessed King *Charles* the First: to implore the mercy of God, that neither the Guilt of that sacred and innocent Blood, nor those other sins, by which God was provoked to deliver up both us and our King into the hands of cruel and unreasonable men, may at any time hereafter be visited upon us or our Posterity' was removed from the *Book of Common Prayer* in 1859. There was a reasonable market for the anniversary sermons (*Joseph Andrews*, I.17), and the office itself was analogous (and printed adjacent) to that for the Gunpowder Treason, mentioned by Partridge in *Tom Jones*, XVI.5, the *Hamlet* chapter.

39. He quotes it at VIII.6, VIII.9, and XIV.3, in each case in a Jacobite context.
40. As Battestin notices in his notes to XII.3; and Lindboe, *art.cit.* (n. 1 above), pp. 310–11, who, however, sees *I Henry IV* merely as providing 'a model for Partridge's cowardice'.
41. New Arden *I Henry IV*, ed. A. R. Humphreys (London: Methuen, 1978), v.i.126–38.
42. For the persistence of the *artes moriendi* into the eighteenth century, see Philippe Ariès, *The Hour of Our Death*, tr. Helen Weaver (Harmondsworth: Penguin, 1983), p.196 and *passim*. Fielding emphasises their importance in connection with Allworthy in v.7.
43. Sandra Gilbert and Susan Gubar, *The Madwoman in the Attic: The Woman Writer and the Nineteenth-Century Literary Imagination* (New Haven and London: Yale U.P., 1979), ch. 1.
44. Schonhorn, *art.cit.* (n. 29 above), esp. pp. 316, 318–21. The question of authority is, of course, the link between Schonhorn's and Battestin's (n. 30 above) apparently diverse readings of the Gypsy episode.
45. Fielding alludes to the idea of a sacrificial *sparagmos*, as in the Osiris and Orpheus myths. The archetypal poet Orpheus appears in *Tom Jones*, XIII.1, through allusion to his mother, Calliope, and the river Hebrus into which his dismembered body was thrown (Ovid, *Metamorphoses*, XI.1–66). For insights into the myth, see W. A. Strauss, *Descent and Return: The Orphic Theme in Modern Literature* (Cambridge, Mass: Harvard U.P., 1971), ch.1.
46. Ariès, *The Hour of Our Death* (n. 42 above), Part I, esp pp. 49, 54; also R. M. Frye, *The Renaissance Hamlet: Issues and Responses in 1600* (Princeton, N.J.: Princeton U.P., 1984) pp. 206–53.
47. Frank Kermode, *The Genesis of Secrecy* (Cambridge, Mass. and London: Harvard U.P., 1979) pp. 6–8.
48. For Mrs Allworthy, beloved and buried 'about five Years before the Time in which this History chooses to set out', see I.2. Fielding's wife, Charlotte, had died in November 1744 and is invoked movingly in XIII.1. Fielding's grief survived his marriage to Mary Daniel (1747). *Tom Jones* was probably one-third written by late summer 1745 and completed around the end of 1748: Battestin (ed.), *Tom Jones*, General Introduction, I.xxxvii–xlii.
49. Cf. XIII.7, the masquerade: '*I don't know you, Sir . . . . Indeed, I don't know your Voice*'. For insights into the way novelists (and critics) in general tend to decode buried cultural and other secrets and thus help their readers to see, or view, the corpse on display in the

morgue of literary history', see A. D. Hutter, 'The Novelist as Resurrectionist: Dickens and the Dilemma of Death', *Dickens Studies Annual*, XII (1983) pp. 10–11 and 35, n. 29. Fielding teases us (and himself) to the ultimate point of tolerance in this respect, suggesting both possibility and impossibility, thus anticipating Derrida's sense of the coffin/crypt as an image of language itself, which holds meaning yet fails, in the end, to hold it sufficiently: Jacques Derrida, 'Fors', *The Georgia Review*, XXXI (1977), 64–116.

50. Abbé Banier, *The Mythology and Fables of the Antients, Explain'd from History*, 4 vols (London, 1739–40), II.553 (Book III, ch. 2), describing the first (winter) festival of three spaced throughout the year. For speculations on the nature of the nocturnal mysteries, see pp. 554–5.

51. On the 'terrible mother' as dragon-devourer of her offspring, see C.G. Jung, *Symbols of Transformation*, II.5. At para. 395 she is interpreted as signifying 'resistance to incest, or the fear of it': tr. R. F. C. Hull, Bollingen Series, XX (New York: Pantheon Books, 1956), p. 259. See also *ibid.*, II.4, para. 264 on the Sphinx as devouring mother.

52. Banier, *Mythology*, II.560, 561 (Book III, ch. 3).

53. The idea of wrath is reinforced by its mention in Horace, *Odes*, I.16, 1.9, the source of the Cybele quotations in XIII.4.

54. *OED, Domino*, 1a, citing Cotgrave, 'a fashion of vaile used by some women that mourne'. On this episode in general, see Robert Folkenflik, 'Tom Jones, the Gypsies, and the Masquerade', *UTQ*, XLIV (1974–5), 224–37; and on eighteenth-century masquerades, Terry Castle's 'Eros and Liberty at the English Masquerade, 1710–90', *ECS*, XVII (1983–4), 156–76 and her *Masquerade and Civilization: The Carnivalesque in Eighteenth-Century English Culture and Fiction* (Stanford: Stanford U.P., 1986).

55. M. W. Latham, *The Elizabethan Fairies: The Fairies of Folklore and the Fairies of Shakespeare* (New York: Columbia U.P., 1930), pp. 104, 181. As Queen of Fairies, Lady Bellaston parodies her virginal feminist relative Diana Western; attempts (but fails) to undo the power of Tom's lunar musings to Sophia in VIII.9: and is equated with Dol Common in Ben Jonson's *Alchemist*, thus reminding us that Tom is, for the moment, the gullible dupe Dapper, imprisoned in stinking darkness, one of the many suffering from *deceptio visus* (Acts III, v). The darkness of this Bellaston phase of the novel suggests, too, that as a planet (*aster*) she is the moon in her Hecate phase, queen of hell and of black magic: Andrew Tooke, *The Pantheon* (London, 1713 edn), pp. 241–4.

56. Perceptively located by H. K. Miller, 'The "Digressive" Tales in Fielding's *Tom Jones*' (n. 15 above), pp. 266–8, in the world of the Restoration stage, and that of the popular 'female' novel with all its psychological and sociological implications (e.g. Ruth Perry, *Women, Letters and the Novel* (New York: AMS Press, 1980)).

57. For text used, see n. 7 above.

Chapter 2

1. John Forster, *The Life of Charles Dickens*, 3 vols (London, 1872–4), III (1874), 329.
2. See, e.g., D. F. Sadoff, 'The Dead Father: *Barnaby Rudge, David Copperfield*, and *Great Expectations*', *PLL*, XVIII (1982), 36–57, and the same author's '*Locus Suspectus*: Narrative, Castration, and the Uncanny', *DSA*, XIII (1984), 207–30, and, more generally, Edmund Wilson's 'Dickens: The Two Scrooges' in *The Wound and the Bow* (Cambridge, Mass.: Houghton Mifflin, 1941). Other readings which complement my own in their emphasis on parental absence are L. J. Dessner's '*Great Expectations*; "the Ghost of a Man's Own Father"', *PMLA*, XCI (1976), 436–49, Steven Connor's heavily Lacanian chapter on the novel in his *Charles Dickens* (Oxford: Basil Blackwell, 1985) and Eiichi Hara's 'Stories Present and Absent in *Great Expectations*', *ELH*, LIII (1986), 593–614. A useful account of trends in psychoanalytic criticism of Dickens is L. F. Manheim's 'Dickens and Psychoanalysis: A Memoir', *DSA*, XI. (1983), 335–45.
3. Sensitive comments on *Hamlet* in *Great Expectations* are to be found in A. L. French, 'Beating and Cringing: *Great Expectations*', *E in C*, XXIV (1974), 147–68, p. 148; David Gervais, 'The Prose and Poetry of *Great Expectations*', *DSA*, XIII (1984), 85–114, p. 95; and W. A. Wilson, 'The Magic Circle of Genius: Dickens' Translations of Shakespearean Drama in *Great Expectations*', *NCF*, XL (1985), 154–75, pp. 158–9 and 162–5. On Dickens and death see especially, for their relevance to the present chapter, Andrew Sanders, *Charles Dickens: Resurrectionist* (London and Basingstoke: Macmillan, 1982) and A. D. Hutter, 'The Novelist as Resurrectionist: Charles Dickens and the Dilemma of Death', *DSA*, XII (1983), 1–39.
4. Quotations from *Great Expectations*, ed. Angus Calder (Harmondsworth: Penguin 1965).
5. So that beating becomes identified with bottle- and spoon-feeding: Dessner, *art. cit.* (n. 2 above), p. 440.
6. The resonances of the word Medium here are discussed by J. O. Jordan, 'The Medium of *Great Expectations*', *DSA*, XI (1983), 73–88. Worth noting in this connection are the faked photographs of apparitions of a dead person's ghostly 'astral body' reproduced from the period in question (1855–65) in Philippe Ariès, *Images of Man and Death*, tr. Janet Lloyd (Cambridge, Mass. and London: Harvard U.P., 1985), plates 251–2, p. 173 (and text p. 175).
7. Dessner, *art. cit.* (n. 2 above), p. 443, and Connor, *op. cit.* (also n. 2 above), pp. 116–7. On the inversions see, e.g., Harry Stone, *Dickens and the Invisible World: Fairy Tales, Fantasy, and Novel-Making* (London and Basingstoke: Macmillan 1980), p. 299. Jane Vogel, *Allegory in Dickens* (University, Alabama: Univ. of Alabama Press, 1977), pp. 82–4 astutely compares Magwitch among the gravestones with Legion in Mark 5 (cf. Luke 8).
8. Illuminating sidelights on this can be found in J. E. Marlow, 'English Cannibalism: Dickens after 1859', *SEL*, XXIII (1983), 647–66, and

Melanie Klein, 'The Psychological Principles of Infant Analysis' (1926) and 'Early Stages of the Oedipus Conflict' (1928), both repr. in *The Selected Melanie Klein*, ed. Juliet Mitchell (Harmondsworth: Penguin, 1986).

9. In L. P. Harley's *The Go-Between* (1953), Prologue.
10. Psychological complement to the terrible mother: see ch. 1 n. 51 above and C. G. Jung, *Symbols of Transformation*, tr. R. F. C. Hull, Bollingen Series xx (New York: Pantheon Books, 1956), pp. 260–2.
11. 'His name meaning, literally, "co-countryman", Compeyson is everyone's secret companion, dark double, diabolical inner voice': E. L. Gilbert, ' "In Primal Sympathy": *Great Expectations* and the Secret Life', *DSA*, xii (1983), 89–113, p. 98.
12. Gilbert, *ibid.*, pp. 101–2, perceptive on the half buried elements of the Christian story in the novel, cites Humphry House's observation that 'the Church was for Dickens a national depository of good-feeling: its establishment allowed for a kind of ancestor-worship, its creeds began with the Fatherhood of God': *The Dickens World* (London: Oxford U.P., 1960), p. 111.
13. Among critics who have noticed that there is some sort of riddle in Pip's letter are Max Byrd, ' "Reading" in *Great Expectations*', *PMLA*, xci (1976), 259–65, and Murray Baumgarten, 'Calligraphy and Code: Writing in *Great Expectations*', *DSA*, xi (1983), 61–72, p. 72. On the quest for authority and authorship in texts that parallel the search for parental authority (as in *Tom Jones*), see Peter Brooks, 'Repetition, Repression, and Return: *Great Expectations* and the Study of Plot', *NLH*, xi (1979–80), 503–26, *passim*, but especially pp. 505–6 and 516–23.
14. For Joe as clown, but with emphasis on Joey Grimaldi rather than Yorick, see E. M. Eiger, 'The Absent Clown in *Great Expectations*', *DSA*, xi (1983), 115–33.
15. The best account of Orlick as Pip's double remains Julian Moynahan's 'The Hero's Guilt: The Case of *Great Expectations*', *E in C*, x (1960), 60–79. On the connection between orphans and doubles see Karl Miller, *Doubles: Studies in Literary History* (Oxford: Oxford U.P., 1985). ch. 3. The connection underlies *Tom Jones*, of course, and Gosse's *Father and Son*.
16. The source of Joe's epitaph is probably Hamlet's 'If thou didst ever hold me in thy heart,/Absent thee from felicity awhile,/And in this harsh world draw thy breath in pain/ To tell my story' (v.ii.351–4).
17. As many have notcied: e.g. J. Hillis Miller, *Charles Dickens: The World of his Novels* (Bloomington and London: Indiana U.P., 1973), p. 273.
18. Cited by D. R. Davis in 'Multiples' (a review of Karl Miller's *Doubles*), *E in C*, xxxvi (1986), 89–94: p. 94.
19. Mary Shelley, *Frankenstein*, ed. Maurice Hindle (Harmondsworth: Penguin, 1985), ch. 5. For a convincing Oedipal reading of the dream, see Mary Jacobus, 'Is there a Woman in this Text?', repr. in her *Reading Woman: Essays in Feminist Criticism* (London: Methuen 1986), pp. 100–3.
20. On Provis see Vogel, *op. cit.* (n. 7 above), p. 85.

21. E.g. Mary Daly, *Gyn/Ecology* (London: The Women's Press, 1987 edn), pp. 49, 176–7, and ch. 10 *passim*; and Rozsika Parker, *The Subversive Stitch* (London: The Women's Press, 1984). Underlying the hypnotic maternal overtones are suggestions of the three Fates, especially the life-thread spinning Fate, Clotho, and the thread-cutting and death-dealing Fate Atropos: cf. the 'three weird old women of transcendent ghastliness, . . . at needlework . . . Witch sisterhood all, stitch, stitch' in Dickens's *Uncommercial Traveller*, ch. 5 (*The Uncommercial Traveller and Reprinted Pieces*, introd. L. C. Staples (London: Oxford U.P., 1958), pp. 50–1) and, of course, the 'knitter' of *A Tale of Two Cities*, II.15,16, and III.14. Miss Havisham gives a 'weird smile' when Pip first encounters her in ch. 8 (p. 91).
22. *Wuthering Heights*, ch. 3, the waif Catherine to Lockwood in his dream.
23. A thoroughgoing Freudian reading of the male fantasy of the female as 'pristine little women and threatening phallic mothers' is offered by Dianne Sadoff, '*Locus Suspectus*' (n. 2 above), p. 214, citing Freud's *Some Psychical Consequences of the Anatomical Distinction between the Sexes* (*SE*, XIX) and *The Dissolution of the Oedipus Complex* (*ibid.*) together with J. Laplanche and J.-B. Pontalis, *The Language of Psycho-Analysis*, tr. D. Nicholson-Smith (New York: W. W. Norton, 1973) pp. 311–12.
24. Andrew Tooke, *The Pantheon, representing the Fabulous Histories of the Heathen Gods and Most Illustrious Heroes* (London, 1824), ch. 8. pp. 155–8; *ibid.*, London 1713 edn, p. 287.
25. See ch. 4, n. 13 below on the Jungian concept of the *anima*. Dirk den Hartog, *Dickens and Romantic Psychology: The Self in Time in Nineteenth-Century Literature* (London and Basingstoke: Macmillan, 1987), p. 141, anticipates me: 'one might argue that whilst Estella, in what she symbolises, is an *anima* figure for Pip . . . the neurotic terms on which his relationship to her inevitably establishes itself, . . . prevent in him any growth through incorporation of "otherness" '.
26. The light-bearer in the Eleusinian mysteries of Ceres and Proserpina is discussed by, e.g., the Abbé Banier, *The Mythology and Fables of the Antients*, 4 vols (London, 1739–40), III.66, Book IV, ch. 11. Tooke, *Pantheon* (1824), p. 160 notes of the Eleusinian rites: 'Lighted torches were used in their sacrifices, because Ceres with them sought Proserpine'. Cf. Sue Bridehead's candles as she reads Swinburne's *Hymn of Proserpine* in Hardy's *Jude the Obscure*, Part II, ch. 3; and see ch. 3, n. 21 below.
27. Georgiana derives, like George, from Graeco-Roman *georgos*, field-labourer (Greek *Gé* = Mother Earth). Joe's name was originally George: T. W. Hill, 'Notes to *Great Expectations*', *The Dickensian*, LIII (1957), 119–26, 184–6.
28. Icongraphically, Dickens's woman in the whiteness of virginity and death seems ultimately to derive from, and be a modification of, the Dormition (Sleep/Death) of the Virgin tradition, for which see Philippe Ariès *Images of Man and Death* (n. 6 above), ch. 3, esp. p. 96, and colour plate I and monochrome plate 149, p. 97. For a visual

correlate, slightly later than Dickens, which suggests the analogy and the extent of the secularization of the Dormition *motif*, see *ibid.*, colour plate IX, George Cochran Lambdin's *The Dead Wife* (North Carolina Museum of Art) and p. 254. Sandra Gilbert and Susan Gubar, *The Madwoman in the Attic* (New Haven and London: Yale U.P., 1979) offer succinct comments on the relationship between the Miss Havisham–Lady of Shalott type and Snow White (pp. 616–21). Miss Havisham's origins in a wandering woman in white whom Dickens saw in Berners Street in his childhood are discussed in Harry Stone, *Dickens and the Invisible World* (n. 7 above), ch. 8. Dickens describes her, significantly, in conjunction with 'a poor demented woman who used to roam about the City, dressed all in black' and 'the rugged walls of Newgate', in *Household Words*, 1 January 1853: in Dickens, *Miscellaneous Papers*, introd. P. J. M. Scott, 2 vols (Millwood, N.Y.: Kraus Reprint, 1983), I. 388–9. On the significance of Ophelia for Victorian myths of female madness, see Elaine Showalter, *The Female Malady: Women, Madness, and English Culture, 1830–1980* (London: Virago, 1987), ch. 3.

29. Vogel, *Allegory in Dickens*, pp. 92 and 325 n. also notices the pun.
30. An attempt at a psychogenesis of *Great Expectations* would have to take into account, among many other details, Dickens's comment in a letter of 19 August 1860 on his senile mother at his brother Alfred's funeral as being 'got up in sables like a female Hamlet' (*The Letters of Charles Dickens*, ed. Walter Dexter, 3 vols (Nonsuch Press, 1938), III.172.) Another clue, preserved in the autobiographical fragment drawn on by Forster and relating to the blacking warehouse days, is his resentment against his mother for wanting him to continue in the warehouse after his father and a cousin had quarrelled about his being there at all: 'My father said, I should go back no more, and should go to school. I do not write resentfully or angrily: for I know how all these things have worked together to make me what I am: but I never afterwards forgot, I shall never forget, I never can forget, that my mother was warm for my being sent back': John Forster, *The Life of Charles Dickens* (n. 1 above), I.49.
31. Cf. Freud, *Remembering, Repeating and Working-Through* (*SE*, XII. 145–56) on repetition and reliving material from the past, encountering it as if it were actually present, as a pyschological event caused by the blocking of recollection by resistance; and Peter Brooks, *art. cit.* (n. 13 above), p. 515. Note also Brooks's comment on the synecdochic quality of the name Pip itself as 'an infinitely repeatable palindrome' (p. 526).
32. Freud, *The Interpretation of Dreams*, *SE*, V. 536, discussed by Jacques Derrida, *Writing and Difference*, tr. Alan Bass (London, Melbourne, Henley: Routledge and Kegan Paul, 1981), pp. 216–17 and 330 n. 18.
33. Roland Barthes, *Camera Lucida*, tr. Richard Howard (London: Fontana, 1984), p. 14. Significantly, at the heart of this book lies the quest for Barthes' dead mother in the month of All Souls: 'Now, one November evening shortly after my mother's death, I was going through some photographs. I had no hope of "finding" her, I

expected nothing from these "photographs of a being before which one recalls less of that being than by merely thinking of him and her". (Proust) . . . ' (p. 63). A. D. Hutter's brilliant 'Dismemberment and Articulation in *Our Mutual Friend'*, *DSA* XI (1983), 135–75, reminds us (pp. 150–1) how fascinated the Victorians generally were by life-like inanimate objects, including *tableaux vivants* and excavated statues, and Ariés, *Images of Man and Death*, p. 247 comments on the Victorian habit of photographing dead children in a seated position (and cf. plates 358, 359).

34. In George Lillo's *George Barnwell* (1731), much printed and performed in the nineteenth century, the apprentice, Barnwell, is seduced by Sarah Millwood into robbing and murdering his uncle and master. They are both caught and hanged. The implications of the play for *Great Expectations* are considerable, not least Barnwell's soliloquy in III.iii: 'Murder my uncle! My father's only brother! who since his death has been to me a father; who took me up an infant and an orphan; reared me with tenderest care' (*George Barnwell*, in *The London Stage*, vol. III (London, 1825)).

35. Freud, *The Theme of the Three Caskets*, in connection with Lear and his daughters: 'We might argue that what is represented here are the three inevitable relations that a man has with a woman – the woman who bears him, the woman who is his mate and the woman who destroys him; or that they are the three forms taken by the figure of the mother in the course of a man's life – the mother herself, the beloved one who is chosen after her pattern, and lastly the Mother Earth who receives him once more' (*SE*, XII.301). Freud makes the link with the Fates that is also present in *Great Expectations*: see n. 21 above.

36. On the excavation of martyrs' remains as recently as March 1849, when 'workmen came upon a heap of unhewn stones, blackened as if by fire, and covered with ashes and human bones, charred and partially consumed' near St Bartholomew's church, see R. Chambers, *The Book of Days*, 2 vols (London and Edinburgh, 1869), I. 371.

37. Hamlet is, of course, imprisoned by pirates as he is by his dead father (IV.vi). His capture by them causes his 'strange return' to Denmark which echoes his father's strange return of the beginning. In the sources of *Hamlet*, the father himself is a pirate, as Avi Erlich has noticed: *Hamlet's Absent Father* (Princeton, N.J.: Princeton U.P., 1977), p. 27.

38. Compare the puns at Paul Dombey's christening: ' "Please to bring the child in quick out of the air there", whispered the beadle, holding open the inner door of the church. Little Paul might have asked with Hamlet "into my grave?" so chill and earthy was the place' (*Dombey and Son*, I.5).

39. *English Dialect Dictionary*, s.v. cag-mag, sb^2 and *adj*. On Jaggers, see ibid., s.v. *Jagger*, *sb* (travelling pedlar) and *Jag(g)*, sb^3 and v^3 (rag or shred of raiment).

40. Freud, *Beyond the Pleasure Principle*, *SE*, XVIII.15.

41. It is the presence of *Hamlet* in *Great Expectations* that insists on the

Ophelian reading of the willow. Out of context, Wemmick's brooch merely repeats contemporary and earlier incongraphical commonplaces: Ariès, *Images of Man and Death*, colour plate VII and monochrome plates 352 and 390.

42. On Barnard's Inn, Holborn, see, e.g., W. J. Loftie, *A History of London*, 2 vols (London, 1884), II.75.
43. Cf. the ambiguity of 'That brings our friends up from the underworld' in Tennyson's 'Tears, idle tears', cited by *OED* as its first instance of *underworld* to signify *antipodes*. The pun became a Victorian commonplace.
44. On Drummle and Orlick, see Moynahan, *art.cit*. (n. 15 above), pp. 73–4.
45. *English Dialect Dictionary*, s.v. Jag(g), v^2 and sb^2.
46. I share Peter Brooks's view of the monotonous repetitiveness of Pip's returns to the locations of his childhood: 'Repetition as return becomes a reproduction and reenactment of infantile experience: not simply a recall of the primal moment, but a reliving of its pain and terror, suggesting the impossibility of escape from the originating scenarios of childhood': *art.cit*. (n. 13 above), p. 514. For an alternative view, which argues that the narrating Pip's humanity, sense of humour, stylistic maturity, and imaginative exuberance announce this novel as 'the summation of Dickens's developing debate with himself about the contrary needs to at once acknowledge and transcend his childhood self', see Dirk den Hartog, *Dickens and Romantic Psychology* (n. 25 above), p. 130 and ch. 4 *passim*.
47. On the 'metalinguistic' applicability to the confessional mode of the novel of the tract given to Pip as he is about to be bound apprentice and entitled 'TO BE READ IN MY CELL' (p. 132), see Jeremy Tambling, 'Prison-Bound: Dickens and Foucault', *E in C*, XXXVI (1986), 11-31, p. 18: 'it comments on the text's sense of the way it should be read, and what Pip thinks it is about'.
48. In metamorphosing this terrible father into his feminine opposite, Pip is also symbolically laying the ghost of what the Freudians call the phallic mother: e.g., the aggressive and dominating Mrs Joe and Miss Havisham (n. 23 above). As Ophelia, the dead Magwitch is, in the above quotation from ch. 54, *composed* (not decomposed), extraordinarily at one with himself as he straddles, then transcends, the gender divide in an image of Pip's own possible liberation from the gender- and difference-ridden Oedipal obsession. For helpful comments on Freud's views on bisexuality, Lacan's modification of them, and subsequent discussion, see Mary Jacobus, *Reading Woman* (n. 19 above), pp. 18–24. At this point in *Great Expectations* Dickens transcends that morbid obsession with drowned Ophelias which he shared with many of his contemporaries: see ch. 3, n. 31 and *The Uncommercial Traveller*, ed. cit (n. 21 above), ch. 19, p. 193: 'Looking over too, I saw, lying on the towing path with her face turned up towards us, a woman, dead a day or two, and under thirty, as I guessed, poorly dressed in black. The feet were lightly crossed at the ankles, and the dark hair, all pushed back from the face, as though

that had been the last action of her desperate hands, streamed over the ground. Dabbled all about her was . . . water and broken ice . . . '.

Chapter 3

1. Ann Thwaite, *Edmund Gosse: A Literary Landscape 1849–1928* (London: Secker and Warburg, 1984), p. 3 (hereafter Thwaite). Gosse's critics are acutely aware of, and subtle in handling, the problem. E.g., E. Pearlman: 'Gosse deploys so many of the familiar stylistic devices of autobiographical novels that we must take every precaution to avoid thinking of *Father and Son* as a work of autonomous fiction' ('Father and Mother in *Father and Son*', *Victorian Newsletter*, LV (1979), 19–23; p. 19). See also Peter Abbs's fine introduction to his Penguin English Library edition *Father and Son* (Harmondsworth, 1983). Wayne Shumaker, *English Autobiography: Its Emergence, Materials, and Form* (Berkeley: Univ. of California Press, 1954), p. 123 observes that *Father and Son* has the form of a brilliant novel. Gosse himself proclaims at the beginning of his Preface: 'At the present hour, when fiction takes forms so ingenious and so spacious, it is perhaps necessary to say that the following narrative, in all its parts, and so far as the punctilious attention of the writer has been able to keep it so, is scrupulously true' (Preface to *Father and Son*, p. 3). The edition cited here and throughout is *Father and Son*, ed. James Hepburn, Oxford English Memoirs and Travels (London, New York, Toronto: Oxford U.P., 1974). Page references will be given in parentheses following quotations in the body of the text.
2. For helpful comments, and disclaimers, see e.g., L. A. Renza, 'The Veto of the Imagination: A Theory of Autobiography', *NLH* IX (1977), 1–26 and John Sturrock, 'The New Model Autobiographer', *ibid.*, 51–63. For a subtle demonstration, using a passage from *Father and Son* as a test case, that 'autobiography is neither memory nor fiction', see B. J. Mandel, 'Full of Life Now' in James Olney (ed.), *Autobiography: Essays Theoretical and Critical* (Princeton, N.J.: Princeton U.P., 1980), pp. 49–72, esp. pp. 58 ff.
3. My approach follows leads given, e.g., by Pearlman, *art.cit.* (n. 1) and Brian Finney, *The Inner I: British Literary Autobriography of the Twentieth Century* (London and Boston: Faber and Faber, 1985), pp. 141–50.
4. On Knowles (1784–1862), see *DNB* and sources cited there.
5. It is thus a classic case of Bloomian poetic misprision, a combination (if we wish to use the terminology) of *tessera* and *kenosis*: Harold Bloom, *The Anxiety of Influence* (New York: Oxford U.P., 1973), pp. 14–15 etc.
6. John Mortimer, *Clinging to the Wreckage: A Part of Life* (London: Weidenfeld and Nicolson, 1982).
7. Evan Charteris, *The Life and Letters of Sir Edmund Gosse* (London: Heinemann, 1931), p. 308 (hereafter, Charteris). James D. Woolf, *Sir*

Edmund Gosse (New York: Twayne, 1972), ch. 5 discusses *Father and Son* as an example of Gosse's 'psychological method', as does Finney, *op. cit.* (n. 3). Another, albeit indirect, link in the chain is offered by Gosse's early tragedy *King Erik*; Woolf, *Sir Edmund Gosse*, p. 45, notes that 'the revenge motive and the Danish setting suggest *Hamlet*, and King Erik's violation of his own decree of justice [against murder] suggests *Oedipus*'. Pearlman, 'Father and Mother in *Father and Son*', (n. 1), p. 23 n. relates the plot of *King Erik* to that of *Father and Son*.

8. Charteris, p. 309.
9. For example, D. L. Gelpi, S.J., *The Divine Mother: A Trinitarian Theology of the Holy Spirit* (Lanham, New York, London: University Press of America, 1984). James D. Woolf, 'The Benevolent Christ in Gosse's *Father and Son*', *Prose Studies*, III (1980), 165–75 offers a fascinating complementary reading to my own in which the son espouses the role of the benevolent Christ in opposition to his father's 'jealous God' (esp. pp. 167–8); and Anna Shipton's narrative suggests that Emily Gosse possessed a kind of double vision in regard to her love for Jesus and her son: 'It was pre-eminently Jesus that she preached; his beauty, his loving-kindness, his tender mercy! . . . Yet all this time she had a mother's eye upon her young son, whom she carefully watched in his amusements and companions' ('*Tell Jesus*.' *Recollections of Emily Gosse*. New edn (London: Morgan and Scott, n. d.), p. 19).
10. The maternal grandfather's 'best trait was his devotion to the education of his children, in which he proclaimed himself a disciple of Rousseau . . .': *Father and Son*, p. 6.
11. Melanie Klein, 'Early Stages of the Oedipus Conflict' (1928), in *The Selected Melanie Klein*, ed. Juliet Mitchell (Harmondsworth: Penguin, 1986), pp. 69–83.
12. Gosse's fondness for the moon seems to be deeply personal. A letter to Hamo Thorneycroft of 6 November 1879, for example, closes: 'It is nearly midnight. I have been out to the post, and seeing the white face of Selene, wondered if yours was upturned to her also' (cit. Charteris, p. 123). This is, of course, the way one writes to one's beloved (*Tom Jones*, VIII.ix), and in what, in effect, might be Gosse's lunar mythology we have perhaps the beginnings of a clue to a vocabulary of homosexuality in Gosse's work. Certainly the preoccupation with death, silence, and ghosts in *Father and Son*, is illuminated by, and belongs to the same imaginative area as, the letter to Swinburne on repression of one's instinctual faults excerpted by Thwaite, pp. 320–21: 'The position of a young person so tormented is really that of a man buried alive and conscious, but deprived of speech. He is doomed, by his own timidity and ignorance, to a repression which amounts to death, because, so far as he can see, it is final, as final as blindness or mutilation could make it. This corpse however is obliged to bustle around and make an appearance every time the feast of life is spread. Happy those who learn to break the cerecloths in time: it is less difficult than might be imagined, with luck and the grace of God'. I have avoided attempting

a homosexual 'reading' of *Father and Son* since it seems to me a speculative and impertinent undertaking. The possibility of one fascinates, however, in the light of this letter and the patterns discussed in this chapter. Nancy Baker Traubitz, 'Heavenly Mother: The Trinity as Structual Device in Edmund Gosse's *Father and Son*', *Journal of Narrative Technique*, IV (1976), 147–54, fails to notice that the 'triune female deity' she so brilliantly discovers in Gosse's text (the mother, the old lady of a midwife, the stepmother) is not so much a deconstruction of the Christian trinity as a revival of the Diana-Lucina-Hecate trinity. Her findings, with which I am completely in sympathy, complement my suggestion above about the female Holy Ghost. The moon shines on a Gosse of homosexual and feminist inclinations.

13. Thwaite, p. 240.
14. Walter Pater, 'Leonardo da Vinci', in *The Renaissance* ed. D. F. Hill (Berkeley, Los Angeles, London: Univ. of California Press, 1980), pp. 97–8.
15. Philip Henry Gosse, *Tenby: A Sea-Side Holiday* (London, 1856), p. 7: 'The lanes of North Devon came strongly up to remembrance, and we could almost fancy ourselves going along the lovely Score Valley, or down the Slade Road near Ilfracombe'. And cf. p. 34.
16. *Tenby*, pp. 289–90.
17. E.g. J. G. Frazer, *The Magic Art and the Evolution of Kings* (*Golden Bough*, vols I and II), 3rd edn (repr. London: Macmillan, 1932), I.14 and II.125.
18. Compare Nancy Traubitz's reading, *art.cit.*, n. 12 above, which, however, omits the Lucina-hound-Diana association. I use the word 'crone' positively, in the sense proposed by Mary Daly in *Gyn/Ecology* (London: The Women's Press, 1987 edn), pp. 14–17, 347–51, etc.
19. Lewis and Short *A Latin Dictionary*, s.v. *almus*.
20. In this quotation I have adopted the reading *Orgyia*, a correction made to the March 1908 printing of the first impression's *orgygia*: Douglas Westheimer, 'Gosse's Corrections to "Father and Son"', 1907–1908', *N and Q*, CCIII (1978), 327–32.
21. Gosse's love for 'the Greek gods' is admitted into *Father and Son* towards the end of ch. 11 (pp. 140–3) and includes the goddesses, but we have to look outside *Father and Son* for further evidence as to how it registered his commitment to the mother goddess: to, for example, his reaction to Swinburne's *Poems and Ballads* as recounted to Austin Dobson. Of the meagre seven poems he admits 'to the first class', two are to the mother goddess and her daughter ('Hymn to Proserpine' and 'The Garden of Proserpine'): Charteris, p. 88. The 'Hymn' is, of course, Sue Bridehead's favourite (*Jude the Obscure*, II.3); inspired by it she creates an Eleusinian shrine in counterpoint to Jude's chanted New Testament and Miss Fontover's scrolls. Walter Pater's long, scholarly and sensitive essay 'The Myth of Demeter and Persephone' is in his *Greek Studies* (1895). The most sensitive account of 'paganism' in *Father and Son*, Philip Dodd's 'The Nature of Edmund

Gosse's *Father and Son*', *English Literature in Transition 1880–1920*, XXII (1979), 270–80, is less interested in the mythology than I am and thus virtually ignores this aspect of the text.

22. Cf. p. 52, where the son's awarenes of blood is related to the father's religious fervour: 'We were not always reading the 'Epistle to the Hebrews', however; not always was my flesh being made to creep by having it insisted upon that "almost all things are by the Law purged with blood, and without blood is no remission of sin".' In addition, the father's obsession with Cain may, by a not unfamilar quirk of illogic, also have led the son to connect him with the murdering brother. Philip rejected the evolutionary theorists like this: to attempt to scale heaven with the ladder of natural history, is nothing less than Cain's religion; it is the presentation of the fruit of the earth, instead of the blood of the Lamb' (P. H. Gosse, *A Year at the Shore* (London, 1865), p. 326); cf. *The Aquarium* (second edn, London, 1856), pp. 203–4: the natural historians, if they ignore God, 'offer Cain's "fruit of the ground", without the blood of Abel's "firstling".' As a man who is professionally involved with dismembered fossil fragments and the examination of the minutiae of biological specimens, the Cain-like father is, as it were, symbolically 'responsible' for the skin trunk as image of dead wife and mother. For comments which illuminate how the text's preoccupation with dismemberment, murder, ghosts, etc may relate to the construction of autobiography itself, see Eugenio Donato, 'The Ruins of Memory: Archaeological Fragments and Textual Artefacts', *MLN*, XCIII (1978), 575–96.

23. Gosse, quoted by Stephen Heath, 'Psychopathia Sexualis: Stevenson's *Strange Case*', *CQ* XXVIII (1986), 93–108 (p. 105). It is at least interesting that Gosse's committed friendship to Stevenson led him, when he heard of his acute illness in California, to think of *Hamlet*: 'He does not think he will recover . . . You cannot think how this has upset me . . . . He is only our age, or a little less. He is exactly like Hamlet's description of Yorick – "a fellow of infinite jest, of most excellent fancy". We never thought of the death of so bright a creation' (letter to Hamo Thorneycroft, 31 December 1879; cit. Charteris, pp. 127–8). *Hamlet* was in Gosse's mind for another reason, too: 'at this time' according to Charteris, but perhaps a little earlier according to Thwaite, he had been invited to see Irving's *Hamlet* at the Lyceum and meet the actor in his dressing room after the performance (Charteris, p. 129: Thwaite, p. 210).

24. Karl Miller, *Doubles: Studies in Literary History* (Oxford: Oxford U.P., 1985), p. 211.

25. When the mother is able to leave her room after her six weeks' confinement the 'occasion . . . was attended by a species of Churching' (p. 8): on the face of it a thanksgiving for mother and son, but subtextually evoking Leviticus 12 on woman's childbearing uncleanness and hence male fear and disgust of the female which reinforces the mother's need to suppress her secret (novelistic) self in the name of her patriarchal religion.

26. For bees and the mother goddess see, e.g., Erich Neumann, *The Great Mother: An Analysis of an Archetype*, tr. Ralph Manheim, Bollingen Series XLVII (New York: Pantheon Books, 1955), pp. 262–7. Hence in part the wit of applying the image (via Virgil's fourth *Georgic*) to the father as he prays with his usual physical exuberance, 'by crackings of the joints of the fingers, by deap breathings, murmurous sounds which seemed just breaking out of silence, like Virgil's bees out of the hive, *magnis clamoribus*' (p. 124).
27. *Dombey and Son*, ch. 8.
28. For the biographical background, see Thwaite, pp. 35 ff. On the Devon mud, compare Philip Gosse's *A Naturalist's Rambles on the Devonshire Coast* (London, 1853): 'we trudged, despite the tenacious red mud that lay ankle-deep, along the narrow lanes around Marychurch and West-hill' (p. 3); 'the red earth, so abundant hereabout as to tinge the clothes of the peasants . . .' (p. 6).
29. John Robinson, *A Theological, Biblical, and Ecclesiastical Dictionary* (London, 1815), s.v. Adam. Like Augustine's *Confessions* (to which *Father and Son* is often compared: e.g., Abbs's Introduction to his Penguin edn, pp. 18–19), *Father and Son* is involved in a dialogue on the relationship between genesis and Genesis. This in turn trails *Paradise Lost* across the text, at p. 62, where the son writes of the hostile reception of *Omphalos*: 'He had been the spoiled darling of the public, the constant favourite of the press, and now, like the dark angels of old, "so huge a rout/Encumbered him with ruin"'. The implications of the quotation are fascinating. They appear to suggest that the son equates the father with Lucifer surrounded by his fallen angels, the victim of God's (and the Son's!) wrath (cf. *Father and Son*, page 63: 'I think he considered the failure of his attempt at the reconciliation of science with religion to have been intended by God as a punishment for something he had done or left undone'). But the lines only indirectly relate to Lucifer, for the 'he' who is 'encumbered . . . with ruin' is actually Chaos (*Paradise Lost*, VI. 874); so that the father-as-Chaos is, in a bitter joke, reduced to the state that preceded the Creation in the Genesis account he is so passionately devoted to defending.
30. For other analyses of the dream see R. J. Porter, 'Edmund Gosse's *Father and Son*: Between Form and Flexibility', *Journal of Narrative Technique* V (1975), 174–95 (pages 84–5) and Vivian and Robert Folkenflik, 'Words and Language in *Father and Son*', *Biography*, II (1979), 157–75, esp. pp. 165–6.
31. Rossetti's case involves exhumation, of course: Oswald Doughty, *A Victorian Romantic: Dante Gabriel Rossetti* (London: Frederick Muller, 1949), pp. 416 ff. The Ophelian overtones of the 'Lady of Shalott' are mentioned by Gilbert and Gubar, *The Madwoman in the Attic*, pp. 617–18. (The whole of their chapter 16, 'A Woman – White: Emily Dickinson's Yarn of Pearl' is relevant to the Ophelia type.) Jerome K. Jerome's drowned Ophelia, accompanied by a Millais-like engraving, is in chapter 16 of *Three Men in a Boat*. For the background see Nina Auerbach, *Woman and the Demon: The Life of a Victorian Myth*

(Cambridge, Mass: Harvard U.P., 1982) and, more especially, Elaine Showalter, *The Female Malady: Women, Madness, and English Culture 1830–1980* (London: Virago, 1987), ch. 3, esp. pp. 90–8.
32. See p. 116 above, and *DNB* entry on Knowles, p. 298.
33. Perhaps with a teasing half-memory of those lines also played on in *Great Expectations*, ch. 54, *Hamlet* II.ii.206–8: 'Will you walk out of the air, my lord?' 'Into my grave?' 'Indeed, that's out of the air'.

Chapter 4

1. *Henry and Cato* (London: Chatto and Windus, 1976), p. 195.
2. *The Good Apprentice* (London: Chatto and Windus, 1985), p. 197.
3. Henry claims to be writing a book about Beckmann, the German Expressionist painter who died in 1950. His paintings are referred to several times (most notably on p. 96), but more importantly the novel's dominant images – of fire, candle light, imprisonment, and violence – are consciously (if not solely) Beckmannesque.
4. Charles worships Shakespeare, has acted the part of Hamlet (*The Sea, The Sea* (London: Chatto and Windus, 1978, p. 38), glimpses a Tibetan Buddhist significance to it when he responds to his cousin James's description of *bardo* with ' "For in that sleep of death what dreams may come" . . .' (p. 384; *Hamlet*, III.i.66), and at the end of the novel notes cryptically: 'Took Miss Kaufman to *Hamlet* and enjoyed it' (p. 501). Elizabeth Dipple, *Iris Murdoch: Work for the Spirit* (London: Methuen, 1982), ch. 10 pursues some of the *Hamlet* clues in *Nuns and Soldiers*, which appeared too late for Richard Todd's *Iris Murdoch: The Shakespearean Interest* (London: Vision Press, 1979), which is perceptive on the earlier fiction.
5. In 1978 she agreed that she 'perhaps identif[ies] with men more than with women, because the ordinary human condition still seems to belong more to a man that to a woman . . . if one writes "as a woman", something about the female predicament may be supposed to emerge. And I'm not very much interested in the female predicament': J. I. Biles, 'An Interview with Iris Murdoch', *Studies in the Literary Imagination*, XI (1978), 115–25; p. 119. The idea of 'mimesis' – assumption of the male personality in order to discover its limitations, structure, etc., with the intention of recovering 'a possible operation of the feminine in language' – is taken from Luce Irigaray, *This Sex Which Is Not One*, tr. Catherine Porter (Ithaca: Cornell U.P. 1985), p. 76, who has also been invoked by Deborah Johnson, *Iris Murdoch* (Brighton: Harvester, 1987), p. 35, in her feminist approach to *The Black Prince*. What astonishes me as a man is the brilliance of Murdoch's mimetic intuitions. It is worth noting, though, that despite her intention (as I see it, anyway) to recover language for the feminine, the narrative structure that Murdoch's fictions perpetuate remain essentially patriarchal in their Oedipal teleology. For other comments on the emergent feminine in her fiction, see Steven Cohan, 'From Subtext to Dream Text: The Brutal

Egoism of Iris Murdoch's Male Narrators', *Women and Literature*, II (1982), 222–42.
6. For Murdoch's Platonism, see W. K. Rose, 'An Interview with Iris Murdoch', *Shenandoah*, XIX (1968), 3–22, and her Platonist essays *The Sovereignty of Good* (London: Routledge and Kegan Paul, 1970) and *The Fire and the Sun: Why Plato Banished the Artists* (Oxford: Clarendon Press, 1977). Her narrative concern with the Oedipus complex is discussed by, e.g., Cohan *art.cit.* (n. 5) pp. 228–31, and P. J. Conradi, *Iris Murdoch: The Saint and the Artist* (London and Basingstoke: Macmillan, 1986), p. 77.
7. *The Anxiety of Influence*, p. 5.
8. *The Black Prince* (Harmondsworth: Penguin, 1975), pp. 17–18. Subsequent quotations are identified by page references within the text.
9. E.g. Jane Sturrock, 'Good and the Gods of *The Black Prince*', *Mosaic: A Journal for the Comparative Study of Literature and Ideas*, X (1977), 133–41, page 136–7: J. F. Stewart, 'Art and Love in Murdoch's *The Black Prince*', *Research Studies*, XLVI (1978), 69–78, pp. 75–6: Elizabeth Dipple, *op. cit.* (n. 4 above), p. 112: Conradi, *op. cit.* (n. 6 above), p. 187 and n.
10. *The Sovereignty of Good* (n. 6 above), pp. 91–2.
11. *The Fire and the Sun* (n. 6 above), pp. 72,76.
12. It is at the centre as 'The Mousetrap' is at the centre of *Hamlet*, and fulfils a similar function of interior duplication and amplification: e.g., Jean Ricardou, *Le nouveau roman* (Paris, 1973), pp. 47–75.
13. On Mercury as quicksilver, and his other meanings, see C. G. Jung, *Alchemical Studies*, tr. R. F. C. Hull, Bollingen Series, XX (Princeton, N.J.: Princeton U.P. 1967), sect. IV. Jung's significance in the novel, probably as an opponent of Freud, is guaranteed by Arnold's 'shadowy' discipleship (p. 187); and Bradley's vows of silence, as novelist and as lover (e.g. pp. 213, 252), are in part Hermetic: see Edgar Wind, *Pagan Mysteries in the Renaissance*, rev. edn (Harmondsworth: Penguin 1967), pp. 12 n. 196 and plate 23 on Hermetic silence as communion with the One. The tradionally hermaphroditic nature of alchemical Hermes points to a Jungian answer to the Oedipus complex within the novel: it is expelled through recognition and assimilation by the male of his feminine *anima*. For the definition of the *anima*, see Jung, *Psychological Types, or the Psychology of Individuation*, tr. H. Godwin Baynes, (London: Kegan Paul, Trench, Trubner, 1923), pp. 588–99, esp. pp. 594–5 and 597–8. The latter states: 'With men the soul, *i.e.* the anima, is usually figured by the unconscious in the person of a woman', and suggests how a failure to project the soul-image can result in homosexuality or narcissism. See also Jung's *Man and His Symbols* (London: Aldus Books and W. H. Allen, 1964), pp. 177–88.
14. *A Fairly Honourable Defeat* (Harmondsworth: Penguin, 1973), p. 41. Wind's discussion of the myth in *Pagan Mysteries*, ch. XI, as a battle between 'the relative powers of Dionysian darkness and Apollonian clarity' is characteristically astute (*ed.cit.*, n. 13 above, p. 173). On the

same page he quotes Dante's prayer to Apollo: 'infuse me with your spirit as you did Marsyas when you tore him from the cover of his limbs'. This view of the myth informs Dipple's reading of the novel (*Work for the Spirit*, pp. 108–32) and, to a large extent, Conradi's (*Saint and Artist*, pp. 187–9).

15. Ovid, *Metamophoses* VI.392–4, tr. F. J. Miller, Loeb edn (London and New York: Heinemann and Putnam's, 1929), p. 315. The political implications of the story – as a battle between the forces of Apollo and the mother goddess – are taken for granted in, e.g., William Smith, *Dictionary of Greek and Roman Biography and Mythology*, 3 vols (London 1862–64), II. 962–3, *s.v.* Marsyas. Note that Plato banishes the flute in *Republic*, 399 D-E, thereby explicitly exalting Apollo over Marsyas.

16. For the dizzying principles of doubling, see Ernest Jones, *Hamlet and Oedipus* (London: Gollancz, 1949), ch. 7, and, for a slightly different approach, Frank Kermode, *Forms of Attention* (Chicago and London: Univ. of Chicago Press, 1985), ch. 2.

17. Fay Weldon, *Down Among the Women* (London: Heinemann, 1971), ch. 1 and Jocelyn's epilogue.

18. As Sturrock and Stewart (see n. 9 above) both noticed without, however, going back to sources.

19. Murdoch, 'Against Dryness', *Encounter*, XVI (1961): repr. in Harold Bloom, ed., *Iris Murdoch* (New York, New Haven, Philadelphia: Chelsea House Publishers, 1986), pp. 9–16; p. 15.

20. Herodotus, Book I, paras 181–2, tr. A. D. Godley, Loeb edn (London and New York: Heinemann and Putnam's, 1931), I.227. Henry in his state of moral myopia in *Henry and Cato* is excited by the idea of Stephanie Whitehouse's past as a prostitute and at one point imagines her as a *hetaira* (p. 165). For Apollo as woman-hater see J. E. Harrison, *Prolegomena to the Study of Greek Religion* (Cleveland and New York: World Publishing Company, 1966), pp. 394–5.

21. *Aeneid*, IV.143–4. Servius's note reads: 'nam constat Apollinem sex mensibus hiemalibus apud Pataram, Lyciae civitatem, dare responsa: unde Patareus Apollo dicitur: et sex mensibus aestivis apud Delum . . .': *Servii Grammatici qui feruntur in Vergilii Carmina Commentarii*, ed. G. Thilo and H. Hagen, 3 vols (Leipzig, 1878–87), I.489.

22. Liddell and Scott, *Greek-English Lexicon*, *s.v.*: 'from Apollo's "crooked", i.e. ambiguous, oracles'.

23. *Oedipus Tyrannus*, l.410 (Tiresias); l.853 (Jocasta); ll.994–6 (Oedipus). Quoted from Loeb *Sophocles* tr. F. Storr, I (London and New York: Heinemann and Macmillan, 1912). The play abounds in epithets and names of Apollo; Loxias is used in these instances and one other neutral instance (by the Chorus, l.1101). Dipple, *Work for the Spirit*, p. 112, misses the Oedipal connection by locating the name in Aeschylus's *Agamemnon*, though Conradi, p. 284, n. 6, suspects the Sophoclean truth.

24. A useful phrase that I have borrowed from Martin Greenberg's *The Hamlet Vocation of Coleridge and Wordsworth* (Iowa City: Univ. of Iowa Press, 1986).

25. See the attack on cosmetics in Juvenal's *Sixth Satire*, ll.457–73 and, for some at least of its influential subsequent history, F.A. Nussbaum, *The Brink of All We Hate: English Satires on Women, 1660–1750* (Lexington: Kentucky U.P., 1984).
26. Bradley identifies Priscilla with their mother on page 82: 'I felt for my misguided mother pain and shame which did not diminish but qualified my love. I was mortally afraid of anyone seeing her as absurd or pathetic, a defeated snob. And later still, after her death, I transferred many of those feelings to Priscilla.'
27. For the Platonist view in Murdoch, see Lynette Hunter, *Rhetorical Stance in Modern Literature: Allegories of Love and Death* (London and Basingstoke: Macmillan 1984), pp. 106–20; for Freud, see *The Theme of the Three Caskets, SE,* xii.301, *cit.* ch. 2, n. 35 above.
28. The classic account of this reading of *Frankenstein* remains that of Gilbert and Gubar, *The Madwoman in the Attic* (New Haven and London: Yale U.P., 1979), ch. 7.
29. The Apollo on whom Bradley models himself is thus not just Apollo the woman-hater (above, n. 20) but Apollo the death-giver, whose name derives from Greek *apollumi*, to destroy: William Smith, *Dictionary* (n. 15 above), i.230. Luce Irigaray's reversal of the Platonic cave myth to show (among other things) how Plato's sun blinds man to the feminine also foregrounds Apollo the destroyer: see ref. in n. 31 below.
30. It is worth noting here that Richard Todd has rightly identified Bradley as a foot fetishist: 'The Plausibility of *The Black Prince*', *Dutch Quarterly*, viii (1978), 82–93.
31. The doves of Aphrodite are a commonplace; for the doves of Dodona as the oracular voices of the wise women see, e.g., Pausanias, *Description of Greece* vii.xxi.2. Murdoch is revisiting here the Jungian archetype of the feminine cave: Johnson, *Iris Murdoch* (above n. 5), ch. 4, discusses its appearance in her fiction and directs attention to the relevance of Luce Irigaray's feminist deconstruction of the Platonic cave-sun metaphor in *Speculum, de l'autre femme* (tr. G. G. Gill (Ithaca: Cornell U.P., 1985)).
32. Hesiod, *Theogony*, l. 120. This is the same Eros that we find in Plato's *Symposium*, 178B.
33. Shakespeare's *Cymbeline*, ii.ii. The further analogy, with Tarquin's rape of Lucretia, is made by Iachimo himself at the beginning of the scene.
34. *Faerie Queene*, iii.iv.18, 23 and, especially, *Pericles* and *The Winter's Tale*.
35. The song resounds hauntingly through *The Sea, The Sea* (e.g. p. 364); Morgan sings (or quotes) it to Peter in *A Fairly Honourable Defeat* as an example of something human that is 'good, ... intact and precious and absolutely beautiful' (Penguin edn (1973), pp. 188–9); to cite only two instances of its relevance to Murdoch's fiction.
36. Murdoch said in a 1978 interview that 'Ideas in art must suffer a sea-change': Bryan Magee, *Men of Ideas: Some Creators of Contemporary Philosophy* (London: BBC, 1978), p. 277; and the idea of the transmuting power of the sea, as well as the sea as source, is

omnipresent in her thinking. Thus, James tells Charles riddlingly, in *The Sea, The Sea*, that 'Plato was descended from Poseidon on his father's side' (p. 176). Interestingly, dreams are a narrative obsession in the novel that followed *The Black Prince*, *The Sacred and Profane Love Machine* (1974).

37. See p. 154 above.
38. Apollo is specifically enemy of the womb, signified by his dragon-opponent Delphyne: see Carl Kerényi, *The Gods of the Greeks*, tr. Norman Cameron (London: Thames and Hudson, 1951), p. 51: *cit*. Mary Daly, *Gyn/Ecology* (London: The Women's Press, 1987), p. 62 and n.
39. On this see, for example, D. J. Gelpi, SJ, *The Divine Mother: A Trinitarian Theology of the Holy Spirit* (Lanham, New York, London: University Press of America, 1984). The 'Jew' pun in Julian's name (which contrasts with Jewish-born Christian's) emphasises the Jewish tradition of feminine spirit here.

Select Bibiliography

Ariès, P. *The Hour of Our Death*, tr. Helen Weaver (Harmondsworth: Penguin, 1983).
——. *Images of Man and Death*, tr. Janet Lloyd (Cambridge, Mass, and London: Harvard U.P., 1985).
Atherton, H. M. *Political Prints in the Age of Hogarth: A Study of the Ideographic Representation of Politics* (Oxford: Clarendon Press, 1974).
Banier, Abbé. *The Mythology, and Fables of the Antients, Explain'd from History*, 4 vols (London, 1739–40).
Barthes, R. *Camera Lucida*, tr. Richard Howard (London: Fontana, 1984).
Biles, J. I. 'An Interview with Iris Murdoch', *Studies in the Literary Imagination*, XI (1978).
Bloom, H. *The Anxiety of Influence: A Theory of Poetry* (New York: Oxford U.P., 1973).
Brooks, P. 'Repitition, Repression, and Return; *Great Expectations* and the Study of Plot', *NLH*, XI (1979–80).
Brooks-Davies, D. *Pope's 'Dunciad' and the Queen of Night: A Study in Emotional Jacobitism* (Manchester and Dover, N. H.: Manchester U.P., 1985).
Byrd, M. '"Reading" in *Great Expectations*', *PMLA*, XCI (1976).
Charteris, E. *The Life and Letters of Sir Edmund Gosse* (London: Heinemann, 1931).
Cixous, H. 'Fictions and Phantoms: A Reading of Freud's *Das Unheimliche* (The "Uncanny")', tr. Robert Dennom, *NLH*, VII (1975–6).
Clarendon, Edward Hyde, first Earl of, *The History of the Rebellion and Civil Wars in England*, 7 vols (Oxford, 1849).
Cohan, S. 'From Subtext to Dream Text: The Brutal Egoism of Iris Murdoch's Male Narrators', *Women and Literature*, II (1982).
Connor, S. *Charles Dickens* (Oxford: Basil Blackwell, 1985).
Conradi, P. J. *Iris Murdoch: The Saint and the Artist* (London and Basingstoke: Macmillan, 1986).
Daly, M. *Gyn/Ecology* (London: The Women's Press, 1987).
Davis, D. R. 'Multiples', *E in C*, XXVI (1986).
Derrida, J. *Writing and Difference*, tr. Alan Bass (London, Melbourne and Henley: Routledge and Kegan Paul, 1981).
——. 'Fors', *The Georgia Review*, XXXI (1977).
Dessner, L. J. '*Great Expectations*: "the Ghost of a Man's Own Father"', *PMLA* XCI (1976).
Dickens, C. *Great Expectations*, ed. Angus Calder (Harmondsworth: Penguin, 1965).
——. *Miscellaneous Papers*, introd. P. J. M. Scott, 2 vols (Millwood, N.Y.: Kraus Reprint, 1983).
——. *The Uncommercial Traveller and Reprinted Pieces*, introd. L. C. Staples (London: Oxford U.P., 1958).

Dipple, E. *Iris Murdoch: Work for the Spirit* (London: Methuen, 1982).
Donato, E. 'The Ruins of Memory: Archeological Fragments and Textual Artefacts', *MLN*, xcIII (1978).
Fielding, H. *The History of Tom Jones, a Foundling*, ed. M. C. Battestin and Fredson Bowers, Wesleyan edn. 2 vols (Oxford: Clarendon Press, 1974).
——. *The Jacobite's Journal and Related Writings*, ed. W. B. Coley, Wesleyan edn (Oxford: Clarendon Press, 1974).
Finney, B. *The Inner I: British Literary Autobiography of the Twentieth Century* (London: Faber and Faber, 1985).
Forster, J. *The Life of Charles Dickens*, 3 vols (London, 1872–4).
Freud, S. *Beyond the Pleasure Principle*, *SE*, xvIII.
——. *The Interpretation of Dreams*, *SE*, IV.
——. *Remembering, Repeating and Working-Through*, *SE*, xII.
——. *The Theme of the Three Caskets*, *SE*, xII.
——. *The Uncanny*, *SE* xvII.
Frye, R. M. *The Renaissance Hamlet: Issues and Responses in 1600* (Princeton U.P., 1984).
Gelpi, D. L. *The Divine Mother: A Trinitarian Theology of the Holy Spirit* (Lanham, New York, Philadelphia; University Press of America, 1984).
Gilbert, E. L. ' "In Primal Sympathy": *Great Expectations* and the Secret Life', *DSA*, xII (1983).
Gilbert, S. and Gubar, S. *The Madwoman in the Attic: The Woman Writer and the Nineteenth-Century Literary Imagination* (New Haven and London: Yale U.P., 1979).
Golden, M. *Fielding's Moral Psychology* (Amherst: University of Massachusetts Press, 1966).
——. 'Public Context and Imagining Self in *Tom Jones*', *PLL*, xx (1984).
Gosse, E. *Father and Son*, ed. James Hepburn, Oxford English Memoirs and Travels (London, New York, Toronto: Oxford U.P., 1974).
——. *Father and Son*, ed. Peter Abbs (Harmondsworth: Penguin, 1983).
Gosse, P. H. *A Naturalist's Rambles on the Devonshire Coast* (London 1853).
——. *The Aquarium*, second edn (London, 1856).
——. *Tenby: A Sea-Side Holiday* (London, 1856).
——. *A Year at the Shore* (London, 1865).
Hartog, D. den. *Dickens and Romantic Psychology: The Self in Time in Nineteenth-Century Literature* (London and Basingstoke: Macmillan, 1987).
Heath, S. 'Psychopathia Sexualis: Stevenson's *Strange Case*', *CQ*, xxvIII (1986).
Hutter, A. D. 'Dismemberment and Articulation in *Our Mutual Friend*', *DSA*, xI (1983).
——. 'The Novelist as Resurrectionist: Dickens and the Dilemma of Death', *DSA*, xII (1983).
Irigaray, L. *Speculum of the Other Woman*, tr. G. G. Gill (Ithaca: Cornell U.P., 1985).
——. *This Sex Which Is Not One*, tr. Catherine Porter (Ithaca: Cornell U.P., 1985).
Jacobus, M. *Reading Woman: Essays in Feminist Criticism* (London: Methuen, 1986).

Select Bibliography

Johnson, D. *Iris Murdoch* (Brighton: Harvester, 1987).
Jones, E. *Hamlet and Oedipus* (London: Gollancz, 1949).
Jung, C. G. *Alchemical Studies*, tr. R. F. C. Hull, Bollingen Series, xx (Princeton: Princeton U.P., 1967).
——.*Psychology and Alchemy*, tr. R. F. C. Hull (London: Routledge and Kegan Paul, 1980).
——. *Psychological Types, or the Psychology of Individuation*, tr. H. Godwin Baynes (London: Kegan Paul, Trench, Trubner, 1923).
——. *Symbols of Transformation*, tr. R. F. C. Hull, Bollingen Series, xx (New York: Pantheon Books, 1956).
Kermode, F. *Forms of Attention* (Chicago and London: University of Chicago Press, 1985).
——. *The Genesis of Secrecy* (Cambridge, Mass. and London: Harvard U.P., 1974).
Klein, M. *The Selected Melanie Klein*, ed. Juliet Mitchell (Harmondsworth: Penguin, 1986).
Lacan, J. *Ecrits: A Selection*, tr. Alan Sheridan (London: Tavistock Publications, 1980).
Manheim, L. F. 'Dickens and Psychoanalysis: A Memoir', *DSA*, xi (1983).
McCrea, B. *Henry Fielding and the Politics of Mid-Eighteenth Century England* (Athens, Ga.: University of Georgia Press, 1981).
Miller, H. K. 'The "Digressive" Tales in Fielding's *Tom Jones* and the Perspective of Romance', *PQ*, LIV (1975).
Miller, J. H. *Charles Dickens: The World of His Novels* (Bloomington and London: Indiana U.P., 1973).
Miller, K. *Doubles: Studies in Literary History* (Oxford: Oxford U.P., 1985).
Mortimer, J. *Clinging to the Wreckage: A Part of Life* (London: Weidenfeld and Nicolson, 1982).
Moynahan, J. 'The Hero's Guilt: The Case of *Great Expectations*', *E in C*, x (1960).
Murdoch, I. *The Black Prince: A Celebration of Love* (Harmandsworth: Penguin, 1975).
——. *The Fire and the Sun: Why Plato Banished the Artists* (Oxford: Clarendon Press, 1977).
——. *The Good Apprentice* (London: Chatto and Windus, 1985).
——. *Henry and Cato* (London: Chatto and Windus, 1976).
——. *Nuns and Soldiers* (London: Chatto and Windus, 1980).
——. *The Sea, The Sea* (London: Chatto and Windus, 1978).
——. *The Sovereignty of Good* (London: Routledge and Kegan Paul, 1970).
Neumann, E. *The Great Mother: An Analysis of an Archetype*, tr. Ralph Manheim, Bollingen Series, XLVII (New York: Pantheon Books, 1955).
Otway, T. *The Orphan: or The Unhappy Marriage*, ed. A. M. Taylor, Regents Restoration Drama Series (London: Edward Arnold, 1977).
Ovid. *Metamorphoses*, tr. F. J. Miller, 2 vols, Loeb (London and New York: Heinemann and Putnam's 1929).
Pearlman, E. 'Father and Mother in *Father and Son*', *Victorian Newsletter*, LV (1979).
Randall, H. W. 'The Rise and Fall of a Martyrology: Sermons on Charles I', *HLQ*, x (1947).

Robinson, J. *A Theological, Biblical, and Ecclesiatical Dictionary* (London, 1815).
Sadoff, D. F. 'The Dead Father: *Barnaby Rudge, David Copperfield*, and *Great Expectations*', *PLL*, XVIII (1982).
———. '*Locus Suspectus*: Narrative, Castration, and the Uncanny', *DSA*, XIII (1984).
Sanders, A. *Charles Dickens: Resurrectionist* (London and Basingstoke: Macmillan, 1982).
Schonhorn, M. 'Fielding's Ecphrastic Moment: Tom Jones and his Egyptian Majesty', *SP*, LXXVIII (1981).
Shelley, M. *Frankenstein*, ed. Maurice Hindle (Harmondsworth: Penguin, 1985).
Shipton, A. '*Tell Jesus*': Recollections of Emily Gosse (London: Morgan and Scott. New edition, n.d.).
Showalter, E. *The Female Malady: Women, Madness, and English Culture, 1830–1980* (London: Virago, 1987).
Sophocles. *Sophocles: The Theban Plays*, tr. E. F.Watling (Harmondsworth: Penguin, 1974).
Stewart, J.F. 'Art and Love in Murdoch's *The Black Prince*', *Research Studies*, XLVI (1978).
Stone, H. *Dickens and the Invisible World: Fairly Tales, Fantasy, and Novel-Making* (London and Basingstoke: Macmillan, 1980).
Sturrock, J. 'Good and the Gods of *The Black Prince*', *Mosaic: A Journal for the Comparative Study of Literature and Ideas*, X (1977).
Tambling, J. 'Prison-Bound: Dickens and Foucault', *E in C*, XXXVI (1986).
Tavor, E. *Scepticism, Society and the Eighteenth-Century Novel* (London and Basingstoke: Macmillan, 1987).
Thwaite, A. *Edmund Gosse: A Literary Landscape 1849–1928* (London: Secker and Warburg, 1984).
Tooke, A. *The Pantheon* (London, 1713).
———. *The Pantheon* (London, 1824).
Traubitz, N. B. 'Heavenly Mother: The Trinity as Structural Device in Edmund Gosse's *Father and Son*', *Journal of Narrative Technique*, VI, (1976).
Virgil. *The Aeneid*, tr. W. F. Jackson Knight (Harmondsworth: Penguin, 1974).
Vogel, J. *Allegory in Dickens* (University, Alabama: Univ. of Alabama Press, 1977).
Weldon, F. *Down Among the Women* (London: Heinemann, 1971).
Wind, E. *Pagan Mysteries in the Renaissance*, revised edition (Harmondsworth: Penguin, 1967).
Woolf, J. D. *Sir Edmund Gosse*, Twayne's English Authors (New York: Twayne, 1972).
Young, R. (ed.) *Untying the Text: A Post-Structuralist Reader* (Boston, London, Henley: Routledge and Kegan Paul, 1981).

Index

Compiled with the help of Mary Nixson

Abbs, Peter   193n., 197n.
Abel   8, 12, 68–9, 71–2, 77, 109,164
Absence (parental)   xii–xiii, xv, 2, 51, 60, 62, 74, 77, 81, 132, 187n.
Achates (in *Aeneid*)   31
Adam   119–20, 138, 140, 150, 197n.
Aeneas (in *Aeneid*)   30–2, 162–3, 181n.
Aeolus (in *Aeneid*)   34
Aeschylus   200n.
Agrippina   23
Anchises (in *Aeneid*)   32, 181n.
Anima (Jungian)   79, 189n., 199n.
Aphrodite   172–3, 201n.
Apollo   xvi, 8, 14, 156–8, 160–3, 171, 173, 179, 199–200n., 201n.
Ariès, Philippe   185n., 187n., 189–90n., 191n.
Ars moriendi   39, 185n.
Ass (symbolism of)   36
Atherton, H. M.   184n.
Atys   49–50
Auerbach, Nina   197n.
Augustine, St   197n.
Authority (authorial)   40–8 *passim*, 188n.
Autobiography (theories of)   115, 117–18, 193n.

Baal   161–2
Bainbridge, Beryl   178
Banier, Abbé   186n., 189n.
Bardo   198n.
Barnard's Inn   94, 192n.
Barthes, Roland   xii, 85–6, 190–1n.
Battestin, M. C.   182n., 183n., 184n., 185n.
Baumgarten, Murray   188n.
Beckett, Samuel   10

Beckmann, Max   152, 198n.
Bees (symbolism of)   136, 196–7n.
Bellona   50
Belshazzar   141
Benjamin (biblical)   10
Bible   10, 33, 67, 77, 109, 112–13, 127, 139, 141, 144, 151–2, 162, 172, 187n., 196n., 197n.
Biles, J. I.   198n.
The Black Prince   xi, xiii; absence (maternal) in 168–9, 177; Apollo and xvi, 156–8, 160–3, 171, 173, 179; Apollo and Marsyas and 158–60, 171, 199–200n.; art (theories of) and 154, 156–7, 160, 175, 179; beginnings in 155, 164; centre (symbolic) in 156–7, 199n.; Christianity in 154, 162, 165, 202n.; cosmetics in 165, 200n.; death-kiss in 170–1; demons in 160, 177; doubling in 159, 164; doves in 172, 201n.; and dreams 175; 'editor's' role in 156, 163, 179; evolutionary theory in 165, 173; female artist in xvi, 154, 160, 170, 179; feminism in xvi, 160, 165, 171–2, 179; foot fetishism in 201n.; and *Frankenstein* 170; ghosts in 164, 167, 169, 177, 179; *Hamlet* in xvi, 151–79 *passim*; idyll in 174; male imitation and xvi, 165, 170, 179; memory in 168–9, 177; Mercury in 157, 159, 199n.; mother goddess in 171–2; names in 158, 202n.; necrophilia in 166, 168, 174, 177; Oedipal patterns in 154, 157–9, 163, 169, 171, 174, 177, 179, 199n.; Ophelia and 158–78 *passim*; Platonism/neo-Platonism in 153–4, 156–8, 160,

169; plot summary of 155–6; remembrance in 176; revenge *motif* in 178; sea symbolism in 174–5, 177, 201n.; separation anxiety in 168; ship symbolism in 168, 176; Virgil's *Aeneid* in 162–3; water symbolism in 167–8, 178; woman (views of) in 154, 164
Blair, Robert 148
Blanchard, F. T. 182n.
Bloom, Harold xvii, 154, 181n., 193n.
Book of Common Prayer 185n.
Brontë, Charlotte 136
Brontë, Emily 76, 176, 189n.
Brooks, Peter 188n., 190n., 192n.
Brooks-Davies, Douglas 183n., 184n.
Brown, N. O. 180n.
Browning, Robert xv
Byrd, Max 188n.

Cain 8, 12, 44, 69, 72–3, 109, 113, 164, 195n.
Calliope 52
Cameron, Jenny 55
Carroll, Lewis 176
Castle, Terry 186n.
Ceres 79, 130–1, 189n., 195n.
Chambers, Robert 191n.
Charles I, King of England 36
Charles, Edward Stuart, Prince (the Young Pretender) 20, 24, 35, 37, 55
Charteris, Evan 193–4n., 195n., 196n.
'Churching' 196n.
Cixous, Hélène xii, 180n.
Clarendon (Edward Hyde, first Earl of) 22, 184n.
Coffin (symbolism of) 36, 39, 43, 184n., 186n.
Cohan, Stephen 198n.
Coleridge, S. T. 182n.
Coley, W. B. 181n., 184n.
Connor, Steven 187n.
Conradi, P. J. 198n., 199n., 200n.
Copts 30

Creation (theories of) 138–9, 197n.
Crone (redefined) 127, 137, 195n.
Cross, W. L. 182n.
Cybele 49–50, 53, 186n.

Daly, Mary 189n., 195n., 202n.
Dance of death 107
Daniel (biblical) 141
Dante 83, 99, 158, 199n.
Darwin, Charles xiii, 116
Davis, D. R. 188n.
Deborah (biblical) 10
Delphyne 201n.
Derrida, Jacques xii, 180n., 182n., 186n., 190n.
Dessner, L. J. 187n.
Diana (goddess) 50, 126, 194n.
Dickens, Charles: autobiographical fragment 190n.; *Bleak House* 132; and Christianity 188n.: and death 187n., 192–3n.; *Dombey and Son* 137, 191n.; *Great Expectations*: *see separate entry*; *Household Words* 190n.; letters cited 60, 190n.; psychoanalytical criticism of 187n.; *A Tale of Two Cities* 189n.; *The Uncommercial Traveller* 189n., 192n.
Dido (in *Aeneid*) 30, 162–3
Dipple, Elizabeth 198n., 199n., 200n.
Dobson, Austin 195n.
Dodd, Philip 195n.
Domino (masquerade costume) 51, 186n.
Donato, Eugenio 196n.
Donne, John 79
Doré, Gustave 83
Doubles/doubling 188n., 200n. *See also The Black Prince; Great Expectations; Tom Jones*
Doughty, Oswald 197n.
Dove (symbolism of) 172, 201n.
Dryden, John 34
Dudley, Edward 183n.
Dworkin, Andrea 181n.
Dykes, D. Oswald 183n.

Egypt 30
Eiger, E. M. 188n.
Eleusinian mysteries 189n., 195n.
  See also Ceres; Proserpina
Ellman, Maud 182n.
Empson, William 3, 182n.
Epigraphy 62, 67, 70
Erlich, Avi 191n.
Eros 172, 201n.
Eurydice 81
Eve 100, 139. See also Great
  Expectations
Evolutionary theories 116, 119,
  138–9, 173

Fates, the three 189n., 191n.
Father: dark 65, 192n.; -as-Law
  xii, xiv, xvii, 59, 83, 102, 142,
  183n.
Father and Son xi, 188n.; Adamic
  symbolism in 138–40, 150,
  197n.; anecdotes in 126–31; as
  autobiography 115–16, 193n.;
  baptism in 121, 143–5; birth
  rites in 127, 137, 143–4; burial in
  129, 146–7; anti-Catholicism in
  136–7; colour symbolism in 140–
  1; Dickens's *Dombey and Son* in
  137; evolution and 116, 119,
  138–9; feminine (symbolism of)
  in 144, 147, 194–5n.; ghostly in
  116, 125–6, 128–31, 135, 139, 143,
  149–50, 194n.; *Hamlet* and 116–
  17, 128–32, 135–6, 139–40, 146,
  149–50; memory acts in 126,
  128–9, 138. 140; Milton's
  Paradise Lost and 197n.; moon
  symbolism in 123–4, 126, 147,
  194–5n.; the mother
  (identification with) in 121–3,
  150; murder *motif* in 131–4;
  mythology in 130–1, 136–8, 139–
  40, 147; naming in 121, 125;
  nightmares in 131–4, 141;
  Oedipal patterns in 116, 131 and
  passim; omphalos and 120–1,
  138; Ophelia and xv, 117, 142–4;
  pleasure principle and 120, 124;
  secrecy in 122–3, 130; silence in

xiii, 142, 146, 150, 194n.;
  suppression of literary source in
  117; trinitarian symbolism in
  120–1, 144, 194n., 195n.
Fielding, Henry; and Catholicism
  5, 25, 182n.; childhood 5, 25,
  182n.; and ghosts 2, 181n.; and
  Jacobitism 25–6, 181n.; on
  tyranny 26–7; wives of 43, 46,
  48, 185n.; *Joseph Andrews* 184n.,
  185n.; *Tom Jones: see separate
  entry*; *The Jacobite's Journal* 25–7,
  34, 181n., 184n.; *The True Patriot*
  25, 183n.
Finney, Brian 193–4n.
Flower maidens 79, 81, 108
Folkenflik, Robert 186n., 197n.
Folkenflik, Vivian 197n.
Forster, John 187n., 190n.
Frazer, Sir J. G. 195n.
French, A. L. 187n.
Freud, Sigmund xi–xii, xv, 85,
  158, 183n., 189n., 192n., 199n.;
  and death 169, 191n.; and
  Hamlet 180n.; the memory trace
  76, 85; Oedipus complex xii,
  180n.; the pleasure principle 92–
  3, 99, 120, 124, 168; thanatos
  and eros 179, 200–1n.; works:
  Beyond the Pleasure Principle 92–
  3, 191n.; *The Dissolution of the
  Oedipus Complex* 189n.; *The
  Interpretation of Dreams* 180n.,
  190n.; *Moses and Monotheism*
  153; *Some Psychical
  Consequences of the Anatomical
  Distinction between the Sexes*
  189n.; *Remembering, Repeating
  and Working-Through* 180n.,
  190n.; *The Theme of the Three
  Caskets* 88, 191n., 201n.; *Totem
  and Taboo* 153; *The Uncanny*
  180n.
Frye, Northrop 182n.
Frye, R. M. 185n.

Garrick, David 2, 181n., 182n.
Gelpi, D. L. 194n., 202n.
George II, King of England 36

Gervais, David 180n., 187n.
Ghosts/ghostly xi, xiv–xv. See
  also *The Black Prince; Father and
  Son*; Fielding: *Great
  Expectations: Tom Jones*
Gilbert, E. L. 188n.
Gilbert. Sandra 40, 185n., 190n.,
  197n., 201n.
Goethe, J. W. xiii
Golden, Morris 182n., 183n.
Golding, William 117
Gosse, Edmund: and
  Hamlet 196n.; and
  homosexuality 194–5n.;
  paganism and 195n.; and
  Swinburne 131, 195n.; *Father
  and Son: see separate entry*; *King
  Erik* 194n.; letters cited 124, 194–
  5n., 196n.; *Life of Philip Henry
  Gosse* 115–16, 119
Gosse, Emily 120–7, 130–46
  passim, 194n.
Gosse, Philip Henry 115–50
  passim, 173, 195–6n.; *The
  Aquarium* 196n.; *A Naturalist's
  Rambles on the Devonshire Coast*
  197n.; *Omphalos* xiv, 119, 128,
  197n.; *Tenby* 125, 195n.; *A Year
  at the Shore* 196n.
Great Expectations xiii–xiv, xvii,
  117, 129–30, 153, 197n.: Abel
  and Cain in 68–9, 71–2, 77, 109,
  113; alphabet in 67–8, 85;
  androgyny in 107, 110–12; and
  autobiography 71, 75, 77, 86;
  Australia in 71, 74; cannibalism
  in 64, 187n.; Ceres myth in 79;
  Christological patterns in 65,
  188n.; confessional mode of
  192n.; cryptography in 67–9, 77,
  188n.; *David Copperfield* and 60,
  76, 85; doubling in 61, 70, 98,
  108–10; dream-work and 78; Eve
  in 76–7, 79, 100; the feminine in
  75–6, 79, 97, 108, 110, 189n.;
  Frankenstein in 73–5, 80, 90, 109;
  gender obsession in 192–3n.;
  and ghosts xi, 61–5, 84, 86–7;
  graves in 61–2, 76–7, 82–3, 85,
  91, 94, 96, 106–7; *Hamlet* and xi,
  60–6, 68, 78–9, 82–5, 87, 90–1,
  93–114 *passim*, 187n., 191–2n.;
  hammer symbol in 70, 72, 83,
  96; hands symbol in 62, 76; and
  hanging 90, 97–8; infanticide in
  76–7; knitting (symbolism of) in
  75–6, 189n.; *Macbeth* and 99–
  100; and maternal loss 66, 73–89,
  95, 104–5; memory in 70, 76, 85;
  mirrors in 81–2; Mother Earth
  in 189n.; mourning iconography
  in 91–3, 111, 192n.; names in 77,
  94, 96, 100, 108; Noah's ark in
  67, 101; numbers (significance
  of) in 76, 106–7; Oedipal
  patterns in 60–1, 64, 68, 79, 80,
  85, 87, 95, 103, 109; Ophelia in
  79–83, 93–9, 104, 107–14 *passim*,
  191–2n.; orphans in 61, 88;
  parentalia and xiv; paternal
  symbolism in 61–7, 71–3, 83, 85,
  90, 96–8, 100, 102; photographs
  and 61–2, 63, 66–8, 71, 85–6;
  prisons and 65, 74, 78, 84, 89;
  remembrance in 66, 70, 73, 75;
  repetition and 90, 101, 113,
  190n., 192n.; softness (concept
  of) in 75, 108–12; and waxworks
  89, 190–1n.; weirdness in 80, 83,
  189n.; zombies in 80, 90
Green, Henry 43
Greenberg, Martin 200n.
Grimaldi, Joey 188n.
Gubar, Susan 40, 185n., 190n.,
  197n., 201n.
Gunpowder plot 185n.

Habeus corpus 17, 183n.
Hall, Sir Edward Marshall 118
Hall, Michael 182n.
Hamlet: appropriations of xiii,
  xv, 180n.; Barnardo in 95;
  cosmetics in 165; doubling in
  200n.; Ghost 2–4, 11–12, 16, 39,
  47, 64–5, 73, 78, 97, 129, 139,
  154, 159, 164; gravediggers 14,
  82, 128, 174; naming in 121;
  misogyny in 51, 153; Oedipal

xiii–xiv, 153–4, 157, 180n.;
Ophelia xv, 33, 42, 51, 58, 60, 66,
111–12, 142–4, 167, 190n., 192–
3n., 197n.; secrecy in 8, 65;
sibling rivalry in 38, 179;
thanatology and 42, 60; Yorick
11, 17, 42, 45, 68, 106–7, 128. See
also The Black Prince; Father and
Son; Great Expectations, Tom
Jones
Hara, Eiichi   187n.
Hardy, Thomas   101, 131, 189n.,
195n.
Harrison, J. E.   200n.
Hartley, L. P.   65
Hartog, K. den   189n., 192n.
Heath, Stephen   196n.
Hecate   127, 186n., 195n.
Heidegger, John   2, 49
Hermes: see Mercury
Hermeticism   43, 157–8, 199n.
Herodotus   161–2, 200n.
Hesiod   201n.
Hill, Susan   117
Hill, T. W.   189n.
Homosexuality   199n. See also
Gosse, Edmund
Horace   39, 186n.
Hound (symbolism of)   126, 195n.
House, Humphry   187n.
Hume, David   182n.
Hunter, Lynette   200–1n.
Hutter, A. D.   186n., 187n., 191n.

Incest   182n., 186n.
Irigaray, Luce   xii, xvi, 180n.,
181n., 198n., 201n.
Irving, Sir Henry   196n.

Jacobites   3–4, 25–7, 30, 35–7,
184n.
Jacobus, Mary   188n,, 192n.
James I, King of England   28
James II, King of England   3, 20,
24–5, 33–4
James Francis Edward Stuart (the
Old Pretender), 'James III'   34
James, Duke of Monmouth   20–1
Jephthah   33–4

Jerome, J. K.   144, 197n.
Jesse, F. T.   178
Johnson, Deborah   xvi, 181n.,
198n., 201n.
Johnson, Maurice   181n.
Johnson, W. S.   xvii, 181n.
Jones, Ernest   xiv, 154, 157, 159,
180n., 200n.
Johnson, Ben   186n.
Jordan, J. O.   187n.
Jung, C. G.   199n., 201n.;
Alchemical Studies 199n.; Man
and his Symbols 199n.;
Psychological Types 199n.;
Psychology and Alchemy 181n.;
Symbols of Transformation 186n.,
187n.; See also Anima
Juno (in Aeneid)   30, 34
Juvenal   165, 200n.

Kafka, Franz   141
Kahrl, G. M.   181n., 182n.
Kerényi, Carl   201n.
Kermode, Frank   43, 185n., 200n.
Klein, Melanie   121, 188n., 194n.
Knitting (symbolism of)   75–6,
189n.
Knowles, J. S.   116, 193n., 197n.
Kristeva, Julia   180n.

Lacan, Jacques   xii–xiv, 180n.,
183n., 187n.; and language xii–
xiii; mirror stage xii; and
prohibiting father xii, 183n.
Laforgue, Jules   xiii
Laius (in Oedipus
Tyrannus)   182n.
Lambdin, G. C.   190n.
Laplanche, J.   189n.
Latham, M. W.   186n.
Legion (biblical)   187n.
Leonardo da Vinci   124
Lillo, George   87, 97, 191n.
Lindboe, B. R.   181n., 185n.
Loftie, W. J.   192n.
Lucina   195n.
Lucretia   201n.
Lyell, Sir Charles   116, 138

Index

Madness (female)   142, 190n.
Magee, Bryan   201n.
Mallarmé, Stéphane   xiii
Mandel, B. J.   193n.
Manheim, L. F.   187n.
Marlow, J. E.   187n.
Marsyas   158–60, 171, 199–200n.
Masquerades   49–50, 186n.
McCrea, Brian   184n.
Memory   52, 85, 115, 138. See also
   The Black Prince; *Father and Son*;
   Freud; *Great Expectations*
Mercury (planetary god)   157, 199n.
Millais, Sir J. E.   173
Miller, H. K.   182n., 183n., 186n.
Miller, J. H.   188n.
Miller, Karl   xiv, 133, 180, 188n.
Milton, John   27, 36, 156, 184n., 197n.
Mnesis   52–3, 57
Moon (symbolism of)   53, 174, 186n. See also *Father and Son*
Moore, George   119, 134
Mortimer, John   117–18
Mother ('terrible')   49–50, 53–4, 99, 186n., 188n., 192n.
Mourning iconography   91–3, 111, 192n.
Moynahan, Julian   188n., 192n.
Murdoch, Iris: 'Against Dryness' 200n.; on art 201n; and dreams 201n.; *A Fairly Honourable Defeat* 158, 201n.; and fathers and sons 151–3, 179; and feminine language 179, 198n.; *The Fire and the Sun* xvi–xvii, 156, 181n., 198n.; *The Good Apprentice* 151–2; and *Hamlet* 151–4, 198n.; *Henry and Cato* 151–3, 165, 198n., 200n.; and male narrator xvi, 153, 198n.; *Nuns and Soldiers* 152–3, 198n.; and Oedipus complex xv–xvi, 154, 198n.; and Platonism xvi–xvii, 156–7, 198n., 200–1n.; prodigal son *motif* and 151–3; *The Sacred and Profane Love Machine* 160–1, 201n.; *The Sea,*
The Sea 152–3, 161, 198n., 201n.; *The Sovereignty of Good* 156, 198n.

Neptune (in *Aeneid*)   34
Nero   23, 28
Neumann, Erich   196n.
Nimrod   20, 184n.
Novak, M. E.   183n.
Nussbaum, F. A.   200n.

Odysseus   10, 183n.
Oedipus   7–8, 14, 16, 182n.
Oedipus complex   xi–xviii, 117,
   See also *The Black Prince*; *Father and Son*; Freud; *Great Expectations*; Murdoch; *Tom Jones*
Olney, James   193n.
Orphanhood   xiv, 188n.
Orpheus   52, 185n.
Osiris   185n.
Otway, Thomas   4–6, 15, 22, 56–8, 182n.
Ovid   181n., 185n., 199n.
Owen, Wilfred   117

Pallas Athene   158, 160
Parentalia   xiv, 180n.
Park, William   182n.
Parker, Rozsika   189n.
Patara   160–3
Pater, Walter   124–5, 131, 195n.
Paulson, Ronald   181n.
Pausanias   201n.
Peacham, Henry   184n.
Pearlman, E.   193–4n.
Perry, Ruth   186n.
Phallogocentrism   179
Photography   61–2, 64, 85–6, 187n., 191n.
Plato   xvi, 156–7, 199–200n., 201n.
Pluto   79
Polyphemus   10
Pope, Alexander   52
Pontalis, J.-B.   189n.
Pornography   xv, 181n.
Porter, R. J.   197n.
Priam (in *Aeneid*)   31–2, 37

Index

Proserpina 79, 81, 189n., 195n.
Pyrrhus (in *Aeneid*) 31–2

Queen of Fairies 53, 186n.
Queen of the night 53
Quillian, W. H. 180n.

Randall, H. W. 184n.
Renza, L. A. 193n.
Ricardou, Jean 199n.
Robinson, John 197n.
Rose, W. K. 198n.
Rossetti, D. G. 144, 173, 197n.
Rousseau, J.-J. 121
Rudnytsky, Peter 180n.

Sadoff, D. F. 187n., 189n.
Sanders, Andrew 187n.
Saussure, Ferdinand de xiii
Schonhorn, Manuel 40, 181n., 184n., 185n.
Scofield, Martin 180n.
Scott, Michael 145–6
Secrecy xiv, 65, 185n. See also Father and Son; Hamlet; Tom Jones
Sells, L. F. 181–2n.
Servius 162, 200n.
Shakespeare, William: *Cymbeline* 174, 201n.; *Hamlet: see separate entry*; *I Henry IV* 37–8, 177, 185n.; *King Lear* 125; *Macbeth* 99–100; *Othello* 45; *Pericles* 201n.; *The Tempest* 116, 175; *The Winter's Tale* 201n.
Shelley, Mary 73–5, 80, 90, 109, 170, 188n., 201n.
Shipton, Anna 194n.
Showalter, Elaine 190n., 197n.
Shumaker, Wayne 193n.
Smithfield 89, 191n.
Snow White 190n.
Sophocles 5, 7–8, 163, 180n., 183n., 200n.
Sparagmos 41, 185n.
Spenser, Edmund 174, 183n., 201n.
Sphinx 186n.
Sterne, Laurence 9, 141–2

Stevenson, R. L. 133, 196n.
Stewart, J. F. 199n., 200n.
Stoicism 16
Stone, G. W. 181n., 182n.
Stone, Harry 187n.
Strauss, W. A. 185n.
Strindberg, August 74
Sturrock, Jane 199n., 200n.
Sturrock, John 193n.
Swinburne, A. C. 131, 189n., 194n., 195n.

Tabbs, Bernard 182n.
Tambling, Jeremy 192n.
Tarquinius Superbus 201n.
Tavor, Eve 182n., 183n.
Tennant, Emma 117
Tennyson, Alfred, Lord 144, 190n., 192., 197n.
Thomas, Keith 181n.
Thorneycroft, Hamo 124, 194n.
Thwaite, Ann 115, 124–5, 193n., 194n., 196n., 197n.
Tiresias 163
Todd, Richard 198n., 201n.
Tom Jones xi, 60, 108, 116–17, 153, 194n.; anti-Catholicism in 25–8; authorial anxiety in 43–8; authority (problem of) in 6, 40–8, 185n.; Calvinism in 183n., 188n.; doubles in 8, 28, 41, 43, 51; and dream-work 23; fathers in 5–6, 8–11, 15–24, 58–9 and *passim*; Mrs Fitzpatrick's tale 54–9; ghosts in 2–3, 11, 15–22, 43, 47, 55; Glorious Revolution and 3, 21, 24; gypsies episode in 28–32, 38, 40, 185n., 186n.; *Hamlet* and 2–4, 11–13, 18, 23, 32–3, 38–9, 41–4, 45, 47, 51–2, 54–5; *I Henry IV* and 37–8, 185n.; incest in 48, 182n.; Jacobites in 2, 25–7, 30, 37, 184n.; Man of the Hill's tale 14–24, 48, 56; masquerade in 49–50, 52, 185n.,186n.; matricide and 23; monarchical absolutism in 29–30, 34–5; mothers in 11, 23, 48–59; names in 7, 9, 16, 50;

'nobody' theme in 9–11, 15, 24, 46; numerical centre of 17, 54; Oedipus complex in 5–6, 8–9, 11, 17, 24, 49, 51, 56; and *Oedipus Tyrannus* 5–8, 16, 182n.; orphanhood and 3, 52, 188n.; Orpheus in 52, 185n.; Thomas Otway and 5, 15, 22, 56; patriarchal conspiracy in 13–14, 55; and primal scenes 30–1; puppet show in 33–6; reprobacy in 9; re-vision in 11–13, 56; revisions for 3rd edition 25; seasonal symbolism in 13–14, 49, 53; secrecy in 6–14 *passim*; sibling rivalry in 12, 17, 24, 38, 44, 54; and Virgil's *Aeneid* 30–4, 37
Tooke, Andrew 186n., 189n.
Traubitz, N. B. 195n.
Trinity (female) 195n.

Vesta (goddess) 136
Villiers, George, first Duke of Buckingham 184n.
Villiers, Sir George 184n.
Virgil 30–4, 37–8, 144–5, 162–3, 181n., 196–7n.
Virgin Mary 77, 189–90n.
Vogel, Jane 187n., 188n., 190n.

Weldon, Fay 154, 178, 200n.
Westheimer, Douglas 195n.
Wild man 16
William III, King of England 21, 24
Wilson, Edmund 187n.
Wilson, W. A. 187n.
Wind, Edgar 199n.
Wood, Thomas 183n.
Woolf, J. D. 193–4n.
Wordsworth, William 142, 146

Young, Edward 147
Young, Robert 180n., 182n.

Zombies: *see Great Expectations*
Zwicker, Steven 184n.

OHIO UNIVERSITY LIBRARY

Please return this ... soon as you
have finished w... ...r to avoid a
fine it must b... latest date
stamped ...